THE NEW SUBJECTIVIST REVOLUTION

THE NEW SUBJECTIVIST REVOLUTION

An Elucidation and Extension of Ludwig von Mises's Contributions to Economic Theory

J. Patrick Gunning

ROWMAN & LITTLEFIELD PUBLISHERS, INC.

ROWMAN & LITTLEFIELD PUBLISHERS, INC.

Published in the United States of America
by Rowman & Littlefield Publishers, Inc.
8705 Bollman Place, Savage, Maryland 20763

British Cataloging in Publication Information Available

Library of Congress Cataloging-in-Publication Data

Gunning, James Patrick.
    The new subjectivist revolution : An elucidation
and extension of Ludwig von Mises's contributions
to economic theory
p.   cm.
Includes bibliographical references.
1. Von Mises, Ludwig, 1881-1973.
2. Austrian school of economists.
I. Title.
HB101.V66G86   1990
330.15'7—dc20   90-8147 CIP

ISBN 0-8476-7622-6 (alk. paper)

5   4   3   2   1

Printed in the United States of America

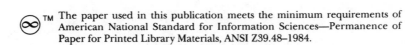

Contents

Preface

The work that resulted in the present book began in 1986. By then, I had been aware of Austrian economics and some of Ludwig von Mises's writings for about ten years. Nevertheless, I had only skimmed Mises's *Human Action*, selecting out the parts that I believed were relevant to my own interests. This piecemeal approach led me to gradually develop a profound respect for Mises's scholarship and his methodological insight. Correspondingly, I came to increasingly use Mises's *Human Action* as a benchmark against which to compare the economic reasoning of both others and myself.

Strangely, Mises's methodological insight did not seem to be fully appreciated by others. First, there were the positivist and historicist critics, who did not seem capable of comprehending his work. Second, there were economists claiming to be Austrians who seemed to go off in a variety of directions without accounting for or dealing with Mises's pivotal discoveries. Third, there were sympathetic late discoverers of Mises's writings like myself who seemed to stop short of a reasonably complete understanding of *Human Action*. Was I mistaken about Mises? Or were the others mistaken? To answer these questions, I had to give *Human Action* the intense reading it seemed to deserve. This book is basically a report of my findings regarding methodology.

It seems worthwhile to tell the reader something about the training and experience that preceded this project. I was trained in a somewhat orthodox, yet non-mathematical economics program, in which methodological individualism and Paretian subjectivism were stressed. It is important to point this out because I believe that one must fully understand the subjective theory of value before one can appreciate the new Misesian subjectivism. This is because the latter is built on the former. It is unlikely that an economist who fails to see the significance of the subjective theory of value will be able to make much sense of *Human Action.*

I cannot say that I was comfortable with the Paretian subjectivism I was taught. I remained unconvinced that the idea of treating the human subject as a utility-maximizing preference unit and the entrepreneur as a profit-maximizing producing unit could get one very far. It seemed to me that elaborate mathematical and verbal models in which individuals are defined in terms of objective functions, are merely shells. The more interesting and significant economic phenomena could only be understood by investigating the "psychology" of the human beings who lay inside the shell. With this in mind, I embarked around 1975 on an independent study of the fields of psychology, philosophy, and sociology in order to determine whether anyone had encountered similar problems and tried to solve them.

Although I scanned numerous books and articles, only a few seemed relevant enough to warrant further study. In psychology, the work of Jean Piaget exhibited a clear understanding of subjectivism. More than that, Piaget's methodological works suggested an unsurpassed understanding of the methods that one must use to form judgments about the values and intellectual abilities of others. In sociology, I was attracted to the writings of Alfred Schuetz. Schuetz, more than any other social theorist I studied, was intimately concerned with the problem of how the social scientist can come to understand and describe the interaction of other human beings. My reading of Schuetz's works led me to the branch of philosophy called phenomenology. In particular, the writings of Husserl and Bergson had a clear subjectivist bent.

At one point in my studies, I envisioned writing a book that would recast economic issues and problems in a Schuetzean light. I even developed the tentative title of "Phenomenological Economics." For various reasons I put this project aside. It is a good thing that I did, since as I became more familiar with Mises's writings, I began to see that he had already written such a book.

As I gradually realized that Mises was dealing with what I believe is the fundamental problem of social science, I was ready to study *Human Action* as a logically consistent whole. My working assumption was that each passage could be related to every other passage. The key to understanding the book, I assumed, was to identify the relationships among the different passages with a view toward what Mises's goals seemed to be. Along with *Human Action,* I acquired other books by Mises and other writings about Mises, especially those that dealt with "human action" themes.

A major initial goal in studying Mises's works was to discover the link between the subjectivism, or phenomenology, of Alfred Schuetz and Misesian economics. A highlight of the early part of my study was the discovery that Schuetz, like Hayek, had participated in Mises's Vienna seminars in the 1920s.[1]

Before I could understand how the different parts of *Human Action* combine to form an integrated whole, I had to work out the theoretical implications of the method that Mises proposed for studying human action in general and economic interaction in particular. This book is essentially a report of this work. My most important discovery by far was that Mises's method of doing economics—which he clearly stated in chapter fourteen—revealed insights and contained implications that appeared nowhere else, not even in the writings of Mises's students. To the best of my knowledge no other economists, including other readers of *Human Action*, have identified the methodological insights described in this book.

This book has two goals. The first is to redirect the energies of economists who associate their work with that of Mises. The second is to inform non-Misesian economists and non-economists of the potential intellectual rewards of learning the new subjectivism. Thus, the new subjectivism is important not only to the small but growing number of Austrian economists. It should be understood by all economists who are interested in learning what they are doing and how to do it better. Beyond this, the book has implications that extend far beyond the rather arbitrary boundaries of economics. The methods Mises discovered are used in all the social sciences and even in psychology. The implications of the methods for these fields have not yet been worked out.

Students of Mises will discover one glaring omission in this book. I have completely neglected Mises's theory of interest, money, and the trade cycle. This might be regarded as an especially dubious omission since Mises seems to have been led to an investigation of methodology by his interest in dealing with the problems of money and the trade cycle.[2] Moreover, in the history of economic thought, Mises is most widely known for his contributions to these fields.

Three reasons can be given for this omission. First, Mises's contribution to methodology, which I shall describe in this book, has not even been discovered, much less appreciated. Second, Mises's theory of money is sufficiently different from his epistemology that his epis-

temology can be treated separately. In other words, a book on Mises's
discovery of the method of economics can stand alone. Third, for
reasons that are too detailed to describe here, I believe that Mises's
integration of the economic method with the theory of money is both
difficult to follow and not entirely successful. Suffice it to say that his
contribution to methodology is so much in need of elucidation and
further development that a book devoted to that subject alone is enough
for me to try to accomplish at this time.

Finally, in light of the ideas of popular economists, it seems worth
saying why this book on methodology is necessary. The reason was
best stated by Mises himself when he recalled his early thinking as a
student at the university. He says:

> [During my early university years], I sought consolation in the thought
> that it matters above all to advance in science and that the problems of
> methodology are of lesser importance. But I soon realized the fallacy of
> this stance. With every problem, the economist faces the basic questions:
> "From whence do these principles come," "What is their significance,"
> "How do they relate to experience and 'reality' "? These are not prob-
> lems of method or even research technique; they are themselves the basic
> questions. Can a deductive system be built without raising the question
> on what to build?

I would add that unless economists are conscious and attentive to
their methods, there is hardly any justification for a special academic
subject of economics.

I would like to thank the University of Central Florida, American
University, and Ohio University for secretarial and materials support
at various times during the preparation of this manuscript.

NOTES

1. See Haberler (1981) "Mises' Private Seminar" *Wirtschaftspolitische Blatter* 4:—. I should mention that Max Weber's work was the focus of some of the Misesian seminars. Thus, it is highly likely that Schuetz and Mises owes a debt to Weber. The link between Mises and Schuetz is also explored in Murry Rothbard's 1973 paper. The interested reader should also consult Walter Block's (1980) systematic defense of Mises against Robert Nozick's attack. Also George Selgin (1988) published his fine paper on praxeology. More recently, Richard Ebeling's work (1986) has come to my attention along with that of Patrick O'Sullivan (1987) and Hans-Hermann Hoppe (1988). I suspect that there are still others who perceive the link but whose writings or thoughts are unfamiliar to me. On the link with Weber see Lachmann (1971).

2. See Mises (1978b, 55–56).

Chapter 1

Introduction

The crowning achievement of Ludwig von Mises was his discovery of the methods of reasoning used in classical and neoclassical economics.[1] These methods, which are partly described in chapter fourteen of Mises's *Human Action*, were not recognized by the economists who used them. As a result, the economists could not effectively defend their interpretations of traditional economic problems and issues.

The ultimate goal of economics is to help individuals understand a particular set of issues and problems that relate to human interaction in a society that uses money. These problems are best understood by referring to an image of the *market economy*. A market economy is an image of economic interaction among normal human beings under the widest range of assumptions about the culture and physical environment. In the image of the market economy, rights to all goods and factors are defined and enforced, and markets have already been created. The culture disposes individuals to peacefully produce, exchange, and use money; but aside from getting disutility from using their labor, the specific goods that individuals want are not significant. The physical environment makes it possible for individuals to survive and to gain from production, exchange, and specialization. But no other particular characteristics are important. When the economist constructs an image of the market economy, she is said to be doing *economic theory*.

The economic theorist is not interested in *behavior* unless it is part of action, that is, unless it is chosen by a normal human being. Nor is the theorist interested in non-monetary action or interaction, such as the production of goods for personal use and barter. Finally, the

1

theorist is not interested in the specific wants, abilities, or knowledge that individuals possess.

The desire to construct an image of the market economy creates a special problem. The economist observes buying and selling in everyday life by individuals who are not normal and by people who behave but do not act. She also observes individuals who produce goods for their own use and who trade by means of barter. Yet, in constructing the image of the market economy, she must try to disregard these observations. Moreover, economic interaction in everyday life takes place within the context of particular cultures, physical environments, and legal structures. Again the theorist must try to ignore the particular culture and physical environment and must assume a legal structure within which a market economy can flourish.

To construct an image of the market economy, the economist must use two methods. First, she must use a method that contrasts (1) a model of behaving robots that simulates economic interaction with (2) an image of how human beings would behave if they faced the situations of the robots. This is because human action can only be *understood* by means of a contrast between (1) behavior that does not entail deliberation and choice, and (2) behavior that does entail these distinctly human characteristics. Such a method is called the method of imaginary constructions. As applied to economics, the author calls it the method of contrasting images of functions. Second, the economist must use a method in which economic interaction has a beginning and an ending point. This is because human action can only be understood by referring to a beginning and ending point of a particular action or class of actions. The author calls this second method the method of economic teleology.

Having constructed an abstract image of the market economy, the economist can proceed to the applied tasks of describing economic interaction under the conditions that prevail in everyday life. To do this, she uses her knowledge of the particular wants, abilities, and knowledge of individuals in everyday life and knowledge of the particular customs, physical environment, and legal structure. Then she combines this knowledge with her image of the hypothetical market economy in order to identify the specifically economic characteristics of interaction in everyday life.

The main purpose of this introduction is to give a preliminary description of the two methods. This is done in Part 1. Part 2 introduces some key methodological issues. Part 3 tries to explain why Mises's revolutionary ideas have not penetrated modern economic thought.

Part 4 tells the plan of this book. The introduction is not intended to document the claim of this book that the new subjectivism, as described here, is contained in Mises's *Human Action*. Although some references are provided, the reader who seeks documentation can find it later in the text.

1. THE METHODS OF ECONOMIC THEORY

Mises employed two complementary methods of constructing an image of the market economy, although it seems that he clearly identified only one. The first, which he referred to repeatedly, was the *method of imaginary constructions*.[2] The second, which he did not clearly identify, was *economic teleology*. Each is discussed in turn.

The Method of Imaginary Constructions

Mises used the method of imaginary constructions both to elucidate individual action in general and specifically to elucidate economic interaction.[3] Consider first how he used it to elucidate action in general. He began by constructing an initial, vague image of action. This image is itself an imaginary construction, as all conceptions of action must be, since the formation of images is the foundation of thought. Next, he used his intuition to identify candidates for what he called the *categories of action*. A category of action is a characteristic that is absolutely necessary for action to occur. Mises proved that ends and means, causality, time, and uncertainty deserved to be called categories of action. He did this by using reason to show that it was impossible to construct an image of action if any one of these categories is absent.[4]

The method of contrasting images of function. Mises used the same method to elucidate economic interaction under the conditions specified in the definition of the market economy. The method begins by constructing an initial, vague image of the market economy. This image is derived from the traditional definition of economics. The traditional definition is used both to describe the conditions that exist in the market economy (rights to goods and factors, existence of markets, and use of money in exchange) and to identify what can be called the *essential characteristics of a fully integrated economic interaction*. These characteristics are consumption, the production of goods, saving, and the supply of factors. A fully integrated initial image of economic interaction must possess these characteristics. Since the characteristics are necessary, they can be called *economic functions*.

Once the economic functions are defined, the method of imaginary constructions is used to show how the categories of action get manifested in the image of a market economy. To do this, the economist makes a *contrast* between two images. The first is an image of an economy in which robots perform the economic functions. In this image, ends are simulated by the consuming behavior of consumer-saving robots. The use of means is simulated by producing and factor-supplying robots. Time and uncertainty are absent in this image. The economist contrasts this image with what he or she can know by intuition and experience to be how real economic actors would perform the economic functions under the conditions specified in the definition of the market economy (rights to goods and factors, existence of markets, and use of money in exchange).

In economics, the distinctly human element involved in dealing with time and uncertainty with the aim of causing the economic functions to be performed is assigned to a particular role, that of the *entrepreneur*. Thus, it can be said that the method of contrasting images of functions enables the economist to identify and elucidate entrepreneurship.

The difference between using the method of imaginary constructions to elucidate action in general and using it to elucidate economic interaction is substantial. Unfortunately, Mises did not emphasize this fact. As a result, his terminology seems to have confused his readers. To avoid this problem, a new phrase is introduced in this book that more accurately describes this economic method. The method is called the *method of contrasting images of functions*. It consists of two parts: (1) constructing a model of function-performing robots, and (2) contrasting the model with an image of normal human beings who perform the same functions. The purpose of the contrast is to elucidate entrepreneurship. Consider each part in turn.

The construction of a model of robots. In a model of economic interaction, the interacting individuals are like robots. The model contains robot consumer-savers, robot producers, and robot factor-suppliers that perform the essential functions, respectively, of consuming, saving, producing, and supplying factors. The robots are said to be related to each other in a way that can be fully deduced from assumptions about wants, resources, and knowledge. Their behavior is performed according to rules, or algorithms, which are fully specified by the economist.

The elucidation of entrepreneurship. A characteristic of economic interaction that cannot be represented by means of models is entrepreneurship. Entrepreneurial action can be said to be comprised of three related parts, or categories: (1) appraisement (identifying factors and estimating relative costs); (2) making decisions about what prospective factors will be used to produce what prospective goods; and (3) bearing the uncertainty connected with such decision making.

The entrepreneur can be regarded as a role. However, the entrepreneur is not a robot and does not behave according to specifiable rules. The entrepreneur is a rule maker. If he follows any rules, it is because he has made a decision to do so. His decisions cannot be represented by an economist's model. The methodological requirement of subjectivism demands that the economist treat entrepreneurship as a characteristic of human interaction that defies exact specification. The behavior of consumer-savers, producers, and factor-suppliers in the economist's models can be described in terms of (or deduced from) the assumptions of a model. The action of entrepreneurs can only be described by means of an appeal to intuition.

The role of the entrepreneur connects the economic functions to the categories of action. Thus, to elucidate the role of the entrepreneur is the same thing as showing how and why human beings produce, consume, save, and supply resources. When the economist understands the role of the entrepreneur, she also understands the significance of means, ends, time, and uncertainty in a market economy.

Included in the concept of entrepreneurship is the idea of entrepreneurial interaction. When individuals act entrepreneurially, they *appraise* what they regard as the prospective factors of production. Then they compare their appraisals with the appraisals of others, which are revealed by price bids. When one entrepreneur's appraisal of a factor is higher than the price bids of others (and, therefore, when he believes that his appraisal is superior) and when he is willing to bear the uncertainty if he is wrong, the entrepreneur bids for the factor in order to control how the factor is used. Among the factors appraised is appraisement ability itself. If an entrepreneur's ability is appraised at a higher value by others than by himself and if someone else is willing and able to bear the uncertainty (or if he can shift the uncertainty to others), he becomes an employee. Entrepreneurial interaction also determines the allocation of rights and responsibilities regarding decisions to produce and sell factors and goods.

Elucidating characteristics of the market economy. Economists have long identified several characteristics of the market economy.

These include competition, consumer sovereignty, the relationship between the prices of goods and the prices of factors of production, that prices are used to signal willingness to buy and sell, and how specialization economizes on the use of knowledge in the production and exchange of factors and goods. The method of contrasting images of functions can be used to elucidate these characteristics also. First a method containing both function-performing robots and "interacting" robot entrepreneurs is constructed. Then the method is contrasted with an image of human entrepreneurs who are assumed to interact under the circumstances assumed in the model.

Economic Teleology

The economist also uses the method of *economic teleology* to identify and elucidate entrepreneurship. In using this method, he assumes that each type of behavior and each relationship among the behaviors is caused by entrepreneurship. To identify the types of decisions made by entrepreneurship, the economist conceives of an endpoint at which a particular set of behaviors is performed. Then he forms hypotheses about the actions that could cause that set of behaviors.

The method of economic teleology can be used at the microeconomic level to show how entrepreneurship creates markets and rights. It can also be used at both the microeconomic and macroeconomic levels simultaneously to show how entrepreneurship leads to coordination and synchronization. When the method is used at the macroeconomic level, it must be supplemented by the method of contrasting images of functions. Doing this helps assure that the entrepreneurial decision(s) he has identified is fully integrated with other entrepreneurial decisions.

2. OTHER ISSUES RELATING TO METHODOLOGY

In using the methods of contrasting images of functions and economic teleology, the economist cannot avoid also using some notion of equilibrium. But this concept is not a mathematical or a mechanical concept; it is a logical one. It means either that economic functions are being repeatedly performed by robots or that individuals have decided independently or collectively to perform a set of separate behaviors.

When the economist tries to construct an image of how individuals would act under particular conditions, she must assume a priori that the individuals possess the categories of action. Then she must try to imagine interchanging positions with them. This is true not only of economics but of all studies of human action. The following discusses these ideas in greater depth.

Equilibrium

The beginning step in using the method of contrasting images of functions and economic teleology is to attempt to conceive of a model of an economy in which there is no entrepreneurship at all. Mises believed that the neoclassical general equilibrium model was such a beginning step. It is important to keep in mind, however, that he interpreted equilibrium as a model in which economic functions were performed and repeated by robots. Good examples are the models used by Joseph Schumpeter and Frank Knight.[5] Beginning with such a model, the economist proceeds to contrast the behavior in the model with what he knows about economic interaction under the conditions specified in the definition of the market economy. Or, he regards the model as an endpoint and investigates the different types of entrepreneurial actions that could result in such an endpoint. Thus, the neoclassical general equilibrium model, properly understood, is an essential part of the economic method.

Logic vs. Mathematics

When modern economists think of equilibrium, they typically have in mind a model in which assumptions and deductions are expressed mathematically. In this form, the concept of equilibrium is hardly usable. To use the concept of equilibrium, the economist must state the conditions of equilibrium in such a way that she can contrast them with the conditions of a market economy. To stress this fact, Mises pointed out that the only proper meaning of equilibrium is what he called a *logical meaning*. Equilibrium should be imagined solely as a logical outcome of human interaction. Nothing is added or saved by using mathematical symbols to represent the conditions of equilibrium. On the contrary, the use of mathematics bodes the potential danger that the economist will altogether ignore the only legitimate uses of the equilibrium concept.[6]

To emphasize his views, Mises avoided the term equilibrium. He dubbed the static equilibrium model of neoclassical economics the *evenly rotating economy* (ERE). In the evenly rotating economy, as Mises defined it, all economic functions are performed by robots; there is no entrepreneurship.

Methodological Apriorism

Methodological apriorism is the procedure of (1) identifying the characteristics that all (normal) human actors undeniably have in common, and (2) using the characteristics so identified to help one make deductions about human action under particular circumstances. In economics, it is manifested in the economist's attempt to identify the categories of entrepreneurial action and the different ways that entrepreneurship causes the economic functions to be performed.

To understand entrepreneurship, the economist must interchange positions with the hypothetical entrepreneur and ask how he would act under similar circumstances. For example, when the economist contrasts the behavior in the evenly rotating economy with the economic interaction in a market economy, she asks herself about the types of entrepreneurial actions that could result in the behavior. To find an answer, she projects herself into the positions of entrepreneurs under the conditions specified in the definition of the market economy and asks what would lead her to act in such a way that the assumed behaviors would result. In making such a projection, the economist necessarily assumes a priori (that is, she knows through introspection and experience) that all human actors possess the categories of action (ends, means, time, and uncertainty). She has precisely identified these categories by using the method of imaginary constructions, as described in Part 1 of this chapter.

Economics and Other Branches of the Study of Human Action

Neoclassical economists knew quite well that their descriptions of economic interaction contained a mix of models of behaving robots and thinking entrepreneurs. They did not appreciate, however, that their descriptions implicitly used methodological apriorism. The unique contribution of Mises to economic methodology was to demonstrate that this was so. In so doing, he developed an impeccable defense of what is called in this book the new subjectivist method. At the same time, he was able to provide a devastating critique of all forms of positivism in the sciences of human action.

Beyond this, Mises recognized that the method developed and used by the neoclassical economists was the only sensible method of all social science and history.[7] Every attempt to describe human action and interaction requires one to begin with a theory of interaction under the widest range of assumptions about particular circumstances. To construct such a theory, one must make an imaginary construct that is based on a contrast between models of behaving robots and images of thinking actors. Mises has the distinction of having shown that the method that economists have used as a matter of course (but which they have not articulated) is, or should be, the method used by all persons who describe human action and interaction. In other words, Mises showed that the method used by the classical and neoclassical economists was the method that all self-proclaimed social scientists use (or should use).

Economics is only one branch of the study of human action, or praxeology. Yet the method of understanding economic interaction that was developed in this branch is the only proper way to describe and understand human interaction in all the branches.

3. THE PREVIOUS FAILURE OF THE NEW SUBJECTIVISM

In this book, the methodology that Mises recognized is called the *new subjectivism*. It is called *subjectivism* because it amounts to defining economic phenomena by accounting for the perspectives, or understandings, possessed by different economic actors, or subjects. It is called *new* in order to distinguish it from the subjectivism of the nineteenth-century subjectivists, while at the same time emphasizing the continuity of thinking.[8]

In the author's view it is impossible to refute Mises's exposition of the method of reasoning used by classical and neoclassical economists. A careful reading of *Human Action* and other works by Mises reveals without a doubt that Mises himself believed that he had provided an irrefutable exposition. It is clear, however, that he was unable to turn the tide of positivism.

There are probably many reasons why the new subjectivism has not been appreciated. Among these are the predispositions of other economists. In modern times, professional economics is hardly an intellectual endeavor in which individuals attempt to understand economic phenomena. It is more an industry that has emerged to supply the demands of politicians with arguments to support or refute one policy or another. It is also partly a competitive game that academics play against each other at the expense of the patrons of the universities with which they are associated. Since Mises used his new subjectivism to criticize practically all of the popular policy arguments and since he also criticized economics in the universities, it is no wonder that many professional economists have rejected the new subjectivism.[9]

There are other reasons for the lack of appreciation, however. First, Mises's new subjectivism was not sufficiently integrated with the old. As a result, he did not consistently elaborate the distinction between the economist as a student of economic interaction and the subject as an interactor. Alfred Schuetz, a participant in Mises's Vienna seminars in the 1920s,[10] was far more competent at making this distinction, although he did not do so for economics.[11] Second, Mises's terminology was confusing. Or at least it is confusing to the modern reader. His uses of the terms "function," "entrepreneur," and "understanding" all contributed to confusion. Third, his use of his methodology contained faults. In particular, in his descriptions of market economy, he employed concepts of profit, loss, income, and wealth that have no subjectivist counterparts. The irony is that although Mises made unrivaled contributions to economic theory, he was unable to adequately describe economic events in a way that manifested his new subjectivism. In a sense, he inadvertently helped to sabotage his own project![12]

Mises's methodological achievements have gone largely unrecognized and perhaps fully unappreciated. Even Mises's students and closest followers seem to have missed the point of them.[13] As a result, in spite of a revival of interest in Austrian economics, Mises's contribution continues to face the prospect of extinction.

4. PLAN OF THIS BOOK

There are at present some excellent descriptions of Mises's "praxeology," which is the foundation of his economics.[14] In the author's view, however, there are no good descriptions of how Mises applied praxeology to economics. On the contrary, all the descriptions of which the author is aware are flawed in the most fundamental respect. They fail to recognize the significance of the methods of imaginary constructions and economic teleology. In consequence they have no way of showing the relationship between the new subjectivist methods and Mises's analyses of economic phenomena. It is this gap that the present book is intended to fill.

Purpose of the Chapters

Several chapters are especially devoted to describing aspects of Misesian economics. These include chapters two, three, and four. Chapter two introduces the new subjectivism as a revolution against positivism and against elitism. It contrasts the new subjectivism with the old. Then it follows Mises in describing the concepts of theory, history, praxeology, economic theory, "applied economics," and hypothesis-testing. Chapter three shows how Mises derived the a priori categories of human action and discusses some issues related to a priori reasoning. Chapter four follows Mises in showing why the method of contrasting images of functions is necessary and describes the initial image of the market economy.

The book does more, however, than merely to describe Mises's contributions to economics. It goes beyond Mises in a number of ways. In chapter five, it clarifies Mises's method of contrasting images of functions by systematically constructing an analogy between the task of describing action in a Crusoe situation and the task of describing economic interaction in a market economy.

In chapter six, the method of contrasting images of functions is used to systematically derive categories of entrepreneurial action. The result is that one can readily see why Mises emphasized the entrepreneurial characteristics of appraisement, the employment of the specific factors, and uncertainty-bearing. Besides this, a number of clarifications and corrections to Mises's descriptions of entrepreneurship are made.

Chapter seven uses the method of contrasting images of functions to elucidate the same characteristics of the market economy described by Mises. These are competition, consumer sovereignty, the relationships among prices at different orders in the structure of production, and the transmission and economization of entrepreneurial knowledge. The difference is that the author tries to make it clear how the description of these characteristics requires one to use the method of contrast. Mises was willing to employ the concept of the entrepreneur in his description of these characteristics without reminding the reader of the need for the method of contrast. To emphasize the method, the author describes the characteristics first in a model of an economy populated only by "robot-entrepreneurs" and then asks the reader to contrast this description with what the reader knows about the way that entrepreneurship, understood on the basis of intuition and experience, would manifest itself under the conditions specified in the definition of the market economy.

Chapter eight deals with the widely misunderstood relationship between the actions of saving and the bearing of intersubjective uncertainty. Of particular interest is a type of economic interaction that Mises seems to have totally neglected—that of providing guaranty. Guaranty is a promise that if a loan is not repaid, the lender will acquire the right to the guarantor's money or to some other property or obligation. It is only by understanding the action of providing guaranty and the economic interaction entailed in getting guaranty provided that one can fully appreciate the relationship between interest, profit, and prices.

By strictly applying the method of contrasting images of functions, chapter nine presents a correct subjectivist understanding of the concepts of profit and loss. This can be contrasted with Mises's own discussions of these concepts in *Human Action*, which are shown to be lacking.

Chapter ten further clarifies the relationship between interest, profit, and prices by showing how entrepreneurship gets manifested in a market economy. Specifically, it shows how entrepreneurship is entailed in buying consumption goods and planning to consume them, in saving, and in supplying factors. It also discusses specialization in appraisement and interaction among undertakers.

Chapters eleven and twelve clarify Mises's use of the method of economic teleology. Mises did not emphasize this method and may have only partly recognized its significance. The method is clarified by using an analogy between the task of describing individual action and that of describing economic interaction. The result appears to be a link between the new subjectivist concept of equilibrium and the concept of equilibrium in modern economics. Specifically, (1) the coordination and synchronization associated with an equilibrium of independently acting robots, and (2) an equilibrium involving simultaneous commitments are described. Chapter thirteen shows how the method of economic teleology can be used to describe entrepreneurial actions at the microeconomic level. It shows how entrepreneurs create markets, legal rights, and the employment agreement that constitutes the essence of the economic firm.

In addition, there are ten appendixes, appearing at the end of the text. The first two are short essays on subjectivism, one relating to positivism and the other discussing Alfred Schuetz. The next six concern the author's interpretation of passages in *Human Action*. They include the topics of *verstehen*, uncertainty, the categories of entrepreneurial action, ideal types, the evenly rotating economy as an endpoint, and external costs. The last two are on the subject of rights-creation. The first includes a discussion of Menger's contribution to the theory of the firm. The second shows the inherent political nature of establishing rights to perform previously unregulated actions that have external effects.

Rationale for Chapter Sequencing

The author's decision to extensively elaborate the method of contrasting images of functions before presenting the method of economic teleology may seem arbitrary. Three reasons for this decision can be given. First, it is easy to misperceive the magnitude of the economic synchronization problem. Unless the reader is first aware of the complexity of the problem and of the only means the economist has to comprehend this complexity (namely, the method of contrasting images of functions), there is a danger that he or she will fail to comprehend economic teleology's limited, yet essential contribution to economic understanding. To avoid this danger, one who reads the chapters in order will start his or her study by taking a macroeconomic view. As a result, the reader will be correctly inclined to associate the actions that contribute to synchronization with appraisement, decisions about factor employment, uncertainty-bearing, and guaranty provision. He or she will be less inclined to use metaphors like the "market process," the "system of prices," and the "order" of "the market." In the author's view, the use of these metaphors detracts and possibly subverts the main message that subjectivism seeks to give.

Second, the core of this book (chapters four through ten) takes off from chapter fourteen of Mises's *Human Action*, which is based on the method of contrasting images of functions. From this base it explores, in greater measure than Mises, the implications of using this method. It would detract from this purpose to interject a discussion of the method of economic teleology.

Third, the method of economic teleology cannot be fully understood unless one adopts the macroeconomic view. This macroeconomic view enables one to more fully comprehend a more complete typology of coordination and synchronization actions. This book does not develop such a typology; it is a first step. A merit of presenting economic teleology later than the contrasting images of functions is that it points the way towards the next step.

NOTES

1. Some readers may object to the use of the terms classical and neoclassical. Indeed, Hicks, who was largely responsible for the term neoclassical, has suggested that it be expunged from the language (Aspromourgos 1986, 269). Rothbard (1973) has used these terms in his interesting history of the "praxeological tradition." Specifically, he calls Say, Cairnes, and Senior classical economists, while Menger, Bohm-Bawerk, Wieser, and Mises are called neoclassical economists. He also identifies Walras and Pareto as members of the positivist-mathematical school. Oddly, Rothbard omits J. B. Clark, Wicksteed, Schumpeter, and Knight. A close reading of these authors indicates that they used the method that Mises elaborated in *Human Action*. Other neoclassical economists like Marshall, Wicksell, and Fisher also used the method, although their expositions were less straightforward and more positivist-mathematical than those of J. B. Clark, Wicksteed, Schumpeter, and Knight. In any event, the use of the terms classical and neoclassical follows Rothbard's lead, although the author has in mind a wider set of authors.

Although Mises did not distinguish between classical and neoclassical, he had this to say:

. . . Until the late nineteenth century political economy remained a science of the "economic" aspects of human action, a theory of wealth and selfishness. . . . The transformation of thought which the classical economists had initiated was brought to its consummation only by modern subjectivist economics, which converted the theory of market prices into a general theory of human choice. (1966, 3)

2. Mises says:

The specific method of economics is the method of imaginary construction.

This method is the method of praxeology. That it has been carefully elaborated and perfected in the field of economic studies in the narrower sense is due to the fact that economics, at least until now, has been the best-developed part of praxeology. Everyone who wants to express an opinion about the problems commonly called economic takes recourse to this method. (1966, 236)

3. See Mises (1966, 237) and other references in *Human Action* to the concept of an imaginary construction.

4. For the use of the method to identify the categories of causality, time, and uncertainty see Mises (1966, 22, 99, and 105, respectively). Also see chapter three of this text.

5. See Knight (1921) and Schumpeter (1934).

6. See Parts 5 and 6 of chapter ten in this text.

7. See Mises's (1981) essay on "Sociology and History."

8. For a description of the old subjectivism, see Mises (1981, chaps. 4 and 5).

9. For a more extensive discussion of the success of positivism in the colleges and universities, see appendix 1.

10. See Haberler (1981).

11. See Schuetz (1943).

12. See Gunning (1989, chaps. 1–6) for a thorough discussion of Mises's shortcomings in presenting the new subjectivism.

13. An example is Ludwig Lachmann, who has frequently extolled the virtues of Mises's conception of the market process. Lachmann says that "[t]he Austrians . . . never were able to show, with the cogency their case required, the incompatibility between the idea of planned action, the very core of Austrian economic thought, and an analytical model which knows no action, but only reaction" (1977, 164). It will be shown in this text that Mises was indeed able to show this.

14. See Rothbard (1973), Block (1980), O'Sullivan (1987), Selgin (1988), and Hoppe (1988).

Chapter 2

The New Subjectivist Revolution of Ludwig von Mises

Methodological individualism refers to the intellectual procedure of interpreting social interaction by referring to the individuals who are involved in it.[1] *Subjectivism* refers to the intellectual procedure of attempting to interpret the behavior of the interacting subjects as the subjects themselves interpret it. Subjectivism requires the social scientist to consider himself and his subjects as having common intellectual characteristics and experiences but also as having different roles and potentially different wants, abilities, and knowledge.

Menger and Jevons are normally credited with having ushered in the subjectivist revolution of the nineteenth century. At best, they only dimly perceived subjectivism as it is defined here. The new subjectivism was introduced to economics and advocated by Ludwig von Mises, albeit under a different name.[2] Its roots are more closely associated with the sociology of Max Weber and his philosopher predecessors than with the neoclassical or nineteenth-century economists.[3]

The new subjectivism, like the old subjectivism, is revolutionary. First, because of the phenomena that it defines as economic, it is a revolution against the positivism that has captivated twentieth-century economists. Second, because it assumes that subjects use the same methods of understanding each other as the economist uses to understand subjects, it is a revolution against elitism.

The purpose of this chapter is to introduce the new subjectivism and to show how it enables one to make a number of subjectivist distinctions. In Part 1, the new subjectivism is contrasted with the old subjectivism. In Part 2, the revolutionary nature of the new subjectivism is discussed. Part 3 further elucidates the new subjectivism by describing some of the distinctions that are associated with it.

1. THE OLD AND NEW SUBJECTIVISM

To Mises, subjectivism referred to the subjective theory of value that was introduced to economics in the mid-nineteenth century.[4] This meaning corresponds to what was called methodological individualism in the opening paragraph of this chapter, as it applies primarily to individual wants. In other words, it is the procedure of interpreting economic interaction by referring to individual wants. After Mises's discoveries, subjectivism acquired a deeper meaning that warrants calling it the new subjectivism. The purpose of this part of the text is to describe the new meaning.

The Old Subjectivism

Prior to Mises's treatise, subjectivism referred to the assumptions that the economist makes about subjects. A simple example is the assumption about subjective *wants*. When the economist assumes that wants are subjective he implies two things. First he implies that the wants of different subjects may be different. Second, he implies that there can be no restrictions on the type of wants that are admissable so long as they represent, or help the economist interpret, some aspect of reality in which he is interested. It is improper, for example, for the economist to maintain that the wants of a sadist should not be accounted for in the same way as the wants of a priest, provided the economist is interested in interactions involving both people.

Besides wants, the old subjectivism may be applied to *expectations*. In this event, the expectations of different individuals may be different. Whatever expectations are reasonable to assume are admissible.[5] Hayek (1945) sought to extend subjectivism at this level to *knowledge* by proposing that different individuals in a market economy have particular knowledge about economic conditions. Lachmann and Kirzner, perhaps following Hayek, have applied the old subjectivism to *plans*.[6]

In the concepts of wants, expectations, knowledge, and plans, one has more-or-less exhausted the characteristics that economists have traditionally employed to distinguish one economic actor from another.

But if it is reasonable to identify other characteristics, they also can be treated subjectively.

The revolutionary nature of the old subjectivism in its time can be seen by comparing it with the view that is usually attributed to the classical economists and that it was intended to replace. In classical economics, the behavior of subjects was thought to be governed by the forces of nature. The classical economists searched for laws of economic interaction—inevitable outcomes of economic interaction that were beyond the control of the actors.

The old subjectivist economists did not deny that there were outcomes of interaction that were beyond the control of any particular actor. But they did not believe that the cause of these outcomes should be described in the same way as an outcome of the forces of nature. On the contrary, they believed that the outcomes could only be understood by attempting to understand why individuals *choose* to interact in particular ways. As they saw it economic interaction is an outcome of the choices of the separate economic actors. To understand a particular outcome, it is necessary to understand the choices of each of the individuals, or subjects, who contribute to that outcome. Hence, the economist's attempt to understand should be conducted from a subjectivist stance.

It is true that no specific individual plans the totality of economic interaction. However, this does not mean that interaction should be attributed to the forces of nature. Instead, the outcome must be regarded as a somewhat unpredictable, yet logical, outcome of the choices of the individuals involved in the interaction.

Some old subjectivists like to emphasize the value neutrality of subjectivism. The old subjectivism limits the freedom of the economist to use his own value judgments, since he must give reasons for whatever assumptions he makes about wants, expectations, and plans.

The New Subjectivism

Mises discovered the new subjectivism by trying to understand the method of the old subjectivists. By learning to understand that method, he was able to discover errors in reasoning and solutions to problems that the old subjectivists had not satisfactorily solved. The old subjectivists took it for granted that they did not know the precise wants, abilities, expectations, knowledge, and plans of subjects. But they did not explain why it was appropriate to assume that subjects *have* these characteristics.

The new subjectivism is derived by asking how an economist decides which characteristics she should attribute to subjects. Careful analysis reveals that she endows subjects with characteristics that she knows from intuition and experience to exist in the minds of human actors.

What does introspection reveal to the economist about the characteristics of economic interaction? A large part of the answer can be known by reflecting on one's own interaction. When you think of interacting with others, what do you think of? Although you think of many things, you organize your thinking around your belief that you can think and choose. Given that you do not regard yourself as superior to others, you must project a similar ability to think and choose into others. By the same token, if economists are to avoid elitism, they must organize their studies around the idea that the other human beings organize their own interaction on the basis of their thinking and choosing.

Thinking, to be *meaningful*, must be connected with some goal. It is therefore a part of choosing. You can fantasize and you can use your memory to conjure up images from the past. You can meditate or contemplate. You can even decide to do these things because you enjoy doing them for their own sake. But when you do them for their own sake, you do not call them thinking. When you are thinking meaningfully, you believe that your thinking may or will help you make a more satisfying choice or choices than if you do not think.

You also share characteristics with other animals, such as physical sensations and instincts. Economists are not interested in these characteristics, since the characteristics are not distinctly human (i.e., part of action).

Thinking and choosing are not two separate activities. They are intimately related. In view of this, the phrase "thinking and choosing" is cumbersome. A simpler term is acting. When Mises wanted to refer to thinking and choosing, he used the term action. When the economist studies subjects, said Mises, she is studying *human actions*.[7]

To describe a human being's actions, the economist makes use of the terms wants, expectations, knowledge, and plans. But the fundamental phenomenon is action. All praxeological and economic concepts must ultimately be derived from (or defined in terms of) one's a priori understanding of the proposition that human beings act. This derivation is accomplished by using the methods of imaginary constructions and teleology.

Methodological Apriorism

Knowledge derived from the idea that human beings act can be called *a priori* knowledge, since every normal human being takes such an idea for granted even though he may not be able to agree with others on a means of elucidating it. A priori knowledge has a status similar to the primitive concepts in mathematics.

Recognizing the a priori nature of knowledge about action, Mises called his approach *methodological apriorism*.[8] Because Mises's methodological apriorism is actually the descendant of the old subjectivist approach to economic phenomena, the author has labelled it the new subjectivism. Thus the new subjectivism and Mises's methodological apriorism are identical.

2. THE REVOLUTIONARY NATURE OF THE NEW SUBJECTIVISM

The new subjectivism is revolutionary in two distinct senses. First, it is a revolution in the definition of economic phenomena. Second, it is a revolution in methodology that holds out the prospect of undermining the elitist approach to studying observable events that is taken by most modern economists. Consider each in turn.

A Revolution in the Definition of Economic Phenomena

Mises revolutionized the definition of economic phenomena by limiting it to subjectively defined rational action. By Mises's definition, all economic phenomena are the consequence of purposeful behavior. He called this purposeful behavior human action. Thus, the title of his treatise in economics reveals his revolutionary definition. He called the theory of human action *praxeology*. Praxeological reasoning consists of using logic (as opposed to mathematics) to reason about human action.

Economic interaction refers to voluntary interaction among actors in which money is a focal point. In defining and describing economic interaction, the new subjectivist economist is primarily interested in how subjects deal with each other. She is only secondarily interested in their physical environment. Indeed, in constructing definitions relating to economic interaction, the new subjectivism requires the economist to try to imagine the interaction in the absence of a specific physical world. Such a procedure results in a theory that is applicable to every imaginable physical world in which individuals interact. Consider, for example, the subjectivist definition of uncertainty. To the subjectivist economist, uncertainty means *intersubjective* uncertainty. This is the uncertainty that individuals have about each others' wants, abilities, and knowledge. The subjectivist economist is only secondarily interested in "uncertainty" about the physical world. The latter is the subject of the natural sciences.

The economist cannot, of course, succeed in abstracting completely from the physical world. The procedure of attempting to do so is of the utmost importance, however. Without using it, abstract economic theory would be impossible.

The new subjectivist also attempts to abstract from the cultural and political environments. Economic theory applies to many imaginable cultural and political environments.

New subjectivism vs. positivism. Mises's Austrian predecessors and many of the neoclassicals developed economic definitions that abstracted from the physical, cultural, and political environments. But they failed to provide sound epistemological foundations. As a result, they could not effectively defend their definitions against the positivist revolution of the twentieth century. One of Mises's major goals was to develop a methodology that could not only be defended against positivism but that also would yield an irrefutable argument against it.

The argument was based on the recognition that whenever one human being describes human behavior to another human being, he makes judgments about the wants, expectations, knowledge, plans, and understandings of the behaver. It is possible to avoid making such judgments and to merely describe the physical movements, but one who does this would fail to recognize the humanness of the behavior. Moreover, he would, in essence, disregard a means of description that is uniquely available to students of human behavior. Thus, positivism is possible but it is unhuman. It is based on a false analogy between natural phenomena, which do not think and choose, and human beings, who do.

The refutation of positivism has become especially relevant in the last forty years. In recent mainstream economics, positivism has manifested itself in three ways. The first is the use of mathematical modelling and statistical definitions of economic phenomena to make predictions about the future. The second is the institutionalist opposition to isolating economic phenomena from the specific political, cultural, and physical environment. The third is historical positivism, which is like institutionalism but that also advocates "holism." The new subjectivism refutes statistical, institutional, and historical positivism in the study of human beings.

A Revolution Against Elitism

The subjectivist revolution is also a revolution against elitist methodology. Economists tend to regard economics as a profession in which economists study subjects. As a student of the behavior of other human beings, the economist sets herself apart. The economist acts as if she is a member of an elite. Mises's new subjectivism destroyed elitism by erasing the distinction between the economist and the economic subject. The economist, as Mises defined her, does not think and choose differently than the subjects studied. She lives and interacts in the same world. She shares the subjects' means of perceiving, conceptualizing, and understanding. She cannot detach the method of interpreting interaction from the method used by her subjects and is likely to make errors if she tries.[9]

One might defend elitism by arguing that the economist must stand aloof from her subject matter in order to achieve a perspective that economic subjects do not or cannot be expected to achieve. Unless the economist stands aloof, the argument goes, she will not be able to obtain the broad perspective needed in order to deal with macroeconomic problems, such as large fluctuations in the purchasing power of money and large fluctuations in the evaluations of factors of production.

There is no quarrel with the argument that the economist has a different role than the economic subject. That the two have different roles, however, implies nothing about whether their methods of thinking should be different. Indeed, it is evident upon reflection that their methods should be the same.

In their interactions, every normal human being recognizes that others have independent wills and the ability to think and choose. When a normal human being attempts to make sense of someone else's behavior, he conceptually interchanges his own ego with that of the other. He first tries to determine whether the behavior is purposeful. Then, assuming that he determines that it is, he tries to understand the actions of the subject by pretending to possess what he assumes to be the subject's wants, abilities, and knowledge. If the number of people the economist is trying to understand is large, she must use the methods of contrasting images of functions and economic teleology. These are precisely the methods that Mises argued economists should and do use.

The goal of the economist—to understand others' actions—is like that of other human beings who interact. The main difference is that the economist is in the vanguard. She identifies with a tradition of economist predecessors, whose studies have revealed ways of reducing the complex interactions of many interacting individuals to simple images that contain essential functions and to hypotheses about how and why the functions came to be performed. The economist's inventiveness lies with her ability to construct realistic yet simple images that are relevant to the issues in which she is interested.

3. THE DEFINITION OF ECONOMICS AND OTHER MISESIAN CONCEPTS

Economics (economic theory) as a system of thought is a branch of the more general theory of human action. Theory is required to make interpretations of human events, or, in other words, to do history. The interpretation of economic events is applied economics. In this section, the relationships among these concepts are discussed.

Theory and History

The abstract idea that individuals act, as distinct from the specific actions they perform, provides the basis for the conceptual separation of theory from the description or prediction of specific actions. *Theory* (or conception) consists of a set of logical deductions or implications derived from the a priori knowledge that human beings act and interact. Theory may be expanded by adding subsidiary assumptions. Doing *history* consists of using theory in conjunction with specific assumptions or hypotheses about the characteristics of individuals and other factors to describe or explain historical events.[10]

In doing history, one makes hypotheses about the specific thinking and choosing that individuals have done. Since it is reasonable to assume that different individuals have different wants, abilities, and knowledge, it can be said roughly that the historian must have *specific* knowledge of the individuals' different wants, abilities, and knowledge. This specific knowledge is distinct from the a priori knowledge that individuals act. The historian knows a priori that his fellow human beings have wants, abilities, knowledge, expectations and plans; the theory he uses is based on this. When he does history, he uses his theory along with his hypotheses about specific wants, and so on, to describe the events in terms of their human causes. Prediction is history pushed into the future.

Praxeology, Economics, and Economic Theory

Praxeology is the theory of human action and interaction. Literally, it is the use of logic to elucidate the meaning and implications of human action. A branch of praxeology is *economics*, which in Mises's terminology means the same thing as *economic theory*. Economics is derived from the traditional subject matter of economists—prices, quantities, types of products and services, and the relations among them.[11] It is a theory of interaction in which choices are assumed to be made on the basis of monetary calculation. Thus, praxeology is broader than economics. It is based on a priori and subsidiary assumptions that may or may not specify that thinking and choosing are performed on the basis of monetary calculation. Praxeology encompasses other branches besides economic theory, although to date other branches have not developed.[12]

Mises used the terms economic theory and economics interchangeably. Since his definition of economic theory differs from that of most modern economists and since many modern economists further distinguish economic theory from economics, Mises's usage can be a source of misinterpretation.

Applied Economics or the Study of Economic History

The relationship between theory and history has an analog in economics in the relationship between economic theory and *applied economics*.[13] Applied economics can be defined as the description and interpretation of real economic phenomena.

To see what this means, it is necessary to construct some definitions. An *economic phenomenon* is defined as the consequence of a set of choices to exchange using money, as opposed to bartering. From the standpoint of the methodologist, it is useful to distinguish two categories of economic phenomena: hypothetical and real. *Hypothetical* economic phenomena refer to those that are represented in the images of the economist. They are deductions based on a priori and subsidiary assumptions relating to action, exchange, and money. *Real* economic phenomena are the economic phenomena of everyday life.[14]

Real economic phenomena never exist in isolation. They are always connected with other, non-economic, *historical* phenomena. Historical phenomena consist of a combination of economic phenomena, non-chosen behavior, coercion, deceit, fraud, barter, non-economic reciprocal action, culture, and natural phenomena. The *economist as theorist* constructs images of hypothetical economic phenomena by making assumptions about the choices that cause them. The goal in building such images is to match the hypothetical economic phenomena with the real economic phenomena that the economist suspects are imbedded in the historical phenomena she can partly observe. Such a match constitutes a description or interpretation of the real economic phenomena.

To construct images of hypothetical economic phenomena, the economist must make four classes of assumptions. First, she must make a priori assumptions about individual action. These include the assumption that individuals think and choose in an environment of time and uncertainty and that subjects are different. A priori assumptions are discussed in chapter three. Second, she must make assumptions about the non-economic environment within which the economic phenomena occur. These are assumptions about non-chosen behavior, culture, coercion, deceit, fraud, barter, self-production, and the physical environment. To make the appropriate assumptions, the economist must step outside the narrow field of economics and use knowledge of biology, psychology, sociology, anthropology, law, politics, war, gamesmanship, one- and two-person production and exchange, and natural science. Third, she must make general economic assumptions. She assumes that individuals experience diminishing marginal utility, that there are diminishing returns to a variable factor of production, that labor yields disutility, that there are gains (defined individually and subjectively) from specialization and the division of labor, that there is existing capital, and that choices are made on the basis of monetary calculation. Fourth, she must make specific assumptions that are dictated by the issue with which she is concerned.[15]

Ideally the applied economist would try to construct an exact duplicate of real economic phenomena. To do this, she would formulate initial assumptions or hypotheses about the wants, abilities, and knowledge of individuals (subjects) who she believes are significant in causing the phenomenon and/or whose actions are effected by it. Then, she would formulate assumptions or hypotheses about the means that the subjects use to coordinate the separate actions. Next, the applied economist would substitute her ego for the egos of the subjects. That is, the economist would put herself in their shoes. The purpose would be to help her judge whether her assumptions or hypotheses about subjects' actions and understandings are reasonable. Then the economist would deduce the consequences, given her assumptions and hypotheses. If she became satisfied that the deduced economic phenomena match the real economic phenomena she had set out to duplicate, and if she believed that the assumptions, hypotheses, and means of coordinating actions were realistic and reasonable, then the economist would conclude that she possessed an understanding of the economic actions of subjects.

The economist might decide that she had not succeeded in duplicating the phenomena in question or that some of her assumptions or hypotheses were not reasonable. In this event, she may redo the second step. An iterative process would ensue in which the economist tries out a number of different assumptions and hypotheses until she is satisfied.

The applied economist can never expect an exact match. One reason is the impossibility of fully detaching the real economic phenomena from non-economic historical phenomena. A second reason is that real economic phenomena are extremely complex in their own right. Because a complete understanding of the economic actions of subjects is out of the question, the applied economist is forced by virtue of her subject matter to pursue a different goal. She must be satisfied to construct simplified images of hypothetical economic phenomena. Such images do not attempt to capture all of the aspects of real economic phenomena. They are meant to illustrate or elucidate some aspects that the economist believes are relevant to issues in which she is interested. They only yield glimpses of some aspects of real economic phenomena.

Judgments and Hypothesis-Testing in Applied Economics

To study economic phenomena, the economist must conceptually separate the economic aspects of historical phenomena from the non-economic aspects. For this reason, although it is correct to say that applied economists study reality in the sense that they study the economic aspects of reality, it is incorrect to say that reality unambiguously reveals whether the economists' descriptions and interpretations of the economic aspects are accurate.

Does this mean that the applied economist cannot test his hypotheses about whether he has indeed identified a real economic phenomenon? Is the applied economist left with only his personal, subjective judgment? Although this is not the case, it does mean that the procedures the applied economist uses must be radically different from those used by natural scientists, who study physical reality. Hypothesis-making in economics consists of contrasting one's images of economic phenomena with reality while, at the same time, making judgments about which aspects of reality are economic. The hypotheses to be tested are whether a hypothetical economic phenomenon matches a real economic phenomenon and how close the match is. To test these hypotheses, one must (1) know economic theory, and (2) know the particular influences relating to culture, politics, and the natural environment, among other things. As in all interpretations of historical phenomena, the only true test is the appeal to the reason of one's peers. The hypothesis passes the test if it can be defended logically and satisfactorily.[16]

CONCLUSION

The main goal of economics is to shed light on some issue or problem in which the economist is interested. To do this, the economist must attempt to understand the economic actions of subjects. Because real economic phenomena are embedded in historical phenomena and because they are so complex, the applied economist must be content to construct simplified images that help to identify and elucidate particular characteristics that are relevant to her main goal. The new subjectivism is the only reasonable means for the applied economist to accomplish her secondary goal. It asserts, among other things, that the assumptions in the economist's images must fall into one of four categories: (1) a priori assumptions, (2) assumptions about the non-economic environment within which the economic phenomena occur, (3) general assumptions that define the phenomena as economic, and (4) specific assumptions that relate to the issue in which the economist is interested. In short, the applied economist must combine economic theory with her knowledge of non-economic facts.

NOTES

1. Methodological individualism has mistakenly been contrasted with methodological holism (Shand 1980, 15–19). Mises demonstrated that there is no alternative in social science to methodological individualism (1966, 41–43; 1978, 80–83). The illusion that methodological holism is an alternative may arise from the analogy that is often drawn between the investigation of natural phenomena and social phenomena (White 1984, p. 24).

2. The place of Mises's work in the history of economic method was systematically presented by Kirzner (1976). Rothbard (1973) provides a complementary treatment. Unfortunately, neither author seems to have appreciated Mises's revolutionary methods, as they are described in this book.

3. Subjectivism is often thought to be synonymous with *verstehen*, a method elucidated by Max Weber and developed further by Ludwig Lachmann (1971). The definition of subjectivism used in this book is deeper than *verstehen*. It recognizes that to apply the procedure of *verstehen*, one must assume that the economist and the subjects she studies have a common procedure for interpreting the world. The interpreter uncovers this common procedure by means of introspection and uses it to develop a framework from which to construct her definitions and to make descriptions. For the source of the author's definition of subjectivism, see Appendix 2. Also see Part 1 of chapter one.

4. The subjectivist revolution of the nineteenth century is different from the so-called marginal utility revolution. See chapter five in Mises (1981).

5. Lachmann (1976, 1983) attributes subjectivism with respect to expectations to Keynes and to Shackle. Lachmann's own paper on expectations (1943) would also seem to qualify.

6. For economic writings that are based on the assumption of the subjectivity of plans, see Kirzner (1966), Lachmann (1978), and Lachmann (1971). The idea for making the plan the foundation for economic analysis may have first been suggested by Felix Kaufmann, another participant in Mises's Vienna seminars. Kaufmann says: "According to the subjective theory of value the central economic problems, i.e., those of price determination, can only be tackled with the prospect of achieving useful results if the economic activity to which they refer is traced back to an economic plan" (1933, 395). The term *plan* was also used in the great socialist planning debate of the 1930s, which involved Mises and Hayek (Vaughn 1980). Hayek frequently used the term *plan* in his first paper on knowledge (Hayek 1937, 41).

7. It is interesting to note a certain ambiguity in the term human action. Human action refers to what economic subjects do, of course. But because it applies to all human beings, it also refers to what economists do. Thus, in a book entitled *Human Action*, one should not be surprised to find descriptions both of what subjects do and of what economists do. The presence of both types of descriptions is one of the distinguishing features of Mises's book. (It

is also a source of confusion to economists who are unaccustomed to this perspective.)

8. See Mises (1966, 32–36 and 64–69).

9. To quote Mises:

> The intellectual methods of science do not differ in kind from those applied by the common man in his daily mundane reasoning. The scientist uses the same tools which the layman uses; he merely uses them more skillfully and cautiously. Understanding is not a privilege of the historians. It is everybody's business. In observing the conditions of his environment everybody is a historian. Everybody uses understanding in dealing with the uncertainty of future events to which he must adjust his own actions. . . . (1966, 58).

10. See Mises (1966, 51–58).

11. See Mises (1966, 232–34).

12. Rothbard (1951) describes other branches of praxeology: (1) the theory of the isolated individual, (2) the theory of hostile action or war, (3) the theory of games, and (4) unknown. In the category he calls economic theory, he includes the theory of barter and theories that concern coercive intervention and abolition of the unhampered market. In addition to economic theory, Mises's *Human Action* (1966) includes the theory of the isolated individual, a theory of barter, a theory of coercive intervention, a theory of the abolition of the unhampered market (socialism), and a theory of war.

13. The author is not aware of Mises's use of the term *applied economics*. Rothbard uses the term. He says: "The praxeologist contrasts, on the one hand, the body of qualitative, nomothetic laws developed by economic theory, and on the other, a myriad of unique, complex historical facts of both the past and the future" (Rothbard 1973, 321). So far as the author can tell, the definition used here is identical to Rothbard's. Mises (1966, 867–68) uses the phrase "the study of economic history."

14. Mises did not use the term *economic phenomenon*. He used the term *characteristic of the market economy* to refer to both real economic phenomena and to hypothetical economic phenomena. As a result, some of his discussion is difficult to follow.

15. Mises does not distinguish between more fundamental subsidiary assumptions and less fundamental ones. For an interpretation that is similar to this one, see White (1984, 18).

16. These points are discussed by Mises (1966, 236–37).

Chapter 3

The A Priori Categories of Human Action

In its everyday interaction with its physical environment, the small child is a personification of the scientific method. From the moment it is born, it begins experimenting with physical objects and discovers how to cause the arrangements to change. This preconscious experimentation, combined with the reality of the physical world, is apparently responsible for the child's development of a conception of time and for its learning that the effects of some actions are more predictable than the effects of others. Thus, it seems, the child is led to acquire a sense of physical causality, time, and uncertainty. All this happens before the child learns to do what is ordinarily called abstract thinking.

Could the conceptions of physical causality, time, and uncertainty that one observes in adults develop without the hands-on preconscious childhood experiences? It is difficult to imagine how. Prior, hands-on experience with the scientific method appears to be a prerequisite for human thought.[1] In short, the human being acts; later she comes to conceptualize her action.

The truth of these remarks is reflected in one's effort to construct a defense of the scientific method in the study of natural phenomena. The usual defense is based on pragmatism. It argues that the method should be used because it has enabled human beings to make great scientific discoveries. People accept the defense partly because of the discoveries but mostly because it is supported by what they already know from experience.

Economics does not deal directly with natural phenomena. Because its principal subject matter is interaction among human beings, its concepts of causality, time, and uncertainty take on a different meaning than they have in the natural sciences. Causality refers not to a person's causing a physical result but to her causing another person to choose differently than otherwise. Time refers not to clock time but to the time that an individual regards as relevant to her decision making. And uncertainty refers not to the fact that a human being cannot fully predict physical events but to the fact that she cannot fully predict the choices that others will make. It is convenient to call these the social concepts of causality, time, and uncertainty.

Like the physical concepts of causality, time, and uncertainty, the social concepts are also used in everyday actions before the developing child learns to conceptualize them. At some point in her development, the child learns to conceptually interchange her position with that of other human beings. Somehow the child learns to predict others' behavior not only as she would predict the behavior of physical objects but also as she would predict her own behavior, which the child knows is strongly influenced by her freedom to choose or not to choose.[2]

Suppose that a person is asked to defend her use of the method of conceptually interchanging positions and her understanding of the social concepts of causality, time, and uncertainty. The person could not refer to scientific successes. The best she could do is to refer to her successes in the social world. One could describe a process used to sell something, to persuade someone to change his mind, to force someone to perform some action, and so on. In addition, one could show how she was able to predict the results of some interaction, such as an athletic contest, a physical confrontation among political groups with opposing points of view, or the shifting of resources from lower-valued uses to higher-valued ones. In these cases, the person would acknowledge that one cannot be certain that what she has described are successes. To know for certain, one would have to be able to verify that the actors themselves perceived and used their ends and means in the way the predictor believes they did. Such knowledge must be speculative, since one person cannot be certain about what is in the minds of others.

The fact that such knowledge is speculative does not mean that the individual is unsure that she possesses it. The human being is probably less sure that she can cause the corner grocer to sell her an apple than that she can hammer a nail. Nevertheless, she is certain that some human beings can cause others to behave differently than they otherwise would and that they can accomplish this by developing a strategy that entails conceptually interchanging positions with them. Thus, the human being also defends her method of interchanging positions and her social concepts of causality, time, and uncertainty, in the social world by referring to successes. But she must ask her colleagues to appreciate her argument by referring to the colleagues' own, intuitively understandable successes in the social world.

When a person acts in the social world, she can choose not to use the ability to conceptually interchange positions. A person can treat others as physical objects, or robots. For this, she would not want or need the social concepts of causality, time, and uncertainty. But to follow this path would indicate a foolish disregard for what she knows to be true. In social interaction, a person takes it for granted that she and others have ends and means and that they share a common meaning of the social concepts of time and uncertainty. She realizes that some people may not use their reasoning abilities in some situations and that other people do not possess such abilities (they are not normal).

Viewing the concepts of physical causality, time, and uncertainty from the standpoint of a developed adult, the student of action simply takes it for granted that she and others possess the concepts. Similarly, the economist takes it for granted that economic subjects possess the social concepts of causality, time, and uncertainty. This taking-for-granted of both the physical and social concepts is called *methodological apriorism*.

The purpose of this chapter is to show how Mises was led to methodological apriorism and to show how he derived the a priori categories. Part 1 introduces the problem of "intersubjective understanding" and shows how Mises was able to solve this problem. Part 2 derives the a priori categories. Part 3 discusses some issues related to methodological apriorism.

1. MISES'S SOLUTION TO THE PROBLEM OF INTERSUBJECTIVE UNDERSTANDING

Every student of human action must face the problem of intersubjective understanding of human actions. This part begins by describing this problem. Mises apparently discovered and resolved the problem by thinking about the debate between Carl Menger and the historicists and by evaluating Max Weber's contribution to the debate. These topics are also discussed in this part.

The Study of Human Action by Human Actors

Whatever else economics is, it is the study of one group by another group of the same species. Because of this, all questions of method, including what to study, how to study it, and how to communicate one's studies, must begin with knowledge or assumptions about the nature of the species (i.e., about human nature).

Human beings have many characteristics. Like all things, they are comprised of chemical substances. Like other living things, human beings respond to stimuli. Finally, as "higher order" mammals, humans have biological drives. There is one aspect of human nature, however, that is uniquely human. This is the ability to think, reason, plan, and choose (or, more simply, to act).

The fact that all normal human beings act means that it is possible at some level of abstraction for one human being to understand other normal human beings merely by contrasting an image of his own action with the others' behaviors.[3] A person can know something about another human being not because of the specific behavior he observes but because he knows that the behavior may be the manifestation of an action that is performed by a being of the same species as himself. He achieves this understanding by conceptually interchanging positions with the other person.

By making hypotheses about their specific wants, abilities, and knowledge, one human being can speculate about the actions that other normal human beings will perform. However, one would never think that such speculations are as accurate as his *general* belief that other human beings have wants, abilities, and knowledge—that is, that they act.

These remarks apply to the praxeologist and economist. Human beings who adopt these roles can employ a method of defining, studying, and describing other human beings that cannot legitimately be used by the physical scientist or biologist. This method consists of projecting assumptions or hypotheses about specific wants, abilities, and knowledge into the subjects they are studying. The economist knows that he is not identical to other human beings, but he also knows that he has in common with others the ability to act. Beginning with this a priori knowledge, the economist can strive to acquire an *intersubjective understanding of actions*.[4]

The subjects studied by the economist also can acquire an intersubjective understanding of actions. The methods of the new subjectivism require the economist to take account of this possibility. Because of this, a more complete description of the economist's goal is that he strives to acquire an intersubjective understanding of individuals' intersubjective understandings of each others' actions and of their understandings. This lengthy expression is implied by the phrase intersubjective understanding of actions.

Historical Antecedents

The reasoning contained in the last subsection is so obviously correct that one must wonder how anyone doing social science or economics could think differently. Yet before Mises, even the best economists failed to appreciate these points. Since Mises, only a handful have followed his lead. Thus it seems worthwhile to trace the probable sources of the development of Mises's thinking about the intersubjective understanding of actions.

Menger vs. the German historicists. Mises seems to have introduced himself to the central issue by studying the nineteenth-century debate between the German historicists and Carl Menger.[5] In that debate, the historicists argued that economics was art, or, worse yet, ideology. They regarded a science of economics, defined as a study that could shed light on historical facts, as impossible. They saw economics as sophistry. Historians, they said, should confine their activities to the mere reporting of facts as they occurred.

Menger argued in opposition that to do history the historian must reconstruct in her mind the human interaction of the past. Such a reconstruction invariably requires the use of logic and imaginary constructions. Logic and imaginary constructions are the essence of economics.

In economics, Menger said, the construction of images enables the economist to deduce *laws*. Such laws are not like the laws in natural science since they cannot be proven by experiment or observation. Instead they are logical laws—deductions made on the basis of fundamental assumptions. To be called laws, the assumptions must be so fundamental and so general that they are widely accepted. Therefore, argued Menger, economics is not ideology. It is the use of logic to derive laws that are useful in interpreting historical events.

Mises on the contradiction of historicism. Although Menger's position was essentially correct, his mode of presentation indicated to Mises that he had not been able to discover the fundamental point at issue. As Mises saw the situation, the arguments advanced by the German historicists did not at all reflect the actual history that the

Germans had done. The German historicists did not merely record facts. If they had, everyone would have realized that the historicists were not doing what was widely understood to be history. As Max Weber and others had pointed out, they typically interpreted the historical facts by referring to the motivations of people in history. Mises recognized that unless the historicists referred to motivations, their reporting of facts could not correctly be called history, that is, it could not be about human beings. When human beings describe the behavior of other human beings, they necessarily make statements about their understandings of the actions of subjects.

The inherent contradiction of historicism is revealed, according to Mises, when one identifies and describes precisely what historians do. What they do, Mises pointed out, is employ methodological apriorism. They make implicit, a priori assumptions about human nature. They add specific assumptions about wants, abilities, and knowledge. Finally, they use assumptions that enable them to construct simplified models of aggregated behavior.[6]

It follows that the arguments of the historicists are contradicted by their very actions. If they are correct in their view that what Menger had called the deduction of economic laws is really ideology, then the history done by the historicists also must be ideology. Yet the historicists claimed to do ideologically free history.

Mises on Weber. Max Weber had also criticized historicism. Thus it was logical that Mises would try to evaluate Weber's criticism and to contrast it with his own.[7] Weber's criticism emerged out of his concern with the issue of whether history could be value-free. He observed what he regarded as biased interpretations of history given by university professors and asked whether the bias could be removed. His answer was based on his view of the methods that he believed must be used to study history. Specifically, he believed that the historian constructs arbitrary *ideal types* to describe the human beings and groups who are involved in historical events. Yet the historian himself can be described as an ideal type who is part of an historical event, namely, the study of history. Thus, the way to understand the methods of history is to try to construct an ideal type of the historian who constructs ideal types to refer to people in history.

By focusing on the ideal type of this historian, Weber achieved a political coup. He effectively recorded his objections against the biased history taught by his colleagues in the university. At the same time, he was able to save history from nihilism. A teacher, following Weber, could seemingly avoid inserting her own values by teaching what various value-oriented historians had said instead of teaching what the historical events were. The teacher who wanted to be regarded as "more value-free" than her colleagues could teach students to use the same methods to understand other historians as the historians used to understand individuals in history.

It is true that the teacher must use her own arbitrary ideal types to classify people as historians. Yet she can seem to rise above the values of the historians. By placing herself at the top of the pyramid comprised of people who construct ideal types, so to speak, the teacher could look down at the values used by those who study others' values. From this vantage point, it is easy for the teacher to claim that her view is less value-laden than that of the historians about whom she teaches.

In assessing Weber's argument, Mises pointed out that Weber had a mistaken and antiquated view of economics. Weber failed to recognize that economists had effectively resolved the value question. Neglecting the positions that Walter Bagehot and Carl Menger had taken during their earlier debate with the German historicists, Weber conceived of economics as a discipline concerned with the study of history. In fact, said Mises, economics is concerned mainly with the deduction of theory on the basis of fundamental characteristics of human beings that no normal human being could deny he possesses. When economists interpret historical events they do not construct ideal types. They attempt to describe the characteristics of those events that must be present if the individuals who interact are normal human beings and if certain other conditions, which comprise the subsidiary assumptions of economic theory, are present. In fact, said Mises, although this method was discovered by economists, it is not confined to economics. It is the method used by sociologists and, indeed, by all actors (who are normal human beings) in society.[8]

The value problem with which Weber was concerned is not an issue for economics, since economics is not directly concerned with the interpretation of historical events. It is true that when the applied economist uses economic theory to try to explain an historical event, he is implicitly claiming that the assumptions of his theory match the actual circumstances that are present. If the economist is wrong, then his theory will not be *relevant*. By introducing the criterion of relevance, Mises was able to resolve the value question raised by Weber.[9]

An economist may erroneously claim that his theory is relevant in the interpretation of an historical event. He may even require his students to repeat such a claim. But such actions should be understood as violating the principle of relevance, not as presenting a biased interpretation of history.

Mises published these ideas in a series of essays written in the 1920s. The essays are in a book titled in English as *Epistemological Problems of Economics* (1981). The same conclusions are contained in the first part of *Human Action* (1966). The latter provides the focus for the discussion in the remainder of this chapter.

2. THE NEW SUBJECTIVISM AND THE A PRIORI CATEGORIES

A priori knowledge "refers to the essential and necessary character of the logical structure of the human mind." Every attempt to prove the presence of the relations in "the logical structure of the human mind . . . must presuppose their validity. It is impossible to explain them to a being who would not possess them on his own account" (Mises 1966, 34).[10] In this part, it is shown how Mises derived the a priori categories.

Prerequisites of Human Action

A prior knowledge begins with the definition of human action. Human action is defined by three prerequisites: (1) the human being's "eagerness to substitute a more satisfactory state of affairs for a less satisfactory," (2) his imagination of "conditions which suit him better," and (3) "the expectation that purposeful behavior has the power to remove or at least alleviate the felt uneasiness" (pp. 13–14). These prerequisites imply a number of characteristics of human action, which Mises called a priori categories. Each is discussed in turn.

Ends and Means

The three prerequisites imply what Mises called the logical relations of the human mind, or a priori categories. The first logical relation, or a priori category, that Mises deduced is that of ends and means: "the end, goal, or aim of any action is always the relief from a felt uneasiness. . . . A thing becomes a means when human reason plans to employ it for the attainment of some end and human action really employs it for this purpose" (p. 93).

Modern economists have replaced the "fluid" notion of ends and means with the static concepts of an order of preference and goods that can be used to satisfy those preferences. From the subjectivist standpoint, when the economist says that a subject has a scale of values or an order of preference, he is merely interpreting or expressing the ultimate given—ends and means—in a particular way. If the economist means something different than that human beings possess ends and means, then his meaning is inconsistent with the aim of economics. "Every notion is always in perfect agreement with the scale of values or wants because these scales are nothing but an instrument for the interpretation of man's acting" (p. 95).[11]

It is sometimes said that economics is a *logic of choice*. Mises defined it as a branch of praxeology, or the *logic of action*. The logic of choice is a part of the logic of action to the extent that its concepts ultimately refer to action. If the concepts of a logic of choice are intended to mean something different, then it is not part of the logic of action or economics. A logic of choice cannot capture the creative, or entrepreneurial, elements of economic interaction. It may, however, help elucidate this element by providing a model with which the economist's initial, intuitive, and experience-based understanding of action can be contrasted.[12]

Does praxeology assume that preferences are consistent, or transitive? If what is meant by this is that the economist can conceive of an individual acting in any way other than in accord with what the economist takes to be the individual's scale of values, the answer is "no." Because the statement that an individual has a scale of values is simply another way of saying that human action implies ends, the concept of consistency, or transitivity, is irrelevant. An individual's preferences need not be consistent or transitive for her to act purposefully.

Causality and Teleology

The second a priori category is what the praxeologist calls *causality*. The human actor must "know" what it means for her choice to cause a state of affairs to be different from what it otherwise would be: "Acting requires and presupposes the category of causality. Only a man who sees the world in the light of causality is fitted to act. In this sense we say that causality is a category of action." (p. 22).

The concept of causality is actually a dual concept. On the one hand, there is the notion that behavior is caused by an act of will. On the other hand, there is the notion that every phenomenon, including an act of will, must have a first cause. In spite of the apparent contradiction of these two ideas, causality and teleology coexist in the mind (pp. 22–25).

Time

The third a priori category is the concept of time: "The notion of change implies the notion of a temporal sequence. . . . The concepts of change and of time are inseparably linked together. . . Human reason is . . . incapable of conceiving the ideas of timeless existence and of timeless action" (p. 99).

There are two concepts of time. The first is time as understood by an actor, or subjective time. The second is clock time, which can be called objective. It is based on the movements of physical objects or forces.

The following subjectivist procedure may help the non-subjectivist understand this distinction. Try to think of a world in which there is no way to tell the objective time. In such a world you can not tell whether it is one o'clock or two o'clock, day or night, January or June. The physical world would be entirely changeless and timeless. Now try to imagine further that in such a world you are still able to act (i.e., to choose a more satisfactory state of affairs than would otherwise exist). If you could put yourself in this imaginary state of mind, you would recognize a system of measuring time that is based entirely on your action. The system would be fully subjective.

Now imagine that you cannot act (i.e., choose). Then no concept of time would be meaningful to you. Even if the physical world still changed, if you could not choose, time would have no meaning to you.

These mental exercises justify the assertion that the relevance of time to human beings—and, therefore, its meaning—derives not from the physical changes but from the fact that human beings possess the three prerequisites. In other words, action implies subjective time.[13]

The same mental exercises enable one to define the concepts of past and future without direct reference to clock time. That is, they enable one to see what would be necessary to define these terms subjectively. The *future* is a "time" at which a state of being that is more satisfactory than otherwise is expected to exist. To envision the future, the human actor conjures up an image of a more satisfactory state along with the image of a sequence of behaviors he must perform to bring it about. Then he defines the future as the point in his images at which the sequence of behaviors is completed. "Man becomes conscious of time when he plans to convert a less satisfactory [anticipated future state] into a more satisfactory future state'' (p. 100).

The same procedure can be used to define the *present* as the contemplation of a sequence of behaviors that is carried out in anticipation of becoming able to achieve a more satisfactory future state. To indicate that the present is a contemplation (i.e., a state of mind), one can use the phrase "extended present."[14] Finally, the *past* refers to the mental image of "[t]hat which can no longer be done because the opportunity for it has passed away . . ." (p. 101).

Note that when the future, present, and past are defined in this way (i.e., subjectively), it is possible to know that another normal human being understands one's references to the future, present, and past merely because the other is a normal human being (who, by definition, acts). No specific knowledge about the other's physical environment is necessary.

From the viewpoint of an applied economist who wants to describe human action and its characteristics, it is often useful to speak of a single action in isolation, such as a choice to buy X instead of Y. In speaking of this choice, it may be useful to say that the subject prefers X over Y. In making such a statement, the applied economist is abstracting from both action and time. Neither an isolated actor nor a person who acts in everyday life experiences an abstract isolated choice. An individual can momentarily direct his attention to some parts of his acting. Indeed, this is one reason why a statement about an isolated action is not incomprehensible. But the individual cannot completely direct his attention away from other parts of his acting that are occurring during the same period of (subjective) time. Another way to put this is to say that action in everyday life entails multiple interrelated ends and interrelated means, all occurring during the same frame (p. 104).

An individual faces multiple opportunities to make his satisfaction higher than it otherwise would be. Because of this, the performance of one action practically always comes at the expense of another. Realizing this, the individual includes the time associated with the production-consumption of a good as part of his ends. When the alternative of good X, which the subject believes will yield satisfaction during a one-year period, is compared with the alternative of good Y, which is believed to yield satisfaction during a two-year period, the difference in time will be important to the individual. This importance was labelled "time preference" by Mises. "Time preference" is evident from the facts that (1) an individual does not devote all of his factors to immediate gratification, and (2) he consumes some goods in the present.[15] The existence of time preference implies a propensity to economize on the use of time.

In a market economy, specialization and exchange lead practically everyone to demand an intersubjectively approved means of comparing the duration of one action with the duration of other actions. This demand is satisfied by clock time, which is derived from the regularity and predictability of physical change. The fact that clock time is used by practically everyone to compare action means that the human scientist practically always finds it useful to understand and describe actions with reference to clock time.

Uncertainty

The fourth a priori category is uncertainty. That the outcome of an action is uncertain is deducible from the fundamental proposition that to act means to have a will. When an actress says that she has a will, she means that she can cause the future to be different from what it otherwise would have been. If one did not believe that she could change the future, she would not be a human being.[16]

The only method that is suitable for defining uncertainty is to attempt to abstract from it entirely by constructing an image of complete certainty. In an environment of complete certainty, an individual would be able to perfectly plan her future actions. A person could benefit by programming her own behavior once and for all, so that it would become completely routinized. In the absence of uncertainty, the individual would not act. She would behave. The individual would carry out the programming that she instituted at some previous time.

There are two categories of sources of uncertainty: nature and the characteristics of human actors. The study of uncertainty in nature is the task of natural science. Uncertainty about the specific characteristics of human actors refers to the fact that future wants, abilities, and knowledge cannot be fully known.[17] Praxeologists are concerned with how individuals deal with this second type of uncertainty.

Uncertainty as an a priori category. In order to assess the claim that uncertainty is a priori category, it seems wise to go beyond Mises and to distinguish three types of uncertainty. The first type is uncertainty about nature, as described in the last paragraph. The second two types are different classes of uncertainty about the characteristics of human actors: *intra*subjective uncertainty and *inter*subjective uncertainty.[18] Intrasubjective uncertainty refers to the uncertainty that a single individual feels about himself. Intersubjective uncertainty refers to the uncertainty that individuals feel about each other.

In making choices in everyday life, all three types of uncertainty are typically present. However, it is possible to imagine making a choice if any two are absent. For example, consider the decision of an isolated individual. Since he is isolated, there can be no intersubjective uncertainty. Assume also that there is no uncertainty in nature. If the individual performs a particular behavior, he is absolutely certain what the physical result of that behavior will be. Even under these circumstances, a choice could occur. The individual may be uncertain about the nature of his future wants and possibly also about his ability to perform the behavior.

Mises points out that the way one knows that a phenomenon is an a priori category of action is to recognize that he cannot imagine action occurring if the phenomenon is absent.[19] However, there are three different types of uncertainty; and as just shown, any two of these may be absent yet action can still be imagined. It follows that action does not imply the presence of any particular one of the three categories. However, action does imply that at least one of the three categories is present.

Intersubjective uncertainty. A close reading of Mises on uncertainty reveals that he was most interested in intersubjective uncertainty.[20] It is worth noting that intersubjective uncertainty is not only about the future. *A* is also uncertain about *B*'s wants, abilities, and knowledge in the present. The idea that the "uncertainty of the future is already implied in the very notion of action" may be less important than the idea that the fact that each individual has a will makes the outcome of one person's interaction with others uncertain.

The economic theorist focuses on the role of entrepreneuriship under the widest variety of natural conditions. Given this focus, she is naturally led, as Mises was, to emphasize actions that require predictions of the future wants, abilities, and knowledge of others. Entrepreneurship in a world where everyone knows everyone else's wants, abilities, and knowledge is incomprehensible.

Errors. Does praxeology assume that individuals can make errors in the choice of means? The answer is "yes." Three types of errors can be identified: scientific errors; errors in one's estimation of his personal wants, abilities, and knowledge; and errors in one's estimation of the future actions of others. The human actor may make any of these errors. The praxeologist and economist must acknowledge such errors by making the appropriate assumptions, if errors are relevant to the issue in which she is interested. Mises said this about scientific errors: "if men do not follow the advice of science, but cling to their fallacious prejudices, these errors are reality and must be dealt with as such" (p. 93).

3. ISSUES RELATED TO METHODOLOGICAL APRIORISM

Other A Priori Categories?

To prove the existence of the a priori categories, Mises appealed to the intuition of the reader. He asked: "Can you imagine yourself existing without, at the same time, recognizing that you possess the a priori categories?" Given that you cannot, you are forced to admit the existence of the categories. One might argue, however, that there are other a priori categories. Consider the following two.

Attending and learning. Is *attending* an a priori category? In the introductory paragraph to his section on the "Prerequisites of Human Action," Mises says:

> . . . Acting man is eager to substitute a more satisfactory state of affairs for a less satisfactory. His mind imagines conditions which suit him better, and his action aims at bringing about the desired state. The incentive that impels man to act is always some uneasiness. (p. 13)

To distinguish his views from those of John Locke, he goes on to say that a "third condition is required: the expectation that purposeful behavior has the power to remove or at least alleviate the felt uneasiness" (pp. 13–14). Now it seems evident from these statements that Mises believed that the actor could not act unless he paid attention to his behavior as well as to other characteristics of the environment that may be relevant to his choice. How could an actor imagine a state of affairs that would be brought about by his purposeful behavior if he did not pay such attention?

The concept of attending is not limited to paying attention to behavior and the environment. The intensity of attending can be chosen. One can presumably attend to his attending. For example, it is possible for an individual to recognize that if he paid greater attention to how he constructs an image of his own purposeful behavior, he would be able to improve his decision making.

Why then did Mises not identify attending as one of the prerequisites of action? One obvious answer is that although attending may improve one's performance, it is not a necessary condition of action. If by attending, one means only the expectation that purposeful behavior has the power to remove uneasiness, then the notion of attending is redundant. On the other hand, if one means by attending that he can improve his ability to perform a particular action, it is unnecessary. Action can occur without it.

The same reasoning applies to the second concept: *learning*. That human beings learn may be undeniable and discoverable through intuition. But it is not a necessary prerequisite of human action. Human action can occur without learning.

Does this mean that attending and learning have no place in economics? The answer depends upon how one defines economics. If, following Mises, one distinguishes economic theory from applied economics, then attending and learning may not be part of economic theory in the pure sense. They are likely to be relevant in applied economics, however, since any realistic description of groups of interacting individuals is likely to contain an implicit recognition of the differences in individuals' abilities and willingness to attend and learn.[21]

The problem of habitual behavior. Consider the problem of describing the observed behavior of an isolated individual. Suppose that the applied praxeologist, or historian, knows that the behavior she observed was once chosen by the actor but that it has since become habitual. Should the behavior be regarded as part of an action? An appropriate answer is that if the actor can, at the moment, choose not to perform it, then it is part of an action. However, if he does not have the ability to choose not to perform it, it should be called inherited behavior. Thus, if an actor cannot now choose not to perform his previously chosen but now habitual behavior, the behavior is not properly called part of an action: It is inherited.

Subjectivism requires that these definitions be constructed from the viewpoint of the subject. Thus, for the behavior under consideration to be a part of an action, it must be behavior that the economist assumes the subject knows he could choose not to perform.

Consider a case where an individual could know that he could choose to perform a behavior if he were only to pay attention. Because the individual does not pay attention, he does not recognize the option. Then, assuming that the individual, from his own point of view, can choose to pay attention, such behavior would be defined as part of an action, although it is obviously different in some measure from the behavior that the individual could directly choose to perform.

Consider a case where an individual could know that he could pay attention to a particular behavior if he were only to pay attention to whether he was paying attention to his behavior. Can the behavior be called chosen? Assuming that the individual knows that he could choose to pay attention to his attending, such behavior should be called part of an action, although it would also be different from directly chosen behavior.

Modes of Presenting Apriorism

Mises's mode of presenting the a priori changed over time. In *Epistemological Problems* ([1933] 1981), he seems to have taken it for granted that his audience would accept his a priori categories. Therefore he merely proceeded to work out their logical implications. In *Human Action* (1966) and *Ultimate Foundations* (1978), he went further by suggesting a process through which the a priori categories could themselves be defined (one is tempted to say derived).

Mises's intention seems to have been to lead an initially skeptical audience to accept the a priori categories by showing that one could not deduce that these categories do not exist. He did this in two ways. The first was to show his appreciation for cognitive development. After saying that he was aware that a priori categories of the human adult were not manifest in the embryo and developing child, he went on to argue that this fact does not imply that one can "learn about" those categories by studying cognitive development. He correctly pointed out that one cannot "learn about" anything without already possessing the a priori categories required for learning (1966, 34).

The second way he dealt with skepticism was to show his appreciation for the theory of evolution by means of natural selection. His 1978 book is the best example. That book contains a section entitled "A Hypothesis About the Origin of A Priori Categories." In that section he ventures the following:

> We are not prevented from assuming that in the long way that led from the nonhuman ancestors of man to the emergence of the species homo sapiens some groups of advanced anthropoids experimented, as it were, with categorical concepts different from those of homo sapiens and tried to use them for the guidance of conduct. But as such pseudo categories were not adjusted to the conditions of reality, behavior directed by a quasi reasoning based upon them was bound to fail and to spell disaster to those committed to it. Only those groups could survive whose members

acted in accordance with the right categories, i.e., with those that were in conformity with reality and therefore—to use the concept of pragmatism—worked. . . . Those primates who had the serviceable (a priori) categories survived, not because, having had the experience that their categories were serviceable, they decided to cling to them. They survived because they did not resort to other categories that would have resulted in their extirpation. (p. 15)

Thus Mises can be said to have explicitly denied the relevance of two sources of information about the a priori categories that other students of human behavior are likely to regard as important: (1) the minds of other human beings, and (2) the prehistorical environments that, in the scientist's mind, preceded and presumably precipitated the emergence of the a priori categories.

Note that these points do not imply that intuition, aided by knowledge of the development of other minds and of prehistory, is irrelevant to the goals of economists. The arguments refer only to the a priori categories and thus apply only to economic theory. Applied economists may want to take account of differences or variations in the ways that human beings acquire wants, abilities, and knowledge or of how differences in wants, abilities, and knowledge help provide motivations for exchange. If so, knowledge of cognitive development and of prehistory may be useful to them.[22]

Value Judgments and Challenges to A Priori Reasoning

An argument is sometimes made that because a coherent deductive system can be constructed on the basis of any set of assumptions, one has a choice among alternative a priori assumptions. Since a choice has to be made, value judgments must be used. It follows, the argument goes, that all deductive systems based on a priori assumptions are "value laden." This argument is a nonsequitur and illustrates a misapplication of the theory of choice. When economists describe economic interaction, they must do so by assuming that the subjects employ value judgments. However, the same reasoning does not apply to the choice of a priori assumptions, since these are derived from the "essential and necessary character of the logical structure of the human mind." To argue convincingly that the choice of a priori assumptions entails value judgments, it is necessary to challenge the set of relations that Mises calls the a priori categories.

An opponent of methodological apriorism can do one of two things.

First she may attempt to show that some other set of relations exist in the human mind and that the use of these would constitute an alternative to Mises's a priori assumptions in the study of economic phenomena. Second, she may attempt to show that the prerequisites of Mises's human action or the logical categories he deduces from them are not essential and necessary. So far as the author is aware, no one has seriously attempted either of these.

NOTES

1. See Piaget (1971, 1974).

2. Piaget has also been a pioneer in research relating to the development of social concepts. His work in this area appears in French. For reports on it, see Kitchener (1981) and Chapman (1986).

3. The term normal human being must be employed to distinguish between members of the human species, as a biologist might define it, and human beings who act in the economist's market economy. In everyday life, many individuals are either unable to act or their functioning is so far below the level of others that they cannot be said to act in any meaningful sense. This class includes minors and many of the mentally and physically disabled, as well as infirm individuals. These individuals typically become dependent on others. On page 252 of *Human Action*, Mises notes that "the minor family members in the market society . . . are . . . themselves not actors."

4. The author has taken the liberty of translating the concept of *verstehen*, or understanding, into the longer and more descriptive phrase intersubjective understanding of actions. Thus, whereas Mises says that the goal of the economist is understanding, and that in achieving this goal the economist employs the method of *verstehen*, the author would say that the economist aims at an intersubjective understanding of others' actions, and that to achieve this goal he must use the methods of the new subjectivism.

The problem with Mises's use of the term understanding is discussed in Appendix 1. The meaning of the intersubjective understanding of actions is described more fully in chapter four of this text.

5. See Mises (1969).

6. Mises pointed out that "[t]he main epistemological problem of the specific understanding [*verstehen*] is: How can a man have any knowledge of the future value judgments and actions of other people?" (1969, 311). It is in answering this question that one is led to the a priori. For more on this, see Mises (1978b, 122–27). This interpretation also reflects Lachmann's (1976, 1982) view.

It is interesting to note that Hayek links the subjectivism of Menger to the concept of *verstehen* as developed by Weber (Hayek 1973, 8). Unfortunately, Hayek's remarks are too sketchy to tell their basis. The author is not aware of any remarks by Hayek on the relationship between Mises's system of thought and *verstehen*. Lachmann (1971, 23–26) explores the link between Menger's subjectivism and *verstehen* in some detail. Also see the recent paper by Ebeling (1986).

7. See Mises (1981, 74–91). The essay that comprises these pages is called "Sociology and History." Mises later regretted that he did not use the term "praxeology" instead of "sociology" (Mises 1978b, 123).

8. Students of Weber might point out that Weber was a professor of economics at two universities. However, what was defined as economics during

that time and in that place was not the neoclassical economics that existed in the writings of Cairnes, Senior, Menger, Bohm-Bawerk, Wicksell, Wicksteed, Schumpeter, and Knight.

9. It follows, in turn, that the theories of economics are indeed value-free, although they need not be *relevant* to the interpretation of a particular historical event.

10. Mises said:

Everybody in his daily behavior again and again bears witness to the immutability and universality of the categories of thought and action. He who addresses his fellow men, who wants to inform and convince them, who asks questions and answers other people's questions, can proceed in this way only because he can appeal to something common to all men—namely, the logical structure of human reason.

The fact that man does not have the creative power to imagine categories at variance with the fundamental logical relations and with the principles of causality and teleology enjoins upon us what may be called methodological apriorism. (Mises, 1966, p. 35).

In addition, see Mises (1966, 40).

11. Also see Mises's discussion of scales of value on page 102 of *Human Action*.

12. The distinction between the logic of choice and the logic of action is further discussed in footnote 11 of chapter eleven.

13. One cannot conceive of existence except with respect to a physical world. Moreover, it is as certain as anything that the physical world existed long before human beings evolved. Given these facts, one can legitimately claim that the source of all conception, including subjective conceptions such as subjective time, is the physical world. This reasonable hypothesis, however, is irrelevant to the point in question. When the author says that the relevance of time derives from human action, he does not mean that human beings created time. He means that in describing the actions and understandings of fellow human beings, the praxeologist must use a concept of time that is derived from the actions of those human beings. The rationale for subjectivist definitions derives from the subject matter of praxeology, not from evolution. In a world without human beings, time would have no meaning. Indeed, nothing would have meaning because meaning can only exist for human beings.

14. Mises (1966, 100) refers to a "real extended present."

15. See Mises's discussion of the miser (1966, 490).

It should be noted that the term "time preference," like the term scale of values, can be misleading. The meaning of time preference must always be implicit in the concept of action that is known a priori. (See the discussion of "ends and means" earlier in the chapter). The a priori evidence of "time preference" is discussed more fully in chapter four of this text.

16. Mises says: "If man knew the future, he would not have to choose and would not act. He would be like an automaton, reacting to stimuli without any will of his own" (p. 105).

17. The phrase uncertainty about the wants, abilities, and knowledge of human actors is the equivalent of uncertainty about what Mises calls the data (Mises 1966, 646).

One way in which Mises distinguished between uncertainty in nature and uncertainty about the characteristics of human actors was to provide an extended discussion of probability. This discussion is summarized in Appendix 4.

18. Mises's most dogmatic statements link action to uncertainty in a general sense. For example, he begins his section on uncertainty with the following paragraph.

> The uncertainty of the future is already implied in the very notion of action. That man acts and that the future is uncertain are by no means two independent matters. They are two different modes of establishing one thing (1966, 105).

It is not clear from statements like these that he is cognizant of the three types of uncertainty (or, at least, that he regards distinguishing between them as important). In any case, it turns out that all of his examples of uncertainty in economics refer to intersubjective uncertainty. In economic interaction, he maintains, each individual's choice is a *speculation*. In particular, he concludes a paragraph on intersubjective uncertainty with the statements: "Every action refers to an unknown future. It is in this sense always a risky speculation" (p. 106).

19. This is Mises's method of imaginary constructions. It is described more fully in Gunning (1989).

20. For example, Mises says:

> Whether [a plan to construct a machine to help supply consumers with the machine's product turns out to be] the appropriate plan depends on the development of future conditions which at the time of the plan's execution cannot be forecast with certainty. . . . Future needs and valuations, the reaction of men to changes in conditions, future scientific technological knowledge, future ideologies and policies can never be foretold with more than a greater or smaller degree of probability (1966, 106).

21. Mises places attending and learning in the category of the "changing content of action" and points out that "[p]raxeology is not concerned with the changing content of acting, but with its pure form and its categorical structure. The study of the accidental and environmental features of human action is the task of history" (1966, 47).

22. To take one example, Piaget claimed to have identified a universal sequence of development of the ability to understand physical causality. This universal sequence enables (properly trained) psychologists to classify individuals according to the stage of development that they have achieved. See Piaget (1930, 1974) and Piaget and Inhelder (1958). The applied economist could use this finding to construct models of exchange and dependence relationships among individuals who are at different stages of development.

Chapter 4

The Method of Contrasting Images of Functions (1): Subjectivism in Macroeconomics and Characteristics of the Initial Image of the Market Economy

The goal of economic theory is to help the economist answer certain questions that relate to economic interaction. The economist decides that some type of interaction is relevant to answering some question. Then he tries to understand the actions and understandings of all the actors who are involved in that type of interaction.

Economists are sometimes interested in questions that relate to interaction among only a few individuals. For example, they may want to describe a particular type of business organization or product market. By far the most important contribution that economics has made over the years, however, has been the help it has given economists in their efforts to comprehend characteristics of economic interaction and change at a general, or macroeconomic, level. These characteristics could not have been grasped without economic theory.

When the applied economist tries to understand the actions and understandings that occur under the conditions specified in the definition of the market economy (i.e., at the macroeconomic level), he is faced with an order of complexity that defies comprehension and description. Upon encountering this complex, the economist soon must admit that he is unable to fully accomplish his goal. It is impossible for him to conceptually interchange his position with those of everyone in the market economy. There are simply too many subjects with too many different characteristics; and the actions that coordinate their interactions are too extensive and complicated. The economist must redirect his energies.

A new goal emerges. It is to develop a method (*a*) that avoids the errors associated with a non-subjectivist approach, but (*b*) that nevertheless enables him to say something useful about the issues in which he is interested.

Mises recognized that the classical and neoclassical economists had developed such a method, although they had not fully understood it. He was the first to describe the method and, in *Human Action*, made it the centerpiece of his economic theory.[1] He called it the *method of imaginary constructions*.

He used this same name to refer to both the method of economics and the method of praxeology. He did this apparently because he wanted to drive home the point that the method of economics is derived from the method of praxeology. Unfortunately, although he showed clearly and convincingly how the method is used in praxeology to derive the fundamental categories of action, his description of how the method is used in economics was less clear and convincing.[2] To overcome this problem, the method, as it is used in economics, is painstakingly clarified in this book. To avoid any confusion, this text uses the term *method of contrasting images of functions* to refer to the method of imaginary constructions as it is used in economics. A further justification for this name is given at the end of chapter five.

The purpose of chapters four through ten is to present the rudiments of this method and to provide some elementary applications of it. This chapter has two purposes. First, Part 1 explains in greater detail why the method of contrasting images of functions is necessary. Second, Part 2 describes the characteristics of the initial image of the market economy: the use of a common denominator of exchange and specialization.

1. THE IMPOSSIBILITY OF DIRECTLY APPLYING SUBJECTIVISM TO MACROECONOMIC ISSUES

The subjectivist knows that it is impossible to construct a complete image of the intersubjective actions and understandings of everyone in a modern economy. So she settles for the next best thing: a model in which economic functions are performed by various puppets, or robots, combined with a vision, based on intuition and experience, of the entrepreneurship that is necessary to cause these functions to be performed. This part explains more fully why this method is necessary.

Intersubjective Understanding of Actions by Subjects

According to the new subjectivism, economic subjects must be assumed capable of possessing all of the characteristics and abilities that one might attribute to an economist.[3] The economist must admit the possibility that the images of economic interaction constructed by subjects can be just as complex, broad, or precise as those used by economists. Whatever understanding the economist may be able to acquire about the actions and understandings of individuals who are labeled as subjects, the subjects themselves must be assumed capable of acquiring at least the same type of understanding of the actions and understandings of each other and of the economist.

When the economist studies the actions of businesspeople, for example, he must admit the possibility that a businessperson may effectively study other businesspeople. Furthermore, the economist must admit the possibility that a businessperson may effectively study the images, understandings, and actions of the economist.

To state this symbolically, suppose that the economist is A and that the subjects are $B, C \ldots N$. When A studies the actions of B, the new subjectivism requires A to have a sufficiently open mind to conceive of the possibility that one of B's actions can consist of studying the actions of $A, C, D \ldots N$. More fully, when A studies the actions of B, $C \ldots N$, he recognizes (1) that B may be studying the actions of $C, D \ldots N$, that C may be studying the actions of $B, D \ldots N$, and so on; and (2) that in their studies $B, C \ldots N$ may know and take account of the fact that A and others are studying their actions.

The main difference between economists and subjects in their efforts to understand actions and understandings is that economists, by definition, choose to use their abilities to understand subjects as a profession. Subjects choose to use their abilities when they perceive a gain from doing so.[4]

Differences Among Subjects

Subjects are different from each other. Moreover, the subjects know that they are different. The crucial problem from the standpoint of the economic theorist is that of choosing how to conceive of such differences. Most importantly, the theorist must decide how to conceive of the differences in abilities to act and to understand the actions and understandings of others. Consider the abilities of subjects to understand each others' actions. First, some subjects are more competent than others in understanding the actions of different categories of cohorts. Second, subjects differ in the assumptions and hypotheses they make in their efforts to understand other subjects' actions.

Where initial differences exist, individuals can cause them to widen. Where initial differences are not obvious, individuals can create them. They do so because they anticipate a net gain. In a market economy, all such differences are manifest in the division of labor, specialization, exchange, and pricing.

Impossibility of Describing Everyone

The complexity of the intersubjective understanding of actions by subjects under the conditions specified in the definition of a market economy, combined with what appear to be realistic assumptions about economic differences among subjects, enables one to easily see the infeasability of detailed descriptions of economic interaction. In a market economy, each individual acquires an understanding of others' actions and understandings that is suitable in her view for the satisfaction of her wants, given her own abilities and knowledge. If the population is large, there are millions of independent yet interdependent, specialized, intersubjective understandings of actions. It would never be possible for a single individual or group (e.g., the economist) to know such understandings. In fact, the idea that one mind could, at any single time, contain a complete image of the separate actions of millions of minds is contradictory. One who seriously believes that detailed descriptions of economic interaction at the macro level are possible is being unrealistic.[5]

What Kind of Descriptions Can the Applied Economist Make?

If the applied economist cannot hope to make a description that contains the intersubjective understandings of the millions of separate individuals, what kind of description can he make and of what use can it be? Both questions can be answered by employing the concept of *function*. The economist conceives of functions that are implied by the definition of economics. Then he constructs models in which the performance of the functions is automatic. When such a model is contrasted with how he believes the functions would come to be performed under the conditions specified in the definition of a market economy, it helps him elucidate the functions and describe how they come to be performed.

The Method of Contrasting Images of Functions

The method used by Mises has been called the method of contrasting images of functions. It consists of three steps. The first is to identify economic functions that are performed in all economies. Such functions are implicit in the definition of economic phenomena. They are: producing, consuming, saving, and supplying factors.[6]

The second step is to construct an image of an economy in which these functions are performed as simply and routinely as possible by robots. The most fundamental image is what Mises called the *evenly rotating economy* (ERE). In the ERE, the basic functions of producing goods and factors, consuming, and saving are performed by robots, who do not act. They merely perform routine behavior according to fixed rules. Therefore there is no entrepreurship.

The third step is to use this image as a basis for constructing other images. These other images are formed by putting oneself into the positions of the robots and asking how their behavior could come to be performed under various conditions. In other words, the images are formed by *contrasting* the image of a robot economy with what one knows about how normal human beings would come to perform the functions under a given set of conditions. The most general conditions are those that are specified in the definition of the market economy. To help describe how the functions would be performed under these conditions, Mises constructed images of economies in which wants change, incomes change, entrepreneurship is present, and/or saving could exceed or fall short of that needed to maintain capital intact.[7] In each of the three steps, the subjectivist economist remains keenly aware of the hazards associated with not accounting for the separate actions and understandings of the subjects.

This can be said in a simpler way. The method of contrasting images of functions entails a contrast between the ERE and economic interaction under the conditions specified in the market economy. Since the former contains no entrepreneurship while the latter does, it can be said that a major reason for such a contrast is to elucidate entrepreneurship.[8]

There is no pretence that an image constructed by the economist depicts all of reality. It is not intended for that purpose and, if it was, the purpose could not be accomplished. Images in economics are constructed in order to help the economist answer particular questions. Aside from the logical requirement that they contain all of the fundamental economic functions, their usefulness must be determined on the basis of whether they indeed help the economist.

Subjectivism in the Method of Contrasting Images of Functions

This subsection has described how Mises explained the use of the method of contrasting images of functions. However, the reader of *Human Action* who focuses only on the parts that deal exclusively with economic issues is unlikely to discover the source of Mises's subjectivism in this method. The method requires one to divide human beings into function-performing robots and entrepreneurs. Unfortunately, this necessary procedure obscures subjectivism. The idea of robots performing economic functions appears to contradict the fundamental subjectivist assumption that every individual acts (i.e., that she has wants, abilities, and knowledge, expectations, and plans). Only one who has a reasonably complete understanding of the nature of complex economic phenomena and of the difficult task of elucidating them recognizes that there is no real contradiction here. Moreover, only such a person can expect to employ the new subjectivist methods without making errors in economic reasoning.

2. CHARACTERISTICS OF THE INITIAL IMAGE OF A MARKET ECONOMY

The definition of the market economy specifies that money is used in all calculations and that there is private ownership of the means of production. It rules out barter, self-production, political interaction (i.e., coercion), non-chosen behavior, and other non-market interaction. Given this definition and the assumptions (*a*) that individuals differ, and (*b*) that they attempt to profit from production and exchange, the economist uses his experience and intuition to make judgments about the nature of economic interaction. The result is his initial image of the market economy.

In this part, the typical judgments that have become a part of economic theory are described. The section begins with a discussion of the assumption that individuals calculate on the basis of money. It explains the assumption by using the concept of a common denominator of exchange. Next it describes some basic concepts in a money-using economy. Finally, specialization and its implications are described.

A Common Denominator for Exchange

A common denominator for exchange is called money. Unless money existed, the personal cost to an individual of evaluating the exchange offers made by others and of deciding what offers to make would be so high that specialization would be severely limited. Individuals would have to rely substantially on barter or self-production.

Imagine an economy in which there is extensive barter but no money. In such an economy, some particularly enlightened individuals would come to recognize the benefits of exchanging commodities with lesser marketability for commodities with greater marketability. The buyers of commodities with greater marketability would use those goods not for their own consumption but as means of obtaining other goods. Other individuals, observing their success, would copy the behavior. Over time, customs would develop in which at least one commodity would be "accepted, not merely by many, but by all economizing individuals in exchange for their own commodities" (Menger 1981, 261; and Mises 1966, 401, 406).

Valuation, appraisement, prices, and profit. The assumption that there is a common denominator of exchange in a market economy means the same thing as the assumption that individuals in a market economy use money to compare goods and to *appraise* factors of production. Individuals acting in the role of the consumer aim for satisfaction by making decisions to buy consumers' goods.[9] They compare the relative satisfactions they expect from different goods with the relative prices of the goods. Such a comparison of goods is called *valuation.*

Individuals acting in the role of entrepreneurs in a market economy buy goods or factors in order to earn money. The aim of an entrepreneurial act is profit. An entrepreneur buys a consumption good if he estimates that the future market value of the good is sufficiently high. He plans to sell the good in the future and expects to profit by doing so. An entrepreneur may buy a factor for the same reason. He may also buy a factor if he estimates that the future market value of the good(s) it can be used to help produce will be greater than the cost of all the factors needed to produce the good(s). The entrepreneur uses what he believes to be superior knowledge of future market conditions to attach a personal subjective price to a good or factor he plans to purchase. The personal subjective price he attaches is called his *appraisal*. If he appraises a good or factor to be greater than the price at which he can buy it, he buys it.[10]

The fact that an exchange occurs implies that two individuals, acting in the entrepreneurial role, have made different appraisals. The price that is paid for a good or factor is an amount of money that is no higher than the buyer's appraisal (or evaluation if he is a consumer, strictly speaking) and no lower than the seller's appraisal.

Specialization

It will be shown in chapter five that the satisfaction of wants in a market economy entails production, consumption, the identification of factors, supply of factors, estimation of relative costs, saving, decision making, and uncertainty-bearing. In a Crusoe situation, the same person must do all of the deliberations, make the decisions, and perform the behaviors. In a market economy, however, individuals can do one or more of these things without doing the others. A person can specialize and pay other people to do other things for her. Thus, *A* may hire *B* and *C* to help produce a factor that had been identified by *D* and whose cost was estimated by *E*. *A* can then trade her factor with *F* for money, which she uses to buy a good that is produced by *G*, who financed her production by borrowing savings from *H*, whose loan is guaranteed by *I*.

Dependence and monopoly power. Consider an individual who is choosing a particular occupation, including whether to work for herself or someone else. From her point of view, every possibility is a specialization. Her choice is an investment. She expects to use some of her time and energy to acquire skills or experience, which she can later use to earn pay. Her anticipated return depends upon the opportunities that she predicts will be available. These opportunities, in turn, depend upon the wants, abilities, and knowledge of others. Thus, when an individual chooses an occupation and/or who her employer will be, she is likely to consider the prospect of future dependence upon others.

Suppose that the individual chooses to become self-employed in a new trade. Then she will become dependent on the prospective buyers of her goods. If she must purchase factors to apply her trade, she may also become dependent on the seller(s) of factors. Finally, her satisfaction will become dependent on the sellers of the goods that she, as a consumer, expects to buy with her income. The individual realizes that unless she can obtain sales and purchase commitments in advance, the prices that others charge and that others pay may be higher or lower than anticipated. In this sense, she becomes dependent on such people.

At the same time, the individual realizes that her choice may make others more dependent on her. In particular, she may choose a specialization that encourages others to make investments elsewhere. The return on such investments may come to depend on her decision not to raise the price of her good or specialized factor above what the others come to expect. Similarly, others may specialize in producing goods that she is expected to buy.

Consider the position held by an individual or individuals upon whom others are dependent for the fruition of their investments. In such a position, a seller of a good or factor can cause the price to be higher and thereby render unprofitable an opportunity that would otherwise be regarded as profitable. Similarly, a buyer of a good or factor upon whom others are dependent can cause the price to be lower and have the same effect. Economists have traditionally referred to such positions as positions of monopoly. In a market economy, everyone occupies positions of monopoly. That is, everyone has some degree of monopoly power over others. Monopoly power is the consequence of specialization. It is another view of dependence.

Occupational choices operate to reduce monopoly power as choosers seek to avoid becoming dependent on others. Also, occupational choices operate to increase monopoly power as choosers seek to establish themselves in monopoly positions and/or as they become willing to subject themselves to being dependent.

Competition: copying and innovating. Monopoly power in a market economy is also affected by what economists have come to call competition. Competition consists of pricing actions that result in copying or in innovating. Consider each in turn. First, specializations where greater monopoly power exists are more attractive than other specializations, other things being equal, because they yield higher incomes. As individuals choose to acquire such specializations they reduce the monopoly power of existing specialists. The behavior of entering a specialization that already exists can be called *copying*. Second, and more fundamentally, most decisions to specialize are made on the basis of the prospective specialist's prediction that the result will be opportunities that buyers will take advantage of. Thus, when A makes a decision to specialize, she expects to provide B with a buying opportunity that he would otherwise not have. From the viewpoint of individuals who would otherwise benefit by selling to B, the availability of the new opportunity constitutes a reduction in their monopoly power. The behavior of entering a new specialization can be called *innovating*.

Collusive monopoly. Individuals may increase others' dependence on them by means of concerted action. For example, a group of specialists may be able to increase the degree of buyers' dependence on each separate specialist by agreeing not to compete against each other. When greater monopoly power is acquired through collusion, the relationship between the specialists and their customers can be called a *collusive monopoly*.

NOTES

1. In the introduction to his chapter in *Human Action* on the scope and method of economics, he says:

> . . . In order to conceive the market fully one is forced to study the action of hypothetical isolated individuals on the one hand and to contrast the market system with an imaginary socialist commonwealth on the other hand. (p. 232)
> . . . Economics is mainly concerned with the analysis of the determination of money prices of goods and services exchanged on the market. In order to accomplish this task it must start from a comprehensive theory of human action. Moreover, it must study not only the market phenomena, but no less the hypothetical conduct of an isolated man and of a socialist community. (p. 234)

The socialist commonwealth (community) to which he refers is the evenly rotating economy. The study of a hypothetical isolated individual is necessary, it will be shown, in order to identify a priori categories so that they can be ultimately translated into the economic functions of the ERE, and entrepreneurship. The first step, which is accomplished in chapter five, is to match the a priori categories of action with a production-consumption decision of an isolated actor.

2. In his brief description of the way to use the method of imaginary constructions, he referred to two such uses. He said:

> The main formula for designing of imaginary constructions is to abstract from the operation of some conditions present in actual action. Then we are in a position to grasp the hypothetical consequences of the absence of these conditions and to conceive the effects of their existence. Thus we conceive the category of action by constructing the image of a state in which there is no action, either because the individual is fully contented and does not feel any uneasiness or because he does not know any procedure from which an improvement in his well-being (state of satisfaction) could be expected. (1966, 237)

3. This is the "postulate of adequacy," described by Alfred Schuetz. See Appendix 2.

4. Modern economic theorists have not seriously attempted to construct images of individuals that assume they have the ability to understand each others' actions. The models they have developed deal with "knowledge" or "information." Many such models simply assume that every subject possesses whatever knowledge or information is specified. More complex models assume that knowledge is dispersed and specialized. Each individual may possess a "parcel" of information about some particular production possibility and/or demand for a good. Hardly any models, however, attempt to specify subjects' knowledge of each others' actions and understandings.

Yet it is evident upon reflection that any attempt to model economic interaction comprehensively requires the economist to take account of subjects' understandings of each others' actions. Unless such understandings are taken into account, the economist cannot construct realistic images of human capital production; market speculation; dependence relationships such as the typical longer-term employment agreement; the operations of an investment house with respect to savers, underwriting, insuring, or agency; and other enterprise activities.

No area of economics theory is in greater need of development than the construction of images of differences in subjects' knowledge and understanding of each others' actions.

5. The point at issue here is identical to the point that detailed central economic planning is logically impossible. The idea that a central economic plan can duplicate the plans of the separate individuals in a free enterprise system is unimaginable.

6. The concept of an economic function was introduced and explained in *Human Action* on pages 251–52. Mises identified five economic functions: entrepreneurship, capitalist-financing, supplying land, supplying labor, and consuming goods. The author has modified Mises's presentation in four ways in order to clarify the method of contrasting images of functions. First, he has omitted all reference to entrepreneurship as a function on the grounds that entrepreneurship is the cause of the performance of the other functions. Second, the author has substituted the term "saver" for capitalist. Saver is more descriptive than capitalist. Moreover, Mises's capitalist is also an entrepreneur (1966, 253). Third, the author has substituted the term "factor supplier" for landowner and worker. There is no need to distinguish between factors because the author is not interested in the policy problem of worker unemployment. Fourth, the author has employed the term "human capital," which is not mentioned by Mises.

7. Mises called his image of an economy in which wants change the stationary economy (1966, 250–51, 294). He called images in which incomes change and in which there is net saving or dis-saving the progressing and retrogressing economies (1966, 294–300). He also used the image of the stationary economy to isolate "pure entrepreneurship" (1966, 155–56). Besides these images to which he gave names, he used the image of the functional distribution (1966, 254) and an image of a changing economy in which individuals have perfect foresight of all future events. In the latter, he pointed out, there would be "neither profits nor losses" (1966, 294). Such an image can be used to help elucidate entrepreneurial profits and losses.

8. This is what Mises (1966) said:

> . . . in order to analyze the problems of change in the data and of unevenly and irregularly varying movement, we must confront them with a fictitious state in which both are hypothetically eliminated. (p. 247)
> . . . There is no means of studying the complex phenomena of action other than first to abstract from change altogether, then to introduce an isolated factor provoking change, and ultimately to analyze its effects under the assumption that other things remain equal. . . . The static method, the employment of the imaginary construction of the evenly rotating economy, is the only adequate method of analyzing the changes concerned without regard to whether they are great or small,

sudden or slow. . . . The [appropriate and indispensible] service which this imaginary construction renders [is the treatment of] the problem of the relation between the prices and products and those of the factors required for their production, and the implied problems of entrepreneurship and of profit and loss. In order to grasp the function of entrepreneurship and the meaning of profit and loss, we construct a system from which they are absent. This image is merely a tool for our thinking. It is not a description of a possible and realizable state of affairs. It is even out of the question to carry the imaginary construction of an evenly rotating system to its ultimate logical consequences. For it is impossible to eliminate the entrepreneur from the picture of the market economy. The various complementary factors of production cannot come together spontaneously. (p. 248)

. . . [W]e need to comprehend in what respects the conditions of a living world in which there is action differ from those of a rigid world. This we can discover only by the *argumentum a contrario* provided by the image of a rigid [evenly rotating] economy. (p. 250)

9. A consumers' good is a good that is immediately consumed by the consumer robot. It differs from a consumption good, which the consumer in a market economy may buy in order to consume at a later time and possibly to resell after she has used it.

10. See Mises (1966, 329–33) for his discussion of valuation and appraisement.

Chapter 5

The Method of Contrasting Images of Functions (2): Using the Method of Contrast to Elucidate Crusonean Action

Discussions of economic method in modern mainstream economics are centered around positivism. Economists know that they construct models of economies, and they give one of two reasons for doing so. The first is a desire to emulate the scientific method of the natural sciences. Those who give this reason regard their model as an approximation of real economic interaction. Their goal is to test the hypothesis that their model approximates what they define as real economic interaction more closely than some alternative. The second reason given for constructing a model is that it is somehow useful to think of the market economy *as if* it was populated by the maximizing robots in the model.

The first reason reflects a misconception of the nature of economics. There is no way to construct a model of robots that approximates the real economic interaction under the conditions specified in the definition of the market economy. A model of robotic behavior can be constructed that approximates the reality of animal colonies. To the extent that human behavior is determined by culture, habit, or obedience to laws, such a model may even simulate the behavior. But such behavior is not necessarily action. As shown in Part 1 of chapter four, the complexity of the human mind and the fact that there are many interacting minds in an economy make it impossible for an economist to construct a model that approximates economic interaction, properly defined.

The second belief is wrong in principle. However, if the principle is not taken seriously, the model has the potential of helping the economist make a contrast. This is so because the notion that the robots in the model behave as if they are human beings is a constant reminder that the robots are *not* human beings. This reminder, in turn, seems to be accompanied by an impulse to explain the difference. If the economist takes this route, he actually comes to use the method of contrasting images of functions, however incompletely and unwittingly.

Too often, however, the modern economist's use of models is motivated by the desire to predict "economic behavior." When a model is used for this purpose, it contributes nothing to the understanding of economic interaction. All that happens is that the observations, which are made to determine whether the prediction is correct, come to be part of the general body of observations on which an economist may draw. Such observations may be useful in identifying economic problems or in constructing theories, but they may also be largely irrelevant because of the failure to identify the truly human part of interaction.

To the author's knowledge, no modern economist realizes that he uses the method of contrasting images of functions. Indeed, most economists have not given much thought to the method they use. As a result, they are likely to resist and even deny that they use the method. They may find some consolation in the fact that the epistemological basis for the method has apparently not been fully demonstrated by anyone, including Mises. Yet the foundation is easy to provide.

When an individual wants to understand and/or describe his own action, he makes a contrast between himself as a behaver, like an animal or mechanical object, and what he knows by intuition and experience to be his true self—a thinker and chooser who has the capacity to deliberate over the outcome, change his mind, and make a decision. The method of describing and understanding the interaction of many individuals must be analogous to this method. If it is not, economists would not be able to capture the essence of human action. Thus, the epistemological foundation for the method is that it is the one and only method that individuals possess to comprehend the truly human part of action.

An economic action occurs within a context of specialization, the division of labor, and the use of money. To understand a particular economic action, the economist constructs models of specialized robots who perform different specialized functions and whose relationship to each other can be expressed in terms of money prices. Then he identifies the role of entrepreneurship, which is defined as the cause of the functional behavior. The economist does this by asking himself how human beings would come to perform the economic functions under the conditions specified in the definition of the market economy. Although the economist's method is more complicated, its epistemological basis is identical to that of the method used by an individual who wants to understand and describe his own action.

The purpose of this chapter is to show how the method of contrasting images of functions is used in the understanding and description of the action of a single individual—of Crusonean action. Because of the economist's interest in production, consumption, and saving, the illustration focuses on a production-consumption action. This focus will provide a reference when the method is used to describe and understand economic interaction in the market economy.

Specifically, this chapter shows how the economist can describe a simple production-consumption action in a Crusoe situation. Part 1 uses the a priori categories of action identified in chapter three as the basis for constructing a complete image of an isolated, individual production-consumption action. Part 2 divides the characteristics of action in a Crusoe situation into two parts: (1) functions that can be performed by a robot, and (2) deliberation, which causes the functions to be performed. Part 3 shows how isolated action is elucidated by contrasting an image of the individual as a robot that performs the functions with one's intuitive understanding of how a real human actor would carry out the deliberation under the circumstances. Then it goes on to reason by analogy that economic interaction in a market economy can be elucidated by contrasting the ERE with one's intuitive understanding of how entrepreneurship would be carried out under the conditions specified in the definition of the market economy.

1. CHARACTERISTICS OF AN ISOLATED PRODUCTION-CONSUMPTION ACTION

Imagine an isolated human being like Crusoe who produces goods only for his own consumption. Such production-consumption action would require Crusoe to identify alternative items to be used in the production of different goods, which he expects to consume at different times. Since Crusoe's choice to use an item to produce one good instead of another requires him to forego the production of another good, he would have to estimate the net benefits of each alternative. Then he would make a decision regarding which goods to produce and when to produce them. Such a decision implicitly contains an element of time and planning, since Crusoe would want to allocate his energies and other resources toward satisfying both distant-future and near-future wants. In addition, the decision contains an element of uncertainty-bearing, since conditions can change after a decision is made.

In this part, these characteristics are systematically described. In order to justify the claim that these are fundamental characteristics of a production-consumption action, each characteristic is linked to one or more of the a priori categories identified in chapter three. As the discussion proceeds, other concepts that are related to the characteristics of action and that also are derived from the a priori categories are identified. Some of these have special importance in a market economy.

Production and Consumption

The first two characteristics are production and consumption. *Production* refers to the behavior that results in the presence of a good. *Consumption* refers to the behavior of using the good in the removal or alleviation of the "felt uneasiness." In an image of a situation in which there is no previous capital and, therefore, no inventory of consumption goods, consumption would refer to the part of an action that occurs after production.

The concepts of consumption, production, and a consumption good are derived from the prerequisites of action and a subsidiary assumption: A consumption good is a means of getting relief from felt uneasiness. Consumption is the act of using a consumption good to get such relief. Production of the consumption good is an action that renders behavior or materials more capable of relieving felt uneasiness. The idea of a produced consumption good is meaningful only with reference to the conditions that would have prevailed if the good had not been produced. The distinction between consumption and production is based on a subsidiary assumption that action can be divided into two parts that are separated by the passage of time. Production occurs before consumption and therefore the two are assumed to not occur simultaneously.[1]

The idea that production occurs through time implies that there is a *period of production*. The period of production equals "working time" plus "maturing time," if any. In a simple agricultural operation that does not entail the production of tools, for example, it equals the amount of working time that it takes to prepare the soil, sow the seeds, and reap the harvest plus the amount of maturing time it takes for the organisms to grow.[2] For some goods, the period of production is variable.

The assumption that some consumer goods are durable enables one to define a different period—the *duration of serviceableness*. This is the time during which a durable good yields services.

The ideas of production and a period of production imply that every choice that Crusoe makes involves an estimation of when the satisfactions of the choice will be realized and what those satisfactions will be. To refer to the time that the individual plans for the satisfactions to be realized, the concept of a *period of provision* is used. The period of provision is "the fraction of future time for which the actor in a definite action wants to provide in some way and to some extent."[3]

Identification of Factors

The third characteristic is the identification of factors. Production consists of a behavior that causes a particular good or goods to be produced at the expense of other goods. Any behavior or physical item that can be used to produce a good is, to Crusoe, a *factor of production*. Before Crusoe could produce any goods, he would have to identify factors. To identify factors, he would estimate his future wants and his abilities to satisfy those wants in different ways.

Identification of factors is derived from the prerequisite of action that an individual must expect purposeful behavior to remove or alleviate felt uneasiness. If Crusoe could not identify factors, he could not expect to remove or alleviate felt uneasiness by means of his choice to produce.

Producing Factors

The fourth characteristic is the production of factors. Some factors, like natural resources and previously produced capital, already exist. Crusoe may choose to produce additional factors or at least to prevent the deterioration of factors he already has. The production of factors is derived partly from the same prerequisite of action as the production of goods. If Crusoe does not produce factors, he may not be able to remove or alleviate felt uneasiness as quickly, as effectively, or at all. More significantly, it is derived from the subsidiary assumption that human beings recognize that factors can be produced.

Types of factors. The factors can be placed into categories. The addition of a subsidiary assumption—that the human being finds it useful to distinguish between *human* and *nonhuman* factors of production—leads to the concept of *labor* as a distinct factor of production. Labor refers to the nonproduced physical behavior that an individual chooses to perform in order to produce a good. That Crusoe makes a distinction between human and nonhuman factors may be based on the subsidiary assumption that the use of labor, in itself, increases uneasiness (i.e., that the use of labor yields disutility). Under this assumption, Crusoe would never use labor unless he believed that the uneasiness removed by the consumption of the good was greater than the uneasiness that is added due to the use of labor.

The addition of another subsidiary assumption allows one to define *capital*. Produced nonhuman factors are called *physical capital*. Produced human factors are called *human capital*. Nonproduced, nonhuman factors are called *land*. The term capital is also used to refer to durable goods that could either be consumed or saved.

At any point in time when Crusoe is making a production decision (i.e., when he is planning), he may take account of the items, abilities, and knowledge that he previously produced but did not consume. That is, he may take account of what he previously regarded as capital. Whether these items are still regarded as capital depends upon the present circumstances. In particular, it depends upon Crusoe's specific current and projected wants and his specific knowledge about his ability to satisfy them by means of various production techniques.

Mises did not use the relatively new term, human capital, in his writings. In the author's view, this is unfortunate. Its use would have helped him avoid some of the ambiguities associated with his uses of the terms labor and entrepreneurship.[4]

Estimating Net Benefits

The fifth characteristic consists of estimating net benefits. In order to make a production-consumption-factor supply choice, Crusoe must estimate the net benefits of producing different goods. Estimating net benefits in this situation can be said to consist of three parts: estimating abilities to produce, estimating valuation, and predicting future knowledge. First, Crusoe must estimate the amounts of labor time and other factors that would be required to produce different goods. In making his estimate, he notes the type of work and intensity of effort that would be required at different stages of the production process. Second, he must estimate his wants for the various goods he could produce, including his like or dislike of different types of labor or other uses of human factors. Because each good may have a different period of provision, the estimates must give due consideration to his expected desire to consume goods and to use labor at different times. Third, he must estimate his future knowledge. If he expects to discover a new and superior method of production, a choice to use an existing method may preclude what would otherwise be future opportunities to satisfy his wants.

Such estimations require Crusoe to envision the future. He constructs a mental image of alternative future states of satisfaction under alternative uses of factors in the various production processes. Because he cannot be certain what his wants, abilities, or knowledge will be after he makes a production decision, his assessments are called estimates instead of determinations. In collecting and using information to make choices, Crusoe never *determines* his net benefits; he always *estimates* them.

The estimation of net benefits is derived from the definition of action and the subsidiary assumption that satisfaction can be obtained in many ways. When there are many options available, the actor tries to determine the net benefits of each in order to find the best uses of his time and energy. The deduction that Crusoe only estimates net benefits and never determines them is derived from the a priori assumption of uncertainty. When a human actor chooses one means over another, the *cost* associated with his choice are the net benefits that he judges will be foregone because he did not choose otherwise.

Saving

The sixth characteristic is saving. *Saving* refers to a broad range of actions that result from a decision (1) not to use existing goods, labor, or nonhuman factors of production to reduce felt uneasiness as soon as possible, and (2) to use them to reduce uneasiness at some later time. Crusoe has four possible different means of saving. First, he can set aside durable consumption goods that have been produced in the past and that have a period of serviceableness that extends beyond the present. Second, he can produce goods that are more durable. Third, he can produce goods that require a longer period of production. Fourth, for some goods, he can shift to more time-consuming methods of production.[5]

That saving in general is derived from the image of action can be seen by contrasting an image of action with an image of non-action.

Action can be said to lie between two extremes of non-action. The first extreme is satiation or bliss. If Crusoe possessed all the goods he wanted, he would not have to save any. He would be satiated. But he would also not experience any felt uneasiness. Consequently, he would not act. The second extreme is a situation in which an individual's decision is dominated entirely by his need to survive. Assume that if Crusoe devotes "all" his energy to his survival in the immediate future, he can justly barely survive. Then he would not save. But there also would be no choice in any meaningful sense. There would be no felt uneasiness. There would be only death or life. Given that action is defined only for cases where there is scarcity and where survival is not at issue, it is difficult to disagree with the assertion that saving is implied by the proposition that human beings act.[6]

Plain saving and capitalist saving.[7] Mises distinguished two purposes for saving. The first is "to provide for the future which the saver currently images could be less amply supplied than in the present." Saving that is done for the first reason is called *plain saving*. The second reason is the fact that saving leads to future goods that are valued more highly. Saving done for the second reason is called *capitalist saving*. It is aimed at earning a premium. To understand more completely what these terms mean, consider the following example.

Suppose that Crusoe lives in the world of Frank Knight's Crusonea plant.[8] Fruit from the plant is the only good that Crusoe can obtain and consume. A decision by Crusoe not to pick a piece of fruit from the plant during any given year would result in 1.05 pieces being available the next year. If the piece is picked, it will not be available next year. Why would Crusoe ever choose to pick the fruit? The answer lies with plain saving. Just as he would never consume all of his fruit today, leaving none for tomorrow, he would never save all of his fruit for the future. This result depends, of course, on his not being satiated or facing the threat of extinction.

Capitalist saving is aimed at earning a return. Since the Crusonea plant yields a 5 percent return, Crusoe might save more than if it only yielded a 4 percent return. If so, the difference would be capitalist saving.

Consider the following simple example, which contains both types of saving. In a two-period model, suppose that Crusoe has fifty-five pieces of fruit and that the rate of return on saving is 0 percent. Assume, at this 0 percent rate, Crusoe would consume five pieces of fruit and save fifty. Assume further that if the rate of return is 5 percent, Crusoe would reduce his consumption to four pieces and raise his saving to fifty-one. Then, at five percent, capitalist saving is one piece of fruit and plain saving is fifty pieces.

Plain saving occurs because Crusoe views his satisfaction through the window of time. In thinking about his satisfaction in the near future and in the distant future, he recognizes that the choice to have more near-future satisfaction implies a result in which he will have less distant-future satisfaction. So he allocates his expected satisfaction over time, so to speak. In his plain saving, Crusoe makes a comparison between his satisfaction at various times. Plain saving would occur regardless of whether saving yielded a return. Capitalist saving is aimed at earning a return.

Capitalist saving may be positive or negative. It all depends upon how a person responds to a positive rate of return on saving. Suppose that Crusoe has the option of producing a good, say X, for near-future consumption or for distant-future consumption. Consider now the proportion of factors Crusoe would devote to the satisfaction of his distant-future want for X relative to the factors he would devote to the satisfaction of near-future want for X. Calculate the proportion under the condition that the rate of return is zero (i.e., if the amount of X that can be produced with a given set of factors in the distant future is the same as the amount that can be produced in the near future). Now compare the proportion calculated in this way with another proportion that is calculated under the assumption that the rate of return is positive. If the latter proportion is greater than the former, then Crusoe's capitalist saving is positive at the rate assumed. If it is less, then capitalist saving is negative.

The purpose of this exercise is mainly pedagogical. Crusoe himself would never care to conduct such a calculation. And an outsider could not hope to answer the questions that must be answered to make the determination.

Plain saving is derived from the image of action. It is a necessary characteristic. Every actor, whether isolated or not, arranges his behavior with regard to the time during which his satisfaction is expected. Capitalist saving is not a characteristic of action. It may occur if Crusoe observes conditions in which a sacrifice of a given amount of time and energy today will yield goods in the distant future that he believes he will value more highly than he would value the goods he can produce in the near future with the same time and energy.

Making Decisions

The seventh characteristic is making decisions. To perform an action, an act of will must be made. Crusoe must consciously decide to use his factors to produce a good, he must consume, and he must save. This act of will is called making a decision. It is distinct from the pre-decision-making characteristics of identifying factors and estimating net benefits.

Decision making may entail a series of behaviors. When Crusoe makes a decision to produce a good, he may be directing himself to gather certain raw materials, to use his labor along with materials to produce capital, and then to use his labor along with other materials and the capital to produce a good. The series may be such that a later behavior is contingent on a particular outcome of an earlier behavior. For example, Crusoe may decide to use technique *A* if the raw materials he is able to gather turn out to be of high quality but to use technique *B* if they turn out to be of low quality.

Uncertainty-Bearing as a Fundamental Characteristic of Action

Uncertainty-bearing is the eighth characteristic of action. Looking ahead to the end of a good's period of provision, Crusoe recognizes that he may not receive the amount of net satisfaction that he expects his decision to yield, according to his best prediction. His wants through time may change during the period or he may discover that his initial knowledge about his abilities was wrong. Crusoe has no alternative but to bear this uncertainty. He may prepare for it by storing durable goods or capital, among other possibilities. In addition, he may be able to reduce his burden of uncertainty by choosing to produce goods for which changes in wants, abilities, and knowledge are more predictable or have a less deleterious effect. But he cannot avoid the uncertainty. *Uncertainty exists in every decision* because normal human beings know that their wants, abilities, and knowledge change in ways that they cannot fully anticipate.

Guaranty. It is worth noting that Crusoe could convert at least part of his uncertainty-bearing into a cost. Imagine that Crusoe calculates the worst possible outcome of a production project. Then, assuming that this might occur, he sets aside durable goods or factors so that, even if the worst possible outcome does occur, he would achieve some targeted level of satisfaction in future periods. The satisfaction sacrificed by the setting aside of goods or factors during the period of provision could be called a personal cost of production. The value to Crusoe of the goods or factors that are set aside for this purpose is called personal *guaranty*. The concept of guaranty is important in a market economy, where the provision of guaranty by one person may entice another to take an uncertain action that he otherwise would not take.

Summary

To summarize, Crusoe's production-consumption action has the following characteristics. Crusoe predicts his wants through time. He identifies both the factors that can be used to produce goods and the possible periods of provision. He supplies his own labor, which he uses to acquire resources and to produce goods. He produces goods and may produce capital. He estimates the net benefits of alternative actions partly by attempting to predict his future wants, abilities, knowledge, and physical environment. Then he decides on a production action. The production decision is at the same time a decision about saving. In making his decision, he must bear uncertainty, although his burden depends upon which actions he chooses. He may offset his burden by providing guaranty.

2. THE ESSENTIAL FUNCTIONS AND DELIBERATION

If Crusoe was faced with the task of describing his action to someone else, he would have to use the method of contrasting images of functions. He would, in essence, contrast his image of a robot that performs what can be called *essential functions* with an image of a human being who performs those functions. The contrast would enable him to identify the distinctively human character of his action. This part shows how Crusoe would proceed.

Crusoe's Description of His Action

Consider how Crusoe could describe his production-consumption action. He could describe some of the characteristics of his action by pointing to the behavior of other animals. He could show how the animals supply factors, produce, consume, and save. But Crusoe also wants to show how his performance of these behaviors differs from that of other animals. To do this he must appeal to the listener to recognize that, as a human being, he possesses characteristics that cannot be fully described by referring to the behavior of animals. These characteristics are the discovery and identification of factors, the estimation of net benefits, making the act of will that constitutes the decision, and bearing the uncertainty.[9] Having identified these latter characteristics of action, Crusoe would proceed to explain how his particular action differs from what it might have been.

Consider more deeply the method that Crusoe would use to describe his action. It is convenient to use the term essential functions to refer to the behaviors of (1) producing, (2) consuming, (3) saving, and (4) supplying factors. The behaviors are called functions because they correspond exactly to the type of action under consideration—that is, the production-consumption action. They are essential, given that one is concerned with this type of action.

To fully describe the essential functions, Crusoe could point to an animal that performs them. Alternatively, he could construct an image of a robot. However, he could not describe the other characteristics of action in this way. To describe them, he would have to contrast an animal, or robot, that performs the essential functions with what he and his listener know intuitively and on the basis of experience to be how a human being would perform a production-consumption action under the conditions specified. In other words, he would have to use the method of contrasting images of functions. By this method, he would be able to set the essential functions apart from the distinctly human characteristics of action.

It is convenient to refer to these distinctly human characteristics as *deliberation* and decision making. In deliberation, an individual apparently constructs a mental image of the alternative behaviors that he can perform and their outcomes. The individual uses his knowledge and reason to choose one over another, keeping in mind that he cannot be certain that the choice made will turn out to be the best one. Neither Crusoe nor the listener could create a complete image of deliberation. Nevertheless, both know intuitively that deliberation must occur in every action.

Identifying Nonessential Characteristics of Deliberation

It may be possible to fully describe a specific difference between you as a deliberating actor and you as a robot. If so, the difference could be made part of a higher-order robot. Suppose that someone asks you to describe how you as a deliberating actor differ from the behavior that is performed in the production-consumption routine of a robot. You may answer in part by specifically identifying some deliberation that is not part of the routine (e.g., the deliberation you performed in creating the routine). Note, however, that to the extent that you fully describe this deliberation process, it can be transformed into a routine. Then it can be combined with the other routine behavior to build a new robot routine that would include the "deliberation behavior" that you claimed distinguished you from a previous robot. The distinctiveness that you claimed to have would now be part of a second generation robot.

The procedure of contrasting the image of a simpler robot routine with one that is more complex can be used to define additional characteristics of an individual's deliberation. Such characteristics are nonessential but they may be present in a particular action. Thus, the praxeologist might construct images of them in order to help the historian make descriptions of action in everyday life. It is important to recognize that all the characteristics of action cannot be defined in this way. In particular, you cannot use this method to define the part of action that consists of using the method itself.

The distinction between essential and nonessential characteristics of deliberation can perhaps best be understood in the following way. Consider the characteristic that has been called the identification of factors. To identify factors, an actor may develop a routine. In the routine are rules that are used to accept or reject a particular factor candidate for further investigation. The routine states that once a candidate is accepted, it is then subjected to several predesigned tests. When the tests are completed, the routine specifies whether the candidate is or is not a factor.

In this example, one could call the routine an identification-of-factor routine. Any behavior that is performed in the process of running the routine would be an aid to deliberation. To the actor, it would be regarded as a characteristic of his specific action—a type of factor. However, it is not an essential characteristic of action as the praxeologist views it. A production-consumption action can be imagined in which the identification-of-factor routine is absent.

Note that even the creation of a routine may be regarded as a nonessential characteristic of deliberation. This would be the case if the subject had previously created a routine for creating identification-of-factor routines. In this case, deliberation would occur during the creation of the prior routine.

The fact is that every behavior you can fully describe is also a behavior that can be modelled and included in a robot routine. You can never fully describe your deliberations. Thus, your identification of factors and estimation of relative net benefits cannot be fully incorporated into a robot routine of any generation.[10]

3. USING THE METHOD OF CONTRASTING IMAGES OF FUNCTIONS

To understand the rationale for using the method of contrasting images of functions, one must appreciate two facts about the nature of economic interaction. The first is the impossibility of directly applying subjectivism to macroeconomic issues. This was discussed in the first part of chapter four. The second is that although entrepreneurship cannot be fully modelled, the method helps one identify and understand it. In this part, the second fact is explored by making an analogy with the use of the method to describe the production-consumption action of an isolated individual.

Using the Evenly Rotating Economy to Elucidate Entrepreneurship

The student of individual action identifies characteristics of deliberation by contrasting a model of herself as a robot with her action in everyday life. Analogously, the economist identifies characteristics of entrepreneurship by first constructing a model of an economy in which essential, non-entrepreneurial economic functions are performed by optimizing robots. Then she contrasts this model with what she can know by intuition and experience about economic interaction under the conditions specified in a market economy.

The student of individual action can *define* nonessential characteristics of action that help in her deliberation by contrasting a simple robot model with a more complex model that contains the robot routines of the simpler model plus the additional routine that represents the characteristics of action that she wishes to define. The economist can define nonessential entrepreneurial characteristics by contrasting the simple model with a more complex model of an economy that contains more and more complex robots that can do everything that the simpler robots can do and then some. Examples of nonessential entrepreneurial characteristics are the behavior performed by hired technicians, which include "the great inventors, the champions in the field of science, the constructors and designers as well as the performers of simple tasks."[11] Another example is the managerial function.[12]

One can imagine identifying more and more nonessential characteristics of entrepreneurship and then defining each newly identified characteristic by contrasting simpler with more complex images of an economy. The definition of entrepreneurship would expand as each new characteristic was added. One would acquire a deeper knowledge of the consequences of entrepreneurship. One would never, however, expect to define entrepreneurship completely. Just as one cannot imagine constructing a robot that would duplicate all of deliberation in an individual action, one cannot imagine constructing robots that would duplicate all of entrepreneurship.

The simplest model of an economy contains only the functions of producing (including capital replacement), consuming, supplying factors, and capitalist saving. These functions are performed routinely by factor-supplier robots and by consumer-saver robots. The factor-supplier robots select particular employment opportunities from among the numerous possibilities. They embody the functions of incurring the disutility of labor, of producing goods, and of maintaining capital. The consumer-saver robots select the goods to consume and the amounts of capital to supply and consume. The consumer-saver robots embody the functions of selecting goods for consumption and of getting wants satisfied through time, as reflected by the saving that enables capital to be retained and produced. In the simplest model, there is no need to single out the producing robots. The function of producing goods is implicit. When factors are combined, production occurs automatically.

The model of an economy that contains only these function-performing robots is called an evenly rotating economy, or ERE, as pointed out in chapter four.[13] In the ERE, no money is demanded or held. Also, no one identifies factors, estimates net benefits, makes decisions, or bears uncertainty. Nevertheless, goods and factors have prices. The prices of factors are such that, when added to the interest on the loan that is necessary to maintain capital, they add up to the prices of products. In the ERE, saving consists only of capitalist saving, since the future is assumed to be no different from the present. Capitalist-saver robots receive *interest*. If they did not receive this, they would allow their capital to be consumed.[14]

The ERE can be thought of as an actionless economy. It is imagined that the same production, consumption, and saving behavior is repeated routinely time and again without any need for entrepreneurship. The model of the ERE as an actionless economy is not only imaginary, it also does not correspond to any experience that one has in everyday life. In the ERE, individuals do not choose to repeat their behavior; they simply repeat it. They behave according to fixed routines.[15] Moreover, their repetitions take no time. In the ERE, all of the functions that correspond to chosen behavior are performed, even though there is no deliberation. Wants get satisfied and resources are used to produce goods. Capital is maintained by means of saving. It is as if the individuals are directed by magic. The magic, of course, is the economist's ability to imagine the robot routines.

Why the Method Is Called the Method of Contrasting Images of Functions

The author has chosen to call the method described in this part the method of contrasting images of functions. The reason for this name is that it reminds the economist that her models of robot economies and her images of economic interaction in the market economy must contain the essential economic functions. It also is suggestive of the method of contrast that must be used to define nonessential economic functions. A danger in this term is that the economist will forget that entrepreneurship itself is not an economic function but a cause of the performance of the economic functions.

NOTES

1. Consumption and production may occur simultaneously in everyday life. An example is a craftsperson who enjoys working. The division of action into production and consumption would not be relevant to such cases. Such cases would either have to be disregarded or be dealt with in an addendum.

2. Mises (1966, 479).

3. Mises (1966, 481).

4. Mises (1966) says only:

> The modern theory of value and prices . . . distinguishes within the class of factors of production the original (nature-given) factors from the produced factors of production (the intermediary products) and furthermore within the class of original factors the nonhuman (external) factors from the human factors (labor). . . . (p. 636)

5. These categories are equivalent to those listed by Mises (1966, 481).

6. Practically all mainstream economists attribute saving to the phenomenon they call time preference. They explain this in terms of impatience or waiting. Impatience, waiting, and similar concepts are ordinarily regarded as psychological. When these terms are used in this way, they do not provide a sufficiently strong epistemological foundation for the idea that saving is a characteristic of action. See Mises's (1966) discussion at the bottom of page 486. When Mises uses the concept of time preference (1966, 483–90), he does not relate it to the psychological phenomenon of waiting.

7. Mises defines these terms in his 1966 book on pages 530–31.

8. See Knight (1944).

9. It is not being maintained here that animals, particularly apes and other higher-functioning mammals, are unable to identify factors, estimate net benefits, make decisions, or bear uncertainty. The point is that the human capacity in these areas is so complex that when Crusoe seeks to describe his own action, he will focus on these characteristics. It may also be appropriate to use the method of contrasting images of functions in the study of higher-functioning mammals. But this only reinforces the idea that the method should be used in the study of human action.

10. For an interesting paper on the contrast between a robot and an individual, which hints at the methodology of the new subjectivism and which clearly recognizes the phenomenological nature of "understanding," see Dennett (1971).

11. Mises (1966, 303).

12. Ibid., 304–09.

13. See Mises (1966, 251–55, 530–31).

14. Mises calls such interest of *originary* interest. In its most general sense, it equals the increase in the money value of a factor due to using the factor in employment X, which takes a long time to complete, instead of using it in employment Y, which takes a shorter time to complete. See Mises (1966, 530–31).

15. Mises says:

. . . Such a rigid system is not peopled with living men making choices liable to error; it is a world of soulless unthinking automatons; it is not a human society, it is an ant hill. (1966, 248)

    . . . [In the evenly rotating economy], automatic reaction is substituted for the conscious striving of thinking man after the removal of uneasiness. (1966, 249)

Chapter 6

The Method of Contrasting Images of Functions (3): The Categories of Entrepreneurial Action

Entrepreneurship is that part of economic interaction under the conditions specified in the definition of the market economy that cannot be represented by robots. It corresponds to the deliberation and decision making that occurs in a Crusonean production-consumption action. However, whereas the individual can come to understand his own deliberation by contrasting with a model of a single robot, the economist must contrast with a model of many robots. Moreover, the fact that the economist must assume that each individual in a market economy can perform actions that are as complex as his own means that the contrast must proceed by means of a step-by-step process. The first step is to construct an image of an economy in which robot consumer-savers and factor-suppliers perform the essential economic functions according to directions from what are called *fully integrated entrepreneurs*.

Such an image enables the economist to clearly identify what are called the *categories of entrepreneurship*. These categories correspond to the characteristics of deliberation and decision making in an image of an individual action. They are performed not because the individual anticipates satisfaction, however, but because the entrepreneur anticipates money earnings. The earnings are called *profit*. Thus, the image that emerges during the first step is of a group of interacting, fully integrated entrepreneurs who direct all of the consumption, saving,

85

factor supply, and production in an effort to earn profit and to avoid loss. This image provides the basis for definitions that the economist uses to communicate the difference between the behavior of robots in a simple robot economy like the ERE and economic interaction in the market economy.

Part 1 of this chapter identifies what will be called the categories, or essential characteristics, of entrepreneurial action. There are three of these: appraisement, undertaking, and uncertainty-bearing. Care is taken to distinguish uncertainty-bearing from risk-bearing. Part 2 shows that these categories are essential and inseparable. A comprehensive image of entrepreneurship that does not contain each of them cannot be formed. Part 3 discusses several related issues: (1) the meaning of uncertainty-bearing, (2) the difference between roles in the ERE and the use of typifications in everyday speech, (3) the hazards of regarding entrepreneurship as a function, (4) the idea that venturesomeness and quickness of perception are characteristics of entrepreneurship, and (5) the production of capital and entrepreneurial ability.

1. THE THREE CATEGORIES

To identify the categories of entrepreneurial action in a market economy, the economist starts with the behavioral routines of robots in the ERE. By contrasting the ERE with her initial image of a market economy, the economist comes to recognize that in a market economy such behavior could not occur by itself. It would have to be caused by deliberation and acts of will. Then she creates a role to perform the deliberation and acts of will that are necessary to "activate" the robot routines of the ERE. The result is an image of an economy that contains all of the economic functions in the ERE in addition to a group of fully integrated entrepreneurs, who are said to cause the functions. This image is used as a reference in making the proper definitions of terms that the economist must use to describe economic interaction. For identification purposes, the image is called the *image of fully integrated entrepreneurs*.

This procedure is analogous to that used in identifying deliberation in a Crusoe situation. The difference is that whereas the goal of an act by Crusoe is the satisfaction of his wants, the goal of an entrepreneurial act is the acquisition of money. The three categories of entrepreneurial action are: appraisement, undertaking, and uncertainty-bearing.[1] The purpose of this part is to introduce these categories.

Appraisement

The first category is *appraisement*. Appraisement encompasses the two deliberative functions that were identified in the Crusoe situation: identifying factors and estimating net benefits. Whereas Crusoe is said to identify factors and to estimate his own net benefits, entrepreneurship appraises factors by acquiring and using knowledge of production possibilities, anticipated factor price offers, and anticipated price offers for goods. A factor is defined as an item or behavior for which an entrepreneur anticipates a money profit if he buys it and employs it to produce a consumers' good.

Consider a decision to buy a set of factors in markets in order to produce a good to be offered for sale at some future time. Before the factors are purchased, the entrepreneur appraises them. When his appraisals are complete, he compares them with the anticipated purchase prices of the factors in order to determine whether he should try to buy the factors and use them. The comparison takes account of the anticipated return on money he can lend or borrow, along with the uncertainty associated with the lending and borrowing.

Undertaking

Entrepreneurship makes decisions as Crusoe does. Both entrepreneurial decisions and Crusoe's decisions involve the employment of factors in specific production projects. The difference is that the entrepreneur obtains her factors by purchasing or renting them in markets. In the special case of labor, employment results in an *employment relation* between the entrepreneur as employer and the factor supplier as employee.

It is useful to call the entrepreneur's decision making *undertaking*. Undertaking refers to an entrepreneur's decision to cause all behavior to be performed that ultimately results in the satisfaction of wants, with the exception of appraisement. Referring to the economic functions in the ERE, undertaking means a decision to employ the factors to produce a good, to direct factors to be used for one purpose instead of another, and to cause the good to be consumed during some specified period of provision. Undertaking implies saving because different goods take different amounts of time to produce and consume, and because factors have alternative time-constrained uses.

Uncertainty-Bearing

Finally, the subjective uncertainty that is borne by Crusoe is replaced by the intersubjective uncertainty borne by the entrepreneur. Intersubjective uncertainty is the uncertainty that each actor in a market economy has about the future wants, abilities, and knowledge of others. The entrepreneur, as a role, bears no intrasubjective uncertainty.

An entrepreneur anticipates a gain from her appraisals and undertaking. *Whether her anticipated gain is realized depends on someone else's future act of will.* For example, the entrepreneur as a producer of a good must predict the actions of a buyer in order to predict her gain. It is evident, however, that the buyer's wants might change, that her abilities to buy might change, or that she might take advantage of other opportunities learned about during the production period. Since such changes are always occurring, entrepreneurial acts are always speculative.

Uncertainty-bearing means putting oneself into a position to accept and bear the responsibility for the outcome of her decision. For the entrepreneur, it means bearing the responsibility for losses if those losses are due to changes in others' wants, abilities, or knowledge. If the decision yields gains, the entrepreneur accepts them. If it yields losses, she bears the responsibility for absorbing them.

Guaranty. The entrepreneur, as a role, hires other factors in advance of the consumption of goods. He must guarantee that the factors get paid regardless of any changes that occur before the planned date of consumption. Because of uncertainty, there is no way to accomplish this except by setting money aside that must be forfeited in the event of an adverse outcome. Such money is called *guaranty*. It is analogous to the goods set aside by Crusoe for the purpose of avoiding a substantial reduction in his consumption if a production project fails. Since entrepreneurial rewards are called, respectively, *profit* and *loss,* this means that the entrepreneur must make up any losses by forfeiting his guaranty. The concepts of uncertainty-bearing, guaranty, profit, loss, and interest are discussed more fully in chapters eight and ten. For the time being, it is sufficient to recognize that appraisement and undertaking are associated with these concepts.

Uncertainty vs. Risk

It is unimportant for Crusoe to make a distinction between uncertainty and risk. For the economist, however, it is essential to distinguish between them. Uncertainty refers to entrepreneurial predictions of wants, abilities, and knowledge. Risk refers to predictions that are made on the basis of scientific or technical knowledge.

Risk-bearing refers to the act of betting a sum of money or property that a particular objective, natural event will occur in the future. The risk-bearer knows that a number of possible events in the same class could occur. But he gambles that only one or one subset of the class will occur. He loses the bet if an event occurs that is not the one (or member of the subset) on which he bets. When this happens, the risk-bearer regards himself as unlucky.[2]

Risk-bearing appears to be like uncertainty-bearing. The money that must be pledged to compensate for lost revenue due to bad luck appears to be similar to the money that an undertaker would lose if, for example, he overestimated future demand and incurred an economic loss. However, to place the two in the same class is to ignore the principle that distinguishes non-entrepreneurial functions from entrepreneurship. Such a confusion threatens to compromise the whole subjectivist approach to the market economy, since entrepreneurship lies at the heart of it.

It is easy to confuse risk-bearing with uncertainty-bearing. Consider the following example. Suppose that a person thinks he knows the probability that an accident will occur. He then makes a bet that the accident will not occur. If the accident occurs, he may attribute it to bad luck and that will be that. However, suppose he discovers that his scientific knowledge was incorrect. The person determines that the actual probability of accident in such a situation is so high that he would not make the bet if the same circumstances arose in the future. In assessing his action, the person will conclude that his appraisal of his scientific or technical knowledge was incorrect. The person will not think of his earlier decision as a bad-luck gamble, which should be repeated under similar circumstances, but as an entrepreneurial decision based on a faulty appraisal, which should not be repeated.

Risk-bearing as a non-entrepreneurial economic function. The distinction between uncertainty-bearing and risk-bearing suggests that another non-entrepreneurial economic function—risk-bearing—exists in a market economy. Risk is present in many if not all actions, since an actor normally recognizes the prospect for accidents of nature. If the physical environment accidentally turns out to be different than expected, the action will not have its expected physical consequences. In a Crusoe situation, the risk cannot be eliminated. Crusoe's risk may be reduced, however, if he can choose a less risky project with a lower expected return over a more risky one with a greater return. When alternatives are available that enable an individual to reduce risk, a risk cost can be calculated.

In a market economy, the risk faced by one person can be shifted to another person. If a gambler and/or someone with superior scientific knowledge agrees to bear the risk associated with producing a good, she may enable a good to be produced that would otherwise be unprofitable. In this event, risk-bearing can be called an economic function.[3]

In a market economy, risks can be pooled, thereby enabling the personal cost of risk-bearing to be spread out over many individuals. Insurers specialize in reducing this cost.

Summary

In contrasting the ERE with a market economy, the economist's attention is directed toward the identification of factors and the estimation of relative money costs and revenues. This is called appraisement. In addition, it is directed toward the decision making, interaction, and uncertainty-bearing of individuals who are designated by the economist to play the role of entrepreneurs. Since entrepreneurial decision making entails the employment of factors, it has been called undertaking. Thus, the three categories of entrepreneurship are called appraisement, undertaking, and uncertainty-bearing.

2. A DERIVATION OF THE CATEGORIES OF ENTREPRENEURIAL ACTION

A phenomenon is a category of entrepreneurial action if its existence cannot be denied, given the a priori and fundamental economic assumptions. The categories of entrepreneurial action are deduced from a combination of a priori categories of action and fundamental economic assumptions. To deduce the categories, the economist asks how the fundamental economic functions come to be performed in a market economy. He uses his intuition and experience to find the answer. His initial image of the market economy plays a part in his search.

No normal human being would use factors to produce a good that he intends to sell without predicting whether he can make a profit. This is the same thing as saying that he would not act entrepreneurially unless he appraised factors. Making the production decision is undertaking.

Since every decision entails uncertainty, it is said that appraisement, undertaking, and uncertainty-bearing are categories of entrepreneurial action.

An economist cannot "prove" either that entrepreneurship itself exists or that a particular phenomena is a category of entrepreneurial action by pointing to an example. Instead, he must appeal to his audience to recognize, by means of intuition and experience, that there are parts of economic interaction that would exist under the conditions specified in the definition of the market economy and that those parts cannot be represented by models of robotic behavior.

Intuition and experience also reveal that the three categories of entrepreneurial action are *inseparable*. As the term is used here, inseparability means that no one in a market economy would bear the uncertainty connected with a decision to produce and/or exchange without basing his decision on his personal appraisals. To prove this inseparability, one begins with an image of economic interaction in which each entrepreneur is assumed to be a fully integrated entrepreneur. Such an entrepreneur exhibits all three categories. However, different entrepreneurs may appraise different classes of factors and make decisions to produce different specific goods with the appraised factors. In other words, they may specialize. Each entrepreneur bears all the uncertainty associated with her undertaking decisions. Using this image as a starting point, one attempts to form another image of economic interaction in which one of the three categories is absent. Inseparability is proven when it is realized that the latter image is impossible to form, given the assumptions about economic functions and given the intuitive and experiential knowledge about economic interaction.

The Fully Integrated Entrepreneur

The fully integrated entrepreneur is an image of a person who borrows from savers while pledging money (guaranty) to pay them the principal and interest that is promised. She then buys factors and fully specifies how the factors are to be used, their length of use, and the pay. The pay is guaranteed by a pledge of guaranty or it is given in advance. In addition, she agrees to compensate workers if there is an adverse change in their disutilities of labor during the period of production. Because the entrepreneur obtains no advance commitments to buy from consumers, she also bears the uncertainty that consumer demands will change. Thus, she provides guaranty for all the producing, consuming, saving, and factor-supplying behavior connected with the undertaking.

The fully integrated entrepreneur combines the factors to produce a consumers' good on the basis of her appraisals. The entrepreneur produces a consumers' good that she thinks will be demanded because she believes that its sale will generate enough revenue to yield a profit. Her uncertainty-bearing consists of her bet of the guaranty. If the worst happens, the entrepreneur knows that she will have to forfeit the guaranty. She bets, however, that she will realize a profit.

An Enterpriser and a Hired Guarantor

In the following discussion, it is useful to employ a new term to refer to the performance of two categories of entrepreneurial action. The term is *enterpriser* and it refers to a *role* that makes undertaking decisions on the basis of appraisals. Thus, the enterpriser both appraises and makes undertaking decisions. However, the enterpriser as such bears no uncertainty (provides no guaranty). For this reason, he differs from the fully integrated entrepreneur.

The question is whether one can form an image of an economy containing all three categories of entrepreneurship but in which the enterpriser role is separated from the role of the uncertainty-bearer. The first step is to try to imagine a class of individuals who provide guaranty for a fee. It is convenient to call a member of this class a *guarantor*. A guarantor would be willing to substitute some of his own money for the guaranty that would otherwise be provided by the fully integrated entrepreneur. The guarantor bets on his ability to appraise the income-earning ability of the fully integrated entrepreneur.

In offering to purchase guaranty, the fully integrated entrepreneur sends a message that he would rather give up some of the expected profit than to bet all of what he believes to be the required amount on his enterprise. The guarantor, when he makes an offer, also sends a message, saying that he is willing to bet the money pledged as guaranty. The willingness to bet (i.e., to bear the uncertainty) stems from his appraisal of the enterprising abilities of the entrepreneur. The appraisal leads him to conclude that this is a good bet.

Suppose that the guarantor provides some amount of guaranty and that the fully integrated entrepreneur incurs a substantial loss. Then the guarantor must forfeit a guaranty that is greater than his fee. But the fully integrated entrepreneur will have succeeded in reducing his loss by shifting some of the uncertainty to the guarantor. Thus, to the fully integrated entrepreneur, the guarantor's fee is a cost. It is paid in order to avoid having to incur the greater loss in the event that his appraisals of factors are incorrect.

There are three differences between individuals that could be used to explain why a trade between the fully integrated entrepreneur and the guarantor would take place. First, the two individuals may have different wealth. The entrepreneur may have no money or wealth to use as guaranty, while the guarantor may have a substantial amount. Second, the fully integrated entrepreneur may be unwilling to bet his wealth on personal enterprising abilities because he has what he believes are better uses for them, while the guarantor is willing to bet on the enterprising abilities because he does not believe that he has better uses for his wealth. Third, the two individuals may appraise the enterprise ability differently. Even if they were both equally willing and able to provide savings and guaranty for a worthwhile project, their appraisals may differ.

An enterpriser who does not bear uncertainty? Now consider the possibility of forming an image of a case where the uncertainty would be removed entirely from enterprise. Suppose that the guarantor in the last subsection offers to pay the entrepreneur a fixed wage to make his appraisals and decisions. In other words, he wants to convert the entrepreneur into an enterpriser. The guarantor would bear all the uncertainty and would earn any profit or loss due to the hired enterpriser.

This arrangement would completely separate enterprise with respect to the factors used by the enterpriser from the uncertainty-bearing. However, the arrangement would not separate enterprise from uncertainty-bearing at a different level. As an economic actor whose goal is profit, the guarantor would never agree to the arrangement unless he had appraised the abilities of the hired enterpriser. In addition, under the trade agreement, the ultimate decision to produce would be made not by the hired enterpriser but by the guarantor who employs him. This ultimate decision would be made at the time when the guarantor agrees to pay the enterpriser a fixed wage. Thus, although the arrangement would transform the entrepreneur into an enterpriser, it would also transform the guarantor into a fully integrated entrepreneur.

The transformed guarantor may not make decisions regarding which nonenterprise factors will be bought and how they will be used. He may also not appraise non-enterprise factors. However, he must make the decision to employ the hired enterprise factor and must appraise this factor.[4]

It follows that the notion that the non-enterprise economic functions could be performed without someone being a fully integrated entrepreneur is untenable.[5] It is not consistent with what one knows by intuition and experience to be the nature of economic interaction. We see then that appraisement, undertaking, and uncertainty-bearing are three essential and inseparable characteristics of entrepreneurship. This qualifies them as categories of entrepreneurial action. It is practically impossible to conceive of entrepreneurial action in which the three categories are not present.

3. RELATED ISSUES

The Meaning of Uncertainty-Bearing

The term uncertainty-bearing has been traditionally used to refer to entrepreneurship's prospect that the anticipated profit of decision making may not be realized. This term should be used cautiously for two reasons. First, it can be easily confused with risk-bearing. As noted in Part 1, risk-bearing is a function performed by one who gambles on widely known probabilities. It may be impossible in some circumstances for an individual in a market economy to shift the risk-bearing to a gambler. If so, the same individual would have to bear both uncertainty and risk. Nevertheless, the two roles must remain distinct in the economist's mind. Uncertainty-bearing concerns the knowledge possessed by entrepreneurship about human wants, abilities, and knowledge, while risk-bearing concerns the knowledge possessed by a natural scientist or technician about natural events.

The second reason why the term uncertainty-bearing should be used cautiously is that it fails to imply the inseparability of the three categories of entrepreneurial action. When inseparability is recognized, uncertainty-bearing is seen to always refer to a *"bet"* that undertaking based on one's personal appraisals of factors will yield profit. The entrepreneur does not bet against anyone; he merely bets on himself. To bear uncertainty means to bet on oneself as an appraiser of factors and as an undertaker.

When uncertainty-bearing is defined as betting on one's appraisement ability, it becomes obvious why the economist must use a subjectivist approach to understand entrepreneurial interaction. Intuition and experience reveal that it would be sheer coincidence if one person's appraisal of his own ability to appraise in a market economy was the same as another person's appraisal of his ability. That different individuals make different appraisals of the same factors, including their own respective abilities to appraise, must be regarded as a fundamental fact of a market economy.[6] Recognition of this fact naturally leads the economist to focus on the relationships that form among appraisers and on the roles that individuals voluntarily adopt (e.g., the guarantor) because they believe they have superior or inferior abilities to make appraisals of different types.[7]

Roles vs. Typifications

It is essential to realize that the term entrepreneur is not a *typification*. It is a role that is based on what a normal human being would regard as an a priori category. A typification is a set of characteristics that are associated with the use of a word in everyday life.

The difference between a typification and a role can be understood by comparing dictionary definitions with economic definitions. One dictionary gives what it calls an "economic" definition of consumer as the buyer or user of commodities and services, as opposed to producer. This definition is presumably based on the lexicographer's interpretation of how the individuals she identifies as economists use the word *consume*. It does not refer to the economic function that has been described in the last two chapters. The consumer as a robot in the ERE stands in opposition to factor-suppliers and savers. The consumer-robot is both buyer and user. The same dictionary defines an entrepreneur as "the person who organizes, manages, and assumes the risks of a business (commercial activity engaged in as a means of livelihood)." This definition does not mention appraisement at all and it refers to the entrepreneur as a person, as opposed to a role.

The difference between the lexicographer and the economist regarding definitions of individuals is that the lexicographer constructs her definitions to reflect accepted usage. She defines individuals in terms of characteristics that are assigned by persons who she believes are most likely to be regarded as authorities by the prospective dictionary users. Such definitions may or may not coincide with an economic function or role. The economic function or role is at best a partial consideration.

The economist defines a role to personify either an economic function or the nonspecific categories of entrepreneurship. When the economist combines all the roles, what emerges is an integrated image of all the assumed functions, the decisions that caused them to be performed, and the deliberation and interaction that preceded the decisions. Such an image does not contain typifications.[8]

Typifications do not belong in economic theory. They are mainly useful only in making provisional, nontheoretical, and/or pragmatic descriptions of one's observations.

Hazards of Regarding Entrepreneurship as a Function

The term "entrepreneurial function" has often been employed to refer to entrepreneurship, and the term entrepreneur has been used to embody the entrepreneurial function. Mises's discussion of entrepreneurship in *Human Action* is a good example.[9] This usage has some didactic benefits but it may also be a significant source of confusion. In the ERE, the non-entrepreneurial functions are performed by robots. Entrepreneurship, however, cannot be performed by robots, by definition. More specifically, in the ERE the terms producer, consumer, saver, and factor-supplier refer to robotic behavior that can be fully and precisely specified by describing the physical movements and an optimizing routine. The term entrepreneur, however, must refer to an image that cannot be fully and precisely specified. The economist can only comprehend it in a general way by using his intuition and experience to judge how individuals would come to perform the other economic functions under the conditions specified in the definition of the market economy. When the economist uses the terms entrepreneur, producer, consumer-saver, and factor-supplier together, he prompts the confusion that entrepreneurship can be modelled like the non-entrepreneurial robotic behavior. To avoid this confusion, he should avoid calling entrepreneurship a function.

Venturesomeness and Quickness of Perception

In *Human Action,* Mises used the term entrepreneurship in two senses. The first and most important sense has already been described: that the term summarizes the difference between (a) the function-performing robots in the image of the evenly rotating economy, and (b) what intuition tells the economist about economic interaction under the conditions specified in the definition of the market economy. The second sense refers to the greater venturesomeness or quickness of perception that some individuals possess. Entrepreneurs, Mises said, "have more initiative, more venturesomeness, and a quicker eye than the crowd."[10]

It is clear that such characteristics can be relevant to entrepreneurship in a market economy. If some individuals get satisfaction from appraising and directing factors in production processes or if they are naturally better appraisers, then individuals acting in the entrepreneurial role will want to monitor the appraisers and directors in order to appraise their characteristics. Although the venturesome people may be no more likely to earn profits than losses, their greater venturesomeness makes it more likely that their actions will uncover knowledge that may be useful to the entrepreneurs in appraising factors.[11] For another example, if fully integrated entrepreneurs can distinguish those individuals who possess a quicker eye than the crowd, the entrepreneurs would be wise to copy their behavior on the assumption that it will be profitable, especially if the copier is unable to improve the quickness of his own appraising ability.

Mises's apparent purpose for using the term entrepreneur in the second sense was to derive what he called the *selective process* in a market economy. At various points in *Human Action,* he points out that competition causes the more venturesome or those with a quicker eye to emerge (i.e., they are selected) in the market as leaders in the process of satisfying consumer wants.[12] It appears, however, that he failed to get to the heart of the matter.

Differences in venturesomeness and quickness of perception do not appear to be either necessary or sufficient to deduce that consumer wants will tend to be satisfied in the market economy. It seems necessary and sufficient to assume that individuals make good bets. That is, if individuals acting in the role of the entrepreneur in a market economy are more likely to be right than wrong in their bets on their appraisement abilities, consumer wants will tend to be satisfied more than not. On the other hand, if such individuals tend to be wrong more than they are right, consumer wants will tend to not be satisfied through the market economy. Whether some individuals are more venturesome or have a quicker eye is irrelevant to consumer satisfaction. Even if everyone had the same venturesomeness and quickness of perception, consumer wants would tend to be satisfied so long as entrepreneurs tended to be right more than wrong in their bets on their appraisals.

It is true that the selective process may be related to differences in venturesomeness and quickness of perception. Yet the way that the more venturesome and quicker are selected out is not by some selective "process." It is by entrepreneurship, which tends to make correct bets on its appraisement abilities. The more venturesome are selected by appraising entrepreneurs who identify them as worth paying more attention to than their conservative counterparts. Those who are quicker of eye are selected by appraising entrepreneurs because their attributes are regarded as more worthy of betting on than the attributes of their slower counterparts.

Production of Human Capital and Entrepreneurial Ability

An individual may act entrepreneurially because she expects to acquire knowledge that will help her earn more income in similar future situations. In other words, the main purpose for the act may be the production of either human capital or entrepreneurial ability. The difference between this case and venturesomeness lies with the entrepreneur's perception. If the entrepreneur believes that something will be learned from her entrepreneurial action that will be an input to a future production process, the desire to produce human capital or entrepreneurial ability motivates her action. If the entrepreneur does not expect to learn anything and if she would buy the factors even if she did not believe that her appraisals were superior, then she is venturesome or curious.

A difficult problem of applied economics is how to use the language of economic theory to describe a person's decision to produce human capital or entrepreneurial ability. If the thing produced is human capital and if there is a market for it, the process can be described in terms that have already been introduced. An example is a person's decision to acquire training in a trade. Suppose that an individual acquires such training by purchasing and employing factors that she has appraised. The individual expects to sell (rent) her "skilled labor" for a price. Then the production is an undertaking performed with the intent of earning profit. She can be said to have appraised factors and to have uniquely decided that they would be more valuable if they were used to produce her training than they would have been if they were used elsewhere. The individual expected to earn profit from the rental of her "skilled labor." Even if she used only her own factors to produce the human capital, the act would be entrepreneurial, since she must have appraised those factors at a higher value than other entrepreneurs. Otherwise, she would have sold the factors.

Suppose, however, that the producer believed she would not be able to sell her "skilled labor" and that it would only be valuable to her in making future appraisals. In this event, it is not clear whether to say that she produced human capital or entrepreneurial ability. On the one hand, the producer's anticipated output could be called entrepreneurial ability because, in her view, it would increase either the superiority of her appraisals or her confidence that the appraisals would be superior. On the other hand, the output could be called human capital because she is capable of appraising it.

It should be evident that in discussing the interaction among entrepreneurs, economists would want to first get a conception of interaction without the complicating possibility that human capital and entrepreneurial ability are produced. Thus, the first step in describing interaction among entrepreneurs is made by assuming that the production of human capital and entrepreneurial ability is not part of the process. The production of human capital and entrepreneurial ability is an extension of the theory of entrepreneurial interaction.

Notes

1. The definition of entrepreneurship in this text is broadly consistent with Grinder and Hagel's conception. They also identify three characteristics of entrepreneurship: "(1) alertness to price discrepancies; (2) control, or ultimate decision making, over the means required to act upon this alertness in the market; and (3) responsibility, or uncertainty-bearing." Unfortunately, their discussion is too sketchy to be certain that they would agree with the characteristics identified here. See Grinder and Hagel (1977, 60).

Mises did not actually identify these categories. For a discussion of their implicit presence in Mises's work, see Appendix 5.

2. This situation is related to what Mises calls class probability. Uncertainty-bearing concerns case probability. See Appendix 4 for a more complete discussion of these terms.

3. The risk-bearing function often occurs in conjunction with entrepreneurial interaction. Suppose that if A were in isolation, he would choose not to produce a good because, according to his scientific knowledge, there is a high probability of accident. B, whose scientific knowledge is different, predicts that the probability of accident is lower. As a result, she offers to insure A for a fee. When the deal is made, A might say that he had been able to shift risk. To him, B's willingness to bear the risk would be regarded as a factor of production, which he purchases for a price.

From B's perspective, however, the situation may be quite different. She possesses scientific knowledge that she appraises at a higher value than A. B may be no more willing to bear risk than A; she may simply believe that her scientific knowledge is superior to A's. In order to bet on her belief that she has made a superior appraisal, B must bear the risk, given the circumstances.

In this case, it is true that some amount of risk has been shifted. Because B still believes that there is some probability of accident, she assumes part of the risk that A perceived. A proper representation of this example, however, would not focus om the shifting of risk. It would focus on the entrepreneurial interaction between A and B, since it is the interaction that causes the risk to be shifted. Without the difference in appraisals of B's scientific knowledge, no risk would be shifted.

4. The transformed guarantor is equivalent to what Mises called a pure entrepreneur. See Mises (1966, 256).

5. This fact was clearly recognized by Frank Knight (1921, 285). Knight pointed out that when entrepreneurship "lacks the means to guarantee the fixed incomes which they contract to pay," the supply of entrepreneurship will be limited. Also, he said:

> . . . In the absence of [knowledge by one person of another person's capabilities] it is clear that no one would put his resources under the direction of another without a valid guarantee of the payment agreed upon, and no one could become an entrepreneur who was not in a position to make such guarantees without assistance,

it being equally clear that no one would make such a guarantee for another. (p. 288–89)

6. This is not meant to imply that it is an a priori fact. It seems possible to imagine action and even economic interaction in an economy in which everyone's appraisement abilities are identical. Moreover, it is not possible for a person to determine through introspection that his appraisement abilities differ from those of others. Parenthetically, it should be noted that in the author's view, the most underdeveloped area of applied subjectivist economics is the identification of the individual differences that are relevant to the economist's understanding of a market economy. The best approach appears to be to study psychology, since it is the task of psychologists to study differences in human intellectual capacities and development.

7. It has become customary in recent non-subjectivist economics to think of betting and uncertainty as though they were quantifiable. Uncertainty-bearing has come to refer to the variability of outcomes in relation to a mathematical mean expected outcome. This thinking seems to be based on a desire to stand the concept of uncertainty in opposition to the concept of certainty. According to this custom, certainty is defined as a designated specific outcome of a choice. Uncertainty in this conception is defined as a range of possible outcomes of a choice.

Such a procedure may be useful in representing the uncertainty-bearer's view of the outcomes of a choice to perform an action. However, it diverts the economist's attention away from the options that individuals have to improve their appraisement abilities. More importantly, there is no reasonable way within such a framework to represent differences among individuals in their abilities to appraise each others' appraisement abilities. The most significant property of uncertainty in economics is not the fact that there is a range of possible outcomes of a choice. It is (1) that the concept reminds the economist of the subjectivity of knowledge of wants, abilities, and knowledge; and (2) that because it is understood to mean intersubjective uncertainty, it focuses the economist's attention on entrepreneurial interaction.

8. It is possible that in describing historical events, the non-economist will use the same role concept as that defined by the economist. Mises says:

. . . The fact that both acting men and historical sciences apply in their reasoning the results of economics and that they construct their ideal types on the basis of and with reference to the categories of [economic] theory, does not modify the radical logical distinction between ideal type [typification] and economic category [role]. The economic categories we are concerned with refer to purely integrated functions, the ideal types refer to historical events. (1966, 252)

Mises's views on ideal types are also discussed in Appendix 6.

9. Mises (1966, 252–54).

10. Mises (1966, 252–55).

11. In fact, Mises seems to recognize this point, although his way of

expressing it is peculiar and his recognition is brief. He says that "the promoter concept refers to a datum . . ." (1966, 255, italics added). To Mises, datum means a characteristic of human actors, such as wants, abilities, and knowledge, which entrepreneurs attempt to discover in order to appraise factors. Unfortunately, he does not develop this idea sufficiently for a reader to be certain what he means.

12. Mises specifically discusses the selective process on pages 311–15 of *Human Action*.

Chapter 7

The Method of Contrasting Images of Functions (4): Elucidating Characteristics of the Market Economy

In his initial image of the market economy, the economist assumes that individuals use price bids to send messages regarding their willingness and abilities to act in various ways. To help him understand these messages, he divides them into three major categories: consumers' goods prices, factor prices, and interest rates on loans.[1] He starts with the ERE, in which the three classes of prices are *pure*. Each specific class exclusively simulates a different type of message. The prices of consumers' goods simulate messages sent between individuals acting in the roles of consumer-savers and producing entrepreneurs. Factor prices simulate messages between individuals acting in the roles of factor-suppliers and producing entrepreneurs. And the interest rate simulates messages between the roles of consumer-savers and loan market entrepreneurs on the one hand and between loan market entrepreneurs and producing entrepreneurs on the other hand.

To help understand these three classes of messages in the market economy, the economist constructs an image of an economy that is more complex than that of the ERE but less complex than the market economy. This is the *image of interacting fully integrated robot entrepreneurs*. In this image, the prices that the economist assumes to exist in the ERE are conceived as having been formed through the interaction of fully integrated robot entrepreneurs. A robot entrepreneur behaves according to what can be called a "robo-profit" maximizing algorithm, which is specified by the economist. It is convenient to use the acronym FIREE to refer to the fully integrated robot entrepreneur economy.

In the FIREE, consumer-saver and factor-supplier robots perform the economic functions of the ERE, as described in chapters four and five. In addition, robot entrepreneurs, which can be called robo-ents for short, behave according to algorithms that simulate entrepreneurial message-sending and decision making. The function of the producing robo-ents is to select the factors and to allocate them among the different industries in order to produce goods. Robo-ents also select savings to be used to finance production.

The algorithms of the robo-ents in the FIREE are constructed in such a way that they cause the emergence of an equilibrium like the ERE.[2] The robo-ents respond to specified signals from consumer, factor-supplier, and lending robots, which they translate into robo-profit calculations. When a robo-ent's calculation indicates that robo-profit can be earned by selecting a different price to offer consumers, factor-suppliers, or lenders, it makes the change. In addition, the robo-ent may choose to produce a different good (i.e., to enter a different industry), to hire different factors, or to borrow a different amount of money for a different period of time.

The FIREE differs from the ERE in that it contains robo-ents who are assumed to maximize robo-profits.[3] Unlike the ERE, the FIREE can be used as a preliminary means of describing entrepreneurship. Whereas a contrast between the ERE and the market economy enables one to identify the categories of entrepreneurship, a contrast between the FIREE and the market economy reminds the economist of the subjectivism required to deal with entrepreneurship in the market economy.

Use of the FIREE enables the economist to elucidate four important characteristics of economic interaction in a market economy: competition, consumer sovereignty, the relationships among prices of goods at different orders in the structure of production, and the use and transfer of entrepreneurial knowledge. At the same time, it raises the potential for confusion, since economists who get accustomed to describing the robo-ents of the FIREE are inclined to treat the human entrepreneurs of the market economy as robots.

Such confusion can be avoided, however, by making a contrast between the FIREE and what one knows by intuition and experience about entrepreneurship under the conditions specified in the definition of the market economy. Such a contrast yields two important results.

First, it enables the economist to recognize parts of the four characteristics that cannot be represented by robot models. Second, it helps the
economist recognize that no price or interest rate in the market
economy is "pure" in the sense described above. Each contains
messages of all types. Individuals acting in the entrepreneurial role try
to separate these messages but they can never fully succeed in doing
so.

The purpose of this chapter is to use the model of the FIREE to help
describe the above-mentioned characteristics of the market economy.
This is done in Part 1. Part 2 contrasts the FIREE with the market
economy, thereby demonstrating the aspects of these characteristics
that cannot be represented in a model. In this way, it helps the
economist avoid errors due to improperly equating the FIREE with
the market economy. Chapter Eight discusses the "impurity" of
market prices.

1. USING THE MODEL OF THE FULLY INTEGRATED ROBOT ENTREPRENEURIAL ECONOMY

To help understand the four characteristics of the market economy,
the economist constructs an image of the FIREE. In the FIREE, robo-
ents are divided into industries. Each one manages a firm that produces
a product similar or identical to that of other firms in its industry. It
also employs factors that are similar or identical to those employed by
other firms. One version of the FIREE assumes that there are two
classes of robo-ents: producing robo-ents and loan market robo-ents.
The simplest way to illustrate the four characteristics is to disregard
the loan market and to assume that each robo-ent both produces goods
and borrows directly from consumer-savers. It is also convenient to
assume initially that each firm produces all goods from start to finish,
although this assumption will have to be dropped in order to understand the relationships among the prices of goods and factors.

Competition

Competition must be distinguished from cooperation. In a market
economy both types of interaction require at least two individuals
acting in the role of entrepreneurs. In competition, the entrepreneurs
use exchange offers to bid against each other for the right to benefit
from trading with individuals acting in the roles of consumers, factor-

suppliers, or lenders. For example, entrepreneurs may compete for customers by means of price bids.

In cooperation, which can also be called *collusion,* the entrepreneurs agree not to compete. They develop a common goal of making as much profit from consumers as possible. To achieve this goal, they adopt a cooperative marketing strategy. Suppose, for example, that there is a single consumer in a goods market. Instead of competing with each other and allowing the consumer to buy at a lower price than otherwise, they agree to charge the highest price that they believe the consumer is willing to pay. Then they share the profit from the sale. If there are many consumers, entrepreneurs may agree to a market-sharing agreement. The agreement assigns each consumer to a specific entrepreneur. Each entrepreneur agrees not to compete for consumers who are assigned to other entrepreneurs.

In this subsection, the FIREE is used to describe competition in the three markets that are implicit in the ERE: goods markets, factor markets, and loan markets. Each is discussed in turn.

Goods markets. To give a preliminary description of competition in goods markets, the economist assumes that each firm is perfectly vertically integrated. Two types of competition can be illustrated. First, there is competition among robo-ents in the same industry. It is assumed that there are several robo-ents in a given industry who bid for customers entirely by offering deals they believe are better than those of their competitors. In the simplest case, it is assumed that each robo-ent produces a good that is identical to that of other robo-ents in the industry. In more complicated cases, robo-ents may compete by offering different characteristics of a particular good. Second, there is competition among robo-ents who can select which industry to be in. It is assumed that in seeking to maximize robo-profits, robo-ents compete for consumers' dollars by sorting themselves into industries, so to speak, on the basis of the robo-profits that can be earned in each one.

Competition is defined in terms of both an outcome and a process. The outcome is called an equilibrium and is said to be caused by the process of robo-ent competition. In the equilibrium, the robo-ents are already sorted into industries. Each is earning its maximum rent, given the competition from the others. In equilibrium, robo-profit is zero since no robo-ent can gain by shifting to an industry that is different from the one it is in.

If it is assumed that each robo-ent faces the same options and that each robo-ent can bid for the right to take the place of any other robo-ent, each robo-ent can be said to earn the same basic entrepreneurial rent in equilibrium. For a given collection of function-performing robots, the size of the rent may be said to depend on the number of robo-ents in the FIREE. Adopting this assumption, one can speak of the demand for and supply of robo-ents. The larger the number of robo-ents, other things being equal, the lower the rent to each.

If it is further assumed that some robo-ents are more productive than others, the economist can impute a *differential rent* to the more productive robo-ents. In other words, the higher incomes of the more productive robo-ents are called differential rent. The income earned by the least productive robo-ent in equilibrium is the basic rent to which the differential rent is added.

In relation to cooperation among robo-ents, competition drives down the prices of consumers' goods. Other things being equal, the greater the competition—that is, the greater the supply of robo-ents—the lower the prices of consumers' goods.

To elucidate the process of competition, it can be assumed initially that no robo-ent has yet selected an industry. A sequence of changes is then specified or derived from a set of assumptions. One sequence is as follows: The first robo-ent selects the industry in which robo-profit is as high as possible. Its choice reduces the profitability to the second robo-ent of selecting that industry. The second robo-ent follows by selecting the most profitable from the remaining alternatives. The second is followed by a third, which is followed by a fourth, and so on until all robo-ents have selected some industry.

When a second robo-ent enters a given industry, it must charge a price that is lower than that of the first entrant. By doing this, it bids some customers away from the first and thereby reduces the first's robo-profit. The first then responds by reducing its own price. A third entrant upsets whatever industry equilibrium might have been reached by the first two and may cause further reductions in price. Such competition is called *price competition.*

Now consider competition among robo-ents in different industries. Instead of producing the same good, a robo-ent may compete for consumers' spending by producing a different good that is a partial substitute for the first. Another way to put this is to say that a competing robo-ent may produce a good that has somewhat different characteristics, which some consumer robots would select over the good offered by the first robo-ent.[4] This kind of competition may be called *characteristic* competition. Characteristic competition gives consumer robots, as a group, a wider range of options.

Factor markets. The robo-ents also compete for factors by bidding prices that are higher than those of their competitors or by offering working conditions or other terms of supply that might "cause" worker robots to select one job over another that gives the same pay. The result is that the price of each factor is raised and working conditions are brought more in line with what factor-suppliers will select. The situation is similar to that of competition in goods markets, except that the traders are not consumer robots but factor-supplying robots.

The process of competition can be represented by imagining an initial situation in which there are no bids for a factor. Then, one by one, robo-ents proceed to bid. Assuming for simplicity that all jobs are the same, a second robo-ent must bid higher than the first in order to obtain the factor's services. Similarly, a third must bid higher than the second, and so on. Through this process, price competition causes an increase in factor prices.

The income earned by factor-supplying robots is rent. If it is assumed that all factor-supplying robots are alike, they each earn the same basic rent. If it is assumed that they differ, some would earn a differential rent. This differential may be partly attributed to their different productivities in helping to produce the same good and partly to the assumption that some factor-suppliers are more capable of helping to produce goods that are in high demand than other factor-suppliers.

Robo-ents may be assumed to be equally competent in arranging deals with factor-suppliers. If so, each will earn the same robo-profit, or basic rent, from such deals. If it is assumed that some robo-ents are more competent at arranging deals than others, then the former will earn a differential rent from their employment of factors.

Loan markets. Robo-ents also compete for savings in loan markets. Their competition causes the interest on savings to be bid up in the same way that competition in factor markets causes factor prices to be bid up.

It may be assumed that robo-ents are equally capable of arranging loans. In this case, each would earn the same rent from arranging the loans. Alternatively, if it is assumed that some entrepreneurs are superior, the superior ones may earn a differential rent.

It may be assumed that there is a separate market for loans of different lengths. In this event, the equilibrium rate of return on a loan of one length may be greater than the rate of return on a loan of a different length. A longer-length loan can be substituted for two successive loans of shorter length with less uncertainty than two successive shorter-length loans can be substituted for a longer-length loan. As a result, it is likely that the rate of return on longer-length loans will be greater than the rate of return on shorter-length ones. One cannot make this deduction on the basis of a priori and fundamental economic assumptions, however. Special, subsidiary assumptions are necessary.

It may be assumed that the cost of administering loans of a given size is smaller than the cost of administering two loans of half the size. Under this assumption, savers of large amounts would receive a higher rate of return than savers of small amounts.

Assume that all loans are of the same length and of the same size. Then, the rate of return on each loan would be the same in equilibrium since a borrowing robo-ent could not be maximizing its robo-profit if it pays a loan rate that is higher than one that is available elsewhere. The rate that would prevail in such an equilibrium is the conceptual equivalent of the rate of interest in the evenly rotating economy. Thus, one can speak of the rate of interest in the FIREE or of different rates of interest on loans of different lengths and different sizes. In the ERE, there can be only one rate of interest.

Consumer Sovereignty[5]

It is alleged that consumer sovereignty is a characteristic of the market economy. Consumer sovereignty literally means that consumers, as opposed to producers or a central authority (sovereign), are the agents responsible for determining which goods are produced, which consumers get the goods, which items are factors, how much the factors are paid, and what the rates of return on loans are. Actually, the claim of consumer sovereignty should not be taken so literally. Sovereignty applies broadly to individuals acting in their roles as consumers, lenders, and factor-suppliers. Thus, a more apt name is individual sovereignty. Nevertheless, the convention of calling it consumer sovereignty will not be changed here.

The selecting behavior of robo-ents in the competitive process has two characteristics that are relevant to consumer sovereignty. First, each selection yields more robo-profit than the best alternative. Second, each selection requires the robo-ent to bid at least one consumer, factor-supplier, and lender away from its best respective alternatives. Thus, each selection yields both robo-profit for the robo-ent and gains to each of the robot consumers, factor-suppliers, and lenders that respond to the robo-ent's bid. This is what is meant by consumer sovereignty.

Consumer sovereignty may be contrasted with sovereignty by a central planner. In a model of a centrally planned system, a single planning robot would be sovereign. The planning robot would decide which suppliers of items used in production would be rewarded, how the items would be used, and who would get the resulting output. In the FIREE, consumer, factor-supplier, and lender robots are the sovereigns in the following sense. In the process of reaching equilibrium, the robo-ent makes selections that enable consumer, factor-supplier, and lender robots to achieve greater robo-utility.[6] This is because the robo-ent's selections make alternatives available that the consumer, factor-suppliers, and lender robots would otherwise not have. Thus, the selection of these otherwise unavailable alternatives in the FIREE simulate gains from exchange in the market economy to individuals who act in the roles of consumer, factor-supplier, and saver.

Externalities and collusion. Conditions may be identified under which consumer sovereignty is not present. For example, there may be externalities due to the high costs of making transactions or of enforcing rights in goods and factors. Externalities mean that selections that yield robo-profit and simulated gains to specific consumer, factor-supplier, and lender robots may also yield simulated gains or losses to other robots. If the economist specifies that these externalities are negative and sufficiently large, he may reach the conclusion that the behavior of robo-ents yields greater simulated losses than simulated gains.

It is sometimes argued that collusion transfers sovereignty from consumers to producers. Relative to competition, this is true. More correctly, producers who succeed in colluding can establish a monopoly price and thereby cause consumers to gain less from the market economy than they would gain if collusion was unsuccessful and if competition prevailed. It is much easier to construct a model of collusion than it is to support the belief that collusion would be an important characteristic of a market economy. Under the conditions specified in the definition of a market economy, collusion that is profitable amounts to an invitation to outsiders to compete with the colluding producers. Although specialized knowledge may forestall such competition for some period of time, human beings appear to be especially able to learn to copy others' actions. To the extent that copying can be successful, collusion will be unsuccessful.

Mises's use of the FIREE. Although Mises did not identify the FIREE, he used an image like it to describe the effects of a change in wants.[7] His description began with an equilibrium in which each robo-ent is making as much robo-profit as possible, given the competition of the other robo-ents. Then there is an increase in the demand for one good, which is accompanied by a decrease in the demand for another good. The change leads robo-ents to expect lower robo-profits in the first industry and higher robo-profits in the second than previously. To maximize robo-profit, some of them must shift factors from the first to the second, thereby causing fewer of the first type of good and more of the second type to be produced. Adjustments in other industries and in the interest rates may also be specified. The important point, however, is that the change in demands gets translated into a change in robo-profit, which "signals" robo-ents to shift factors from the lower-demand industry to the higher-demand industry.

The Prices of Higher-Order Goods[8]

The image of the FIREE can be used to elucidate the relationship between the prices of first-order, or consumer, goods and the prices of second, third, fourth-order, and so on, goods (factors of production).[9] To do this, one must construct a model of an economy in which some producing robo-ents are in industries that produce the factors used by other producing robo-ents. Assuming that there is competition among robo-ents, equilibrium must have the property that the difference between the price of a good of a given order and the sum of the costs of each factor used to produce it cannot be so great for one good relative to another good that it is profitable for producers to shift from one industry to another. This, in turn, implies that the sum of the prices of the factors used to produce a particular good, including the robo-profit and taking account of interest, must be approximately equal to the price of the product. In other words, the price of a lower-order good is approximately equal to the sum of the prices of higher-order goods that are used for its production.

Students have sometimes argued that factors have a value independent of entrepreneurial appraisement. It is evident, however, that without the robo-ents to establish prices according to the algorithms specified by the economist in the FIREE, factors could not be used to produce goods or earn income. The factors could have no market value. This suggests that the market value of factors in the market economy is caused by entrepreneurship.

Students sometimes interpret the relationship between the price of a lower-order good and the prices of higher-order goods as a relationship between current prices. Proper use of the FIREE requires the economist to focus first on the relationship between the current prices bid by robo-ents for factors and robo-ents' expectations of future first-order goods' prices. The equilibrium relationship between the current prices of goods of different orders is deduced from the economist's specific assumptions about the way that the assumed expectations get coordinated and synchronized. When the economist contrasts the FIREE with the market economy, however, he sees that the assumptions about robo-ent expectations, coordination, and synchronization cannot duplicate entrepreneurial appraisals. The economist, as a subjectivist, knows that he cannot fully specify the methods used by entrepreneurship in the market economy to make appraisals. Thus, the correct interpretation of the price relationships in the market economy is that there is a relationship between prices currently bid for higher-order goods and entrepreneurial judgments about what the future price of the relevant lower-order goods is likely to be.[10]

The Transmission and Economization of Entrepreneurial Knowledge

The image of the FIREE is useful in demonstrating how entrepreneurial knowledge is transmitted and economized in a market economy. By isolating the different markets and prices, it helps the economist to distinguish different types of messages. It is sometimes said that prices are signals. For example, one might say that the prices in goods markets signal consumer robots about the relative costs of producing different goods. However, the operations of the algorithms of robot consumers do not depend on their having received signals about relative costs. It is sufficient that they be confronted with prices at which goods can be bought. Thus it is more accurate to say that prices in the FIREE *economize* on the use of "entrepreneurial knowledge." The consumer robots do not need to "know" relative costs because robo-ents are assumed to "know" them.

Of course there is no knowledge, as such, in the FIREE. There is only the knowledge of the economist, which is manifest in the behavioral routines of the robots. Nevertheless, the FIREE can be contrasted with the market economy. Such a contrast suggests that offers to sell in the market economy enable consumers to get their wants satisfied without having to compare the relative costs of production.

By means of this contrast, the economist can submit that the price system economizes on the use of entrepreneurial knowledge.

Similar reasoning applies to individuals acting in the roles of factor-suppliers and lenders. The prices of factors bid by robo-ents in the FIREE simulate messages about the contribution of the factors to the production and sale of consumers' goods. Interest rate bids simulate messages about the difference between the expected prices of lower-order goods and the current prices of higher-order goods.

2. CHARACTERISTICS OF THE MARKET ECONOMY THAT CANNOT BE FULLY REPRESENTED IN A MODEL

In this part, intuitive and experience-based knowledge is used to describe how the interaction of robo-ents in the FIREE differs from the interaction of human entrepreneurs under the conditions specified in the definition of the market economy. Broadly speaking, entrepreneurs differ from robo-ents in that they bet that their projects are superior to those that have been previously offered to individuals in the role of consumer-savers and factor suppliers. The economist's intuition tells her that an entrepreneur is more likely to be correct than incorrect. Accordingly, the economist describes the entrepreneur's action in terms of how it makes available to consumer-savers and factor suppliers opportunities that they would not otherwise have. Such opportunities may be totally new or they may only be new to the particular consumer-savers and factors suppliers under consideration.[11] Part 2 follows the same order of topics as Part 1.

Competition

A producer in a market economy may compete in goods markets with other producers by offering goods that were previously unknown to consumers, by offering combinations of goods that consumers did not previously use together, or by using methods of production that were previously not used because they were either previously unknown or regarded as inferior. Similarly, the producer may compete in factor markets by offering conditions of work or combinations of factors both that are more desirable to workers and that were previously unknown or unavailable to them. In the case of capital, a producer who rents the capital may offer previously unavailable conditions of supply that lead to less deterioration or to a particular type of deterioration that is less

objectionable to the owner. Entrepreneurs in loan markets may compete by identifying terms or conditions of paying out and collecting
interest that were previously unavailable and that are more suitable to
particular producers and savers. Although a model can be constructed
that could represent each of these behaviors, no model can fully
represent the process of competitive entrepreneurial discovery since
this process is partly unknowable to the economist.

An economist who gets too accustomed to using models of robo-ent
behavior is inclined to overlook the ways that entrepreneurs in the
market economy can combine their exchange offers. As an employer,
an entrepreneur may offer employees discounts on merchandise. The
employer may borrow from the employees by deferring some portion
of their wages. The employer may shift uncertainty-bearing to the
employees by making the payment of deferred wages contingent on the
continued profitability or solvency of the employer as a producer. An
employer may offer free or low-cost services to employees in an effort
to promote loyalty to the firm or comradery among its employees.
Generally speaking, the employer can combine the actions of supplying
goods and services, attracting factor-suppliers, and attracting lenders
in an indefinite number of ways.

An example that is especially useful in illustrating economists'
limitations in representing competition is that of copying. It is easy for
the modeller to specify that when A earns a robo-profit, B can compete
with him by copying A's behavior. In the market economy, however,
the action of a profit-making entrepreneur who is copied may be so
complex that it can neither be modelled nor understood by the economist. Nevertheless, another entrepreneur may be able to model it or
understand it sufficiently to earn a profit himself. In a case like this,
although the model of behavior copying is useful, it obviously cannot
fully represent the phenomenon of copying in a market economy.

Consumer Sovereignty

The economist can "prove" that consumer sovereignty is present in
the market economy only by appealing to a reader's intuition and
experience. She must convince her audience that individuals acting in
the role of entrepreneurs tend to profit by making decisions that enable
those who act in the roles of consumers, factor suppliers, and lenders,
to gain. In the process of reaching equilibrium in the FIREE, robo-
ents are assumed to earn robo-profit by taking advantage of opportunities that are specified by the economist. That they will earn robo-

profit when they do this is absolutely certain. When all opportunities are availed, the equilibrium is reached. At that stage robo-ents cannot earn robo-profit; they earn rent due to their continuing and repetitive behavior of borrowing and producing. In the market economy, individuals acting in the role of the entrepreneur earn "real" profit by betting that they know of previously unknown and unavailable opportunities to benefit consumers, factor-suppliers, and lenders. There is no certainty among entrepreneurs and equilibrium in the market economy cannot exist. Entrepreneurial action is characterized not by repetition of behavior that the economist specifies as maximizing but by inventiveness, alertness, and a willingness and ability to bet on one's beliefs about possible gains.

Entrepreneurial actions may have external effects. In describing externalities in the FIREE, the economist merely specifies them. In the market economy, the presence of external effects implies either that those affected are unaware of their source or that, if they are aware, they are powerless to change matters. The economist's image of entrepreneurship regarding external effects is focused on the individual's incentives to discover and implement rearrangements of rights and obligations for which he believes other individuals will pay.

Prices of Higher-Order Goods

That price relationships cannot be fully represented in a model is evident from the fact that the relationships in question are among future prices of goods, as anticipated by entrepreneurs, and the current price bids that are made by prospective producers. The anticipated prices are in the minds of the producers. How they arrive at them in a market economy must remain partly a mystery to an economist, since each individual must be assumed to possibly possess a unique method of making appraisals that partly eludes the economist.

Transmission and Economization
of Entrepreneurial Knowledge

The model of the FIREE can be used to represent the economization of the use of entrepreneurial knowledge, as shown in Part 1 of this chapter. It cannot, however, represent the solicitations and acceptances of knowledge among entrepreneurs that result in the provision of and shifting of uncertainty-bearing, since the FIREE contains no uncertainty. In this subsection, two different types of knowledge transmission are considered in turn: (1) between producing entrepreneurs and financier entrepreneurs, and (2) between producing entrepreneurs and individuals acting in the roles of consumers and factor-suppliers.

Knowledge transmission between producing entrepreneurs and financiers. The more obvious cases of the transmission of knowledge related to uncertainty-shifting in the market economy involve producing entrepreneurs and financiers. To see this, consider the image of fully integrated entrepreneurs. Each entrepreneur possesses some amount of wealth that he can use to finance production projects. Each entrepreneur also has particular knowledge of at least one production project, but no entrepreneur has the knowledge needed to implement all of the profitable production projects. Some entrepreneurs have wealth but little knowledge of a profitable production project. Others have substantial knowledge but little wealth. Under the circumstances, entrepreneurs with knowledge would communicate at least part of it to prospective financiers. The knowledgeable entrepreneurs would use part of their wealth to finance their solicitations, and they would plan to use the remainder either as guaranty for a loan or as part of the assets of an enterprise that is entered into jointly with a financier. Prospective financiers would solicit knowledge of profit-making opportunities so that they could better judge whether a return could be earned by financing the production projects.

Precisely what is entailed in the knowledge-transmission process cannot be completely specified. The economist must assume that she may not know or be able to comprehend the knowledge of the producing entrepreneur or the financier. It follows that the economist must assume that she may also not be able to specify the nature of the knowledge-transmission process.

It would be possible to construct a model in which units of information are regarded by robo-ents as inputs to the production process. In such a model the robot enterprisers would possess the bits of information, while the robot financiers would possess the funds necessary to finance projects that used the information bits. Such a model could not capture the process through which one human being learns and evaluates the knowledge possessed by another human being. To actors in the market economy, knowledge is not a unit of information.

Besides this, such a model could not capture the economist's intuitive confidence that individuals who bet that their knowledge is superior are more likely to be correct than incorrect. Consider this example. Imagine a prospective hired enterpriser who possesses knowledge of a production project. The enterpriser does not have the funds to finance the project. However, even if he did, he would not finance the project, since he does not believe it is profitable. In spite of this, the enterpriser believes that if he describes his plan to a prospective financier, the financier may agree to finance it and to pay him a sizeable salary to direct it. With this prospect in mind, the enterpriser solicits the financier to finance the project. Suppose that the financier accepts. In deciding to finance the project, the financier bets on his belief that the project will yield profit.

In this example, the beliefs of the two parties differ. A difference of this sort might be represented by a model of robo-ents in which different robo-ents had different expectations. In such a model, however, it would seem arbitrary to claim that one of the two is correct while the other is wrong. Yet the economist's intuition tells her that the financier, who is willing to bet that his knowledge is correct, is more likely to actually be correct, other things being equal, than the enterpriser. Such an intuition about entrepreneurship in a market economy corresponds to the more general intuition that a human being who can choose is more likely to satisfy her wants (remove felt uneasiness) than one who cannot choose.

Relationships involving consumers and factor-suppliers. There are numerous, more subtle ways in which the economization of knowledge-use relating to uncertainty-bearing plays a part in a market economy. Consider first the economization of knowledge transmission involving consumers. Every profitable production-consumption action in a market economy is a joint undertaking. It involves at least one individual acting in the role of the consumer and another individual acting in the role of the producer. Both individuals contribute to the uncertainty of the undertaking. The consumer's wants, abilities, and knowledge may change, as well as the producer's. Because the undertaking is joint, the uncertainties are also joined together. Some allocation of uncertainty must be arrived at. One of the parties can take it on himself to voluntarily accept the full burden of uncertainty. Many producers in everyday life appear to take on this burden by producing goods before receiving a commitment from consumers to buy them. Alternatively, the parties can attempt to work out an uncertainty-bearing agreement. Whichever method is adopted, at least one of the parties will accept the burden of uncertainty on the basis of his bet that his knowledge of the consumer's wants is superior to that of others.

The case that corresponds most closely to textbook teaching on this issue is one in which a producer finances the production of a substantial amount of a good, which he expects to sell to a number of consumers. In this case, the producer bears all the uncertainty. But a variety of other arrangements are possible. A producer may require payment in advance of production or a commitment from consumers to buy the product when it is produced and made available. If there is uncertainty about the price or availability of raw materials, the producer may even require the consumer to agree to pay a price that depends upon some measure of the producer's cost. In the extreme, the producer may require that the consumer agree to pay whatever price the producer eventually decides to charge, within limits, of course. In making whatever agreement is eventually reached, the parties try to find a mutually acceptable allocation of uncertainty-bearing. In this sense, the agreement can be said to economize on the acquisition, use, and transmission of knowledge.

Uncertainty-bearing agreements between employers and employees are typically more complicated than this. Typically, the employer agrees to pay the members of a team of employees at intervals while they work. This is so even though the revenue derived from their work is not expected until the future and even though the project may turn out to be unprofitable. At least past of the money that is paid in advance is used to shift uncertainty-bearing from the workers to the employer. If the employees had to share the uncertainty of the project, they would either decline to work or they would want to acquire enough knowledge about the project to have confidence that the plan would succeed. Because the usual agreement between an employer and her employees greatly reduces the employees' desire to acquire entrepreneurial knowledge, the agreement can be said to economize on the use and transmission of such knowledge.

NOTES

1. A fourth price that is disregarded here is the price of insurance against risk.

2. The equilibrium may be the ERE but it may also be an economy in which different goods take different time periods to produce.

3. The typical textbook in modern microeconomics describes competition among entrepreneurs as if it were the same thing as competition among robo-ents. In such a discussion, the term "profit" is used to describe the income the robo-ents earn. This text reserves the term profit to refer to the income of the entrepreneur, properly defined as the role that performs the categories of entrepreneurial action described in chapter six.

4. A model of competition among goods with slightly different character-istics has been presented by Professor Lancaster (1966).

5. Mises discusses consumer sovereignty in general terms in *Human Action* on page 269–73.

6. This "utility" is *defined* in relation to the algorithms according to which each consumer-saver robot is assumed to behave. It is a purely mathematical conception. The economist may define it in such a way that the utilities of different individuals are comparable or she may define it so that the utilities are not comparable. A tenet of the old subjectivism is that elucidations of market economy characteristics should not be made on the basis of the assumptions that the utilities are comparable. Under the new subjectivism, the economist goes further. She recognizes that while the utilities of robot con-sumer-savers are intended to simulate utilities (removal of felt uneasiness) in the market economy, they refer entirely and only to each individual's separate motivation to act. The idea that it is meaningful to quantify the utility of even a single individual is improper.

7. See Mises (1966, 251). Also see his discussion of the prices of higher order goods (p. 333–39). Among other things, he points out that "[t]he entrepreneur is the agency that prevents the persistence of a state of produc-tion unsuitable to fill the most urgent wants of the consumers in the cheapest way" (p. 336).

8. Mises (1966) discusses the prices of higher-order goods on page 333–39.

9. The image of the FIREE corresponds to the method described by Mises in his discussion of the "tasks incumbent upon the theory of the prices of factors of production" (1966, 334).

10. Mises (1966, 334–37).

11. In this discussion, it is important to keep in mind that consumer-savers and factor suppliers are roles. In the market economy, the introduction of a new product, for example, requires the entrepreneurship of both the inventor-producer and the consumer. A consumer cannot come to know that a previ-ously unknown product can yield satisfaction without exercising her own entrepreneurship.

Chapter 8

The Method of Contrasting Images of Functions (5): Saving, Uncertainty-Bearing, Guaranty, and Interest in a Market Economy

An individual in everyday life has the option of saving in two ways: privately in the form of goods or money and socially by lending money to someone else. Generally speaking, private saving is not relevant to the concerns of this book.[1] When an individual saves socially, he turns some money—savings—over to other entrepreneurs. By so doing, he takes advantage of the investment opportunities of which only the other entrepreneurs are initially aware. He is a lender. It is convenient to use the word economic to refer to such saving.

Economic saving necessarily entails uncertainty. The uncertainty of a lender is ordinarily greater than the uncertainty of a producer who finances production from her own savings. This is because a lender does not normally have as much knowledge of the investment project as the entrepreneur to whom he lends. Still, there are ways for a lender to reduce uncertainty.

A common way for a lender of money to avoid some uncertainty is to shift it to someone else who is willing to provide guaranty. The guarantor may be the borrower himself who posts collateral, which he agrees to forfeit in the event of nonpayment of the loan. Alternatively, the guarantor may be a third party who promises that in the event of default, she will either pay off some part of the loan or forfeit the property or money posted. The willingness and ability of some individuals to provide guaranty gives savers an opportunity to lend to producers to whom they otherwise would not lend. In this way, the savers can earn a higher rate of return on their loans.

Guaranty ordinarily consists of property or ownership claims to property, including money, although it may also include IOUs and even promises to work. The value of guaranty in terms of money is determined by appraisers. Every reliance made by a lender on guaranty requires the lender's appraisal of the guaranty. Even guaranty in the form of money may require an appraisal, since the same money guaranty may be used for more than one loan. Thus, a lender can never be absolutely certain that he will be repaid the amount he lends even if guaranty is provided on the money lent.

When an individual in a market economy saves money instead of spending it, she can ordinarily earn a rate of return. Part of this return is interest. Interest is the rate of return a saver would earn (a) if no entrepreneurship was necessary to create the loan market and to administer loans, and (b) if the saver was absolutely guaranteed that the money saved would be returned to her.[2] These conditions are never present under the conditions specified in the definition of the market economy. Loan markets must be created by price-bidding entrepreneurs, loans must be administered, and no loan can ever be completely guaranteed. In the market economy, some part of a saver's earnings must be profit or loss for the lender.[3] Indeed, when a producing entrepreneur finances a production project by means of borrowing instead of using his own funds, he shifts some uncertainty from himself to the lender.

Besides interest and profit or loss, the money a lender is paid back in a market economy practically always has different purchasing power than the money he lends. Accordingly, the rate of return may also include what Mises called a *price premium*.[4] The price premium is disregarded here, since we are not concerned with Mises's ideas on money and credit.

The main purpose of this chapter is to explore the relationship between saving, uncertainty-bearing, and providing guaranty in a market economy. The exploration proceeds systematically. Part 1 describes the saving, uncertainty-bearing, and guaranty of an isolated actor. Part 2 does the same for individuals in the market economy. An additional purpose of the chapter is to show how the phenomenon of interest gets reflected in market prices. This is done in Part 3.

1. SAVING, UNCERTAINTY-BEARING, AND GUARANTY OF AN ISOLATED ACTOR

On the basis of the discussion of saving in chapter five, the proper image of an isolated actress is that of an individual who divides her labor time among a number of different production projects, the goods from which she expects to consume at different future times. The actress both discovers and implements a plan to allocate her labor and human capital among some production projects instead of others. She knows that the projects take different amounts of time. In some cases, the actress may not be able to directly link a project she chooses to the production of a specific good. She believes, however, that the project will benefit her in some way.

Saving and the Burden of Uncertainty

In this image, the isolated actress both saves and bears uncertainty every time she decides to use her labor to produce a good. First consider saving. There are two reasons why every allocation of an actress's labor implies saving. First, her labor, which is assumed to yield disutility, could be used to yield immediate satisfaction in the form of leisure. Second, when choosing to forgo production of a good that she could have consumed sooner, she saves. Next, consider uncertainty-bearing. Every decision to use labor to produce a good entails the prospect that at the end of the period of provision the decision will yield less satisfaction than expected. If the satisfaction is sufficiently less than expected, the actress would like to be able to return to the time before the decision was made, since she believes that the loss could have been avoided by choosing a different alternative. More succinctly, every decision by an isolated actress to use her labor entails the prospect of loss. The loss could be expressed entirely in terms of the disutility of labor and forgone satisfaction. It is useful to note that both saving and uncertainty-bearing are measured by the isolated actress in the same terms—a sacrifice or loss of satisfaction.

Let the portion of her leisure and other forgone satisfaction that the isolated actress believes she might lose be called the *burden of uncertainty*. Similarly, let the portion for which there is no uncertainty be called *pure saving*. Is it consistent with intuition and experience to assume that when the isolated actress makes a decision to produce a particular good she could draw the line between the burden of uncertainty and pure saving? This question must be answered in steps.

Saving is always uncertain. The first step is to assure oneself that the isolated individual's saving cannot be certain. Saving is an action intended to satisfy future wants. As such it must be uncertain. To see this, consider a simple example. Suppose that Crusoe has durable goods, say nuts, and that he stores them away for a given period of time. Because he cannot possess certain knowledge about the forces of nature, he cannot be certain that the nuts will survive through the entire period that he plans to save them. Even if he could be certain that the stored nuts would not be lost in some way, his wants may change during the period. In this event, the satisfaction he expects from consuming them may fall drastically. Additionally, in the meantime he may discover so large a cache of nuts that nuts would no longer be scarce. Thus, even if he is absolutely certain about the physical environment, Crusoe's plans to save may be frustrated by a change in either his wants or his abilities to produce. In this event, part or all of the work and other resources that he had previously devoted to producing the nuts would be lost. He would lose the satisfaction that he would have expected to gain if he had used his resources in their best alternative uses. Thus, Crusoe cannot even set aside durable goods without bearing uncertainty.

The second step is to consider a case of investment. An example of hunting seems useful. Suppose that Crusoe plans an expedition to hunt meat. He plans to take a store of nuts, which will function as provisions. He also plans to use his labor in the hunt. In this venture, Crusoe would face not only the uncertainty connected with the prospect that his wants or abilities to produce different goods might change while he carries out the hunt. He would also face the uncertainty that the hunt itself would not be as successful as he planned. He might lose (a) the expected satisfaction from the goods he could have produced if he had applied his labor elsewhere, and (b) whatever alternative satisfaction he had to give up due to his production of the provisions he consumes during the hunt.

The nuts in this example have customarily been called capital. When Crusoe chooses to devote them to his hunting venture, he bears the uncertainty that his capital will be consumed and not replaced with other goods of equivalent value to him.

Consider a variant of this example in which Crusoe is absolutely certain that he can be at least minimally successful in the hunt. In other words, he is certain that he will return with some minimum amount of meat. The only uncertainty he faces is how much more than the minimum the hunt will produce. Then it might be said that the minimum amount is Crusoe's saving. He could have abandoned the planned hunt and consumed his nuts. Instead, he chose to exchange the nuts and his labor for a minimum amount of meat and possibly an additional amount. Even this saving would be uncertain, since his wants could change, his abilities to produce may change, or he may discover new goods or methods of production that render his initial plan obsolete. The possibility that nature would guarantee a given minimum of product resulting from the performance of a given behavior does not mean that there is no uncertainty regarding the value of that minimum amount.

Subjectivity of Saving

An outsider cannot know for certain how Crusoe envisions a planned action. The most that can be said is that Crusoe himself may be able to distinguish between a portion of his investment that he expects to conserve and a portion that he may totally lose. The first portion can be called saving, although it is still always linked to uncertainty-bearing; the rest can be called the burden of uncertainty. In other words, the amount of saving and the burden of uncertainty are subjective.

Note that although the outsider cannot measure saving and the burden of uncertainty, she is as certain as anything that a normal human being in the position of Crusoe would both save and bear uncertainty. The outsider knows this a priori.

Personal Guaranty

As a final example, suppose that Crusoe knows that his hunt may be completely unsuccessful. In order to avoid a drastic reduction in his wealth, he delays plans for the hunt until he has put aside enough nuts not only to maintain him during his trip but also to sustain him for a period of time after he returns. These nuts can be called his personal guaranty. Crusoe does not expect to have to consume them. However, he puts them aside just in case his hunting plan does not succeed, so that he will not have to endure a drastic reduction in his level of satisfaction at the end of an unsuccessful production period.

Conclusion

It can be concluded that an isolated actor would not be able to distinguish between the part of his saving action that is pure saving and the part that entails a burden of uncertainty. Given this fact, the economist cannot legitimately form an image of an isolated actor who purely saves and does not bear uncertainty. The economist knows on the basis of experience and intuition that what she defines as action always entails a burden of uncertainty. It is nevertheless true that the economist can form an image of pure saving. To do this, she converts an actor into a maximizing robot by assuming (1) that wants, abilities, and knowledge do not change, and (2) that there is scientific certainty that goods that are set aside will not deteriorate or be destroyed. Such a robot has a timeless existence yet, as contradictory as it seems, the robot can be said to save. Indeed, if it is to maintain its capital, it must save.

2. SAVING, UNCERTAINTY-BEARING, AND GUARANTY IN THE MARKET ECONOMY

In a market economy, individuals who want to save can take advantage of the investment opportunities that other producing entrepreneurs have available to them. Similarly, the producing entrepreneurs are able to carry out production projects that they themselves are unwilling or unable to finance. These possibilities exist because of loan markets.

In the ERE, the FIREE, and the image of fully integrated entrepreneurs, savers are robots. They can earn interest on their saving without having to bear any uncertainty. They can engage in pure saving. A saver in a market economy, however, cannot avoid uncertainty. Whether she lends directly or indirectly to a producing entrepreneur, her saving entails a burden of uncertainty.

In a market economy, a saver may be able to reduce her uncertainty in a loan by requiring the borrower to post collateral or by requiring the borrower to get another individual to promise either to pay off the loan or to forfeit property in the event the loan is not paid. In either case, it is said that guaranty is provided. A producing entrepreneur who wishes to reduce the uncertainty of his action may borrow from someone who agrees that the repayment of the debt will depend upon how profitable the production project turns out to be. In this case, the lender deliberately bears some of the uncertainty in order to earn what he bets will be a higher return.

The Role of Guaranty Provision in the Market Economy

Guaranty defined. Guaranty is an amount of money or other property, including promises of work, that is pledged as security for a loan. The guarantor does not finance a production project. Instead, he promises to pay off at least a part of the loan or to forfeit the guaranty if the project fails.

It is important to keep the actions of lending and providing guaranty separate. Lending is a means of shifting uncertainty from a producing entrepreneur to a lender. Providing guaranty is a means of shifting uncertainty from a lender to the guarantor.

An image of an economy with lending but no guaranty. To understand the significance of guaranty in a market economy, the economist begins with an image in which it does not exist. In a market economy in which there was no guaranty, every saver would be a financier. She would be an entrepreneur who possesses some wealth, which has been earmarked for financing production projects, but who has no profitable projects personally available to her. The saver could minimize her uncertainty-bearing by lending to producing entrepreneurs who propose projects that she regards as less uncertain than others. But her uncertainty could never be eliminated. In this image, some financiers would be willing to bear only a small amount of uncertainty in their loans, while others would bear greater uncertainty.

Consider an image of a market economy in which saving entrepreneurs had made loans such that they were bearing precisely the amount and types of uncertainty that they wished to bear, given the options available and the competition from other saving entrepreneurs. No exchange would be possible in which two savers could be better off in their own reckoning by switching loans of the same amount of money. Also no additional loan could be made by a saver to a producing or factor-supplying entrepreneur in which both would gain. Such an image contains some shifting of uncertainty-bearing but no guaranty.

In this image, no saving entrepreneur could, by her determination, reduce uncertainty further and still get the same prospect of return. Similarly, no producing entrepreneur could shift uncertainty further, in her estimation, without giving up more valuable rights to the profit. No prospects for profit from borrowing and relending could exist.

Suppose that, in this economy, A had decided not to carry out or participate in a production project because the prospect of a return was not sufficient to compensate for her perceived increase in uncertainty. A would have investigated the possibility of borrowing and of making repayment of her loan contingent on the success of the production project. But either no one would be willing to make a loan or no one would regard the conditions of the loan as suitable.

Gains due to guaranty. In order to understand how individuals in such an economy would be able to gain from making trades that involve guaranty provision, consider the following situation. Suppose that *B,* a saving entrepreneur, could make a one-year loan to *A,* a producing entrepreneur. *B* chooses not to do so because, in his judgment, the likelihood that he will be repaid is too low. *C,* however, believes that *A* is more likely to repay than *B* does. However, *C* either has what, in his estimation, are more profitable loan opportunities or he has what he regards as better uses for his money. In this circumstance, *A* could not get a loan from *B* or *C*.

Suppose now that *C* can provide guaranty. In particular, suppose that *C* owns property. He could sell the property in order to obtain the money necessary to lend to *A*. However, he would rather keep the property and earn the guaranty income. Given that his confidence in *A*'s repaying the loan is sufficiently great, *C* may agree to pledge his property as guaranty for *B*'s loan to *A*. He promises to give up the title to his property after the year if *A* does not repay *B*. This pledge may be sufficient to entice *B* to loan to *A*. In this event, the provision of guaranty by *C* would enable *A*'s production project to be carried out. All three parties would expect to gain from the combination of actions that the provision of guaranty helps to bring about.[5]

More on the concept of guaranty. In retrospect, the guarantor who provides guaranty for a successful production project both "has his cake and eats it too." In prospect, however, "having the cake" is uncertain. Only the guarantor is willing to bet his cake (i.e., the cake he expects to still own in the future) that the production project will be successful.

It is important to realize that property ownership alone does not constitute guaranty. It must be combined with the owner's willingness to use his property to make a bet that a production project will yield enough money to repay a loan.

Lending, Guaranty, and Team Production

Lending may enable team production to occur. Team production means that more than one individual is used to produce a good. In team production, the cause/responsibility for production is shared by team members. Consider a production team that is proposed by a prospective employer. Suppose that some prospective team members are unwilling to bear the uncertainty connected with having their share of the proceeds depend upon how successful the project turns out to be. The team could form if one team member adopts the role of employer and agrees to pay wages in advance. The employer would exchange an advance payment of wages for what would otherwise be the employees' rights to the expected profit.[6] In essence, the employer in this exchange makes the employees a loan, the repayment of which is contingent on the profitability of the production project. By doing so, she agrees to bear uncertainty that they otherwise would have to bear.[7] If the employer does not have enough funds to make the loan, she may borrow the necessary funds from savers. In this event, the uncertainty is shifted from the team members to the savers.[8]

Types of Guaranty

It is worthwhile to consider the different items that may be regarded as guaranty. Five types can be identified: real property, debts, rights to profit from existing production projects (stock certificates), promises to work, and money. The discussion here is divided into two parts: non-money guaranty and money guaranty.

Non-money guaranty. Suppose a loan is guaranteed by real property. The guarantor agrees that the property will be turned over to the lender in the event of default. To the lender, the value of the property is equal to the anticipated future market value minus the administrative costs of completing the transfer. The lender must estimate these market values on the basis of his predictions about future wants, abilities, and knowledge of others. In addition, there is some prospect that the promise to turn over the property will not be kept either because the guarantor is untrustworthy or because the guarantor's ownership of the property depends upon his success in other entrepreneurial ventures. If the lender knows this, his estimate of the resale value will be lower. Thus, the use of property as guaranty amounts to a partial substitution of the uncertainty connected with predicting the value of the guaranty promise for that connected with predicting the success of the borrower's production project.

Similar reasoning applies to the next three types of guaranty. If debts are used as guaranty, the lender must estimate the money value of the debts, and must now bear the uncertainty connected with the debts. If stock certificates are used as guaranty, the lender must estimate the money value of these. This requires him to estimate the profit-making potential of the producers who issued the stock. The lender who accepts work as guaranty must appraise the work as well as make a prediction about the willingness and ability of the promisor to actually perform the work if the loan is not repaid.

Money guaranty. The use of money as guaranty requires special consideration. For one thing, if a guarantor actually sets money aside as guaranty, then the money is, by definition, idle. Except for the possibility that a lender may erroneously believe that more money is set aside than actually is, it would always be more financially profitable for the guarantor to become a lender herself, since she is responsible for the uncertainty connected with the loan in any event.

The significance of money as guaranty arises from the fact that the cost of appraising a promise of money is so much lower than the cost of appraising non-money guaranty. As a result, a guarantor finds a greater demand for pledges of a given sum of money than for a given amount of non-money guaranty that would be appraised at the same value. Because of this, it is more likely that a given amount of money will be used as guaranty for more than one loan. Suppose that a guarantor has $1,000. Then, he or she may agree to provide guaranty for ten loans of $1,000 for a total of $10,000. Of course, lenders will not accept such a pledge unless they have confidence that the money pledged will be available in the event of a default on their loan. However, if a guarantor has knowledge of repayment prospects that is sufficiently superior to that of the lenders, she may be able to acquire a reputation for always keeping her pledges. This may be sufficient to give many lenders the confidence to make loans that they otherwise would be unwilling to make.

The Error of Confusing Uncertainty with Risk

Both a lender and an economist may make the error of confusing uncertainty with risk. Consider what would happen if a lender regarded the guaranty for his loan as insurance against risk. To such a lender, money that is pledged as guaranty for loans that have a greater face value than the money would be like an insurance fund. Assuming that the lender knows that the loans exceed the guaranty, he may mistakenly believe that the amount of a guarantor can expect to be required to pay out for defaulted loans during a given time is normally (or predictably) distributed about a mean. So long as the guaranty reserve is large enough, the probability that the fund would be insufficient to make the required payoffs would appear so low that it can be disregarded. This is true even though the fund is a small fraction of the sum of the face value of the loans that are guaranteed.

Uncertainty is not risk, however. The failure of one particularly crucial business in a market economy may lead to the failure of other businesses. Whole sectors may be replaced by new and superior sectors, leaving guarantors of loans to producing entrepreneurs in the old sectors to bear the losses. In an age of specialization, this may mean that a particular guaranty fund is quickly depleted, leaving many lenders unable to collect from the guarantor.[9]

An economist who fails to properly distinguish between uncertainty and risk may mistakenly believe that savers can be insulated from uncertainty and protected from their entrepreneurial errors by making a law that requires money guarantors to keep a minimum percent of the face value of loans in a money reserve. No reserve requirement short of a 100 percent cash reserve can protect savers, and a 100 percent requirement would eliminate the gains that would otherwise result in cases where individuals with limited funds have superior knowledge of repayment prospects by borrowers.[10]

Mises on Guaranty

To the author's knowledge. Mises did not clearly distinguish between saving and guaranty. Indeed, it is not evident that he even identified a concept like guaranty. He clearly understood entrepreneurial uncertainty, but his discussion of it was confined to his observation of the fact that entrepreneurs face the prospect of profit or loss. The idea that an entrepreneur would have to possess wealth in order to finance an undertaking or in order to provide guaranty for the savings borrowed from others was not a significant consideration in his analysis. On the other hand, his discussion of interest clearly indicated he recognized— indeed he discovered—that the phenomenon of interest cannot be clearly conceived except by constructing images like the ERE and FIREE. It is precisely such images that enable one to conceptually distinguish between guaranty and saving.

3. INTEREST IN THE MARKET ECONOMY

In the image of interacting fully integrated entrepreneurs, the artificial separation of entrepreneurship from the economic functions entails an equally artificial separation of profit from interest. When describing this image, one can speak of a *pure rate of interest*. The pure rate of interest is a hypothetical return on pure saving—that is, saving without uncertainty-bearing or guaranty provision. It is received by the robot savers.[11]

In the market economy, entrepreneurial profit and the hypothetical pure rate of interest are inseparable. From the standpoint of the lender, the rate of return she earns in the market must be sufficiently higher than the rate she could earn in her own production to compensate her for the additional uncertainty-bearing. Besides this, the rate must compensate her for any market-creating costs she may have to incur. When these factors are considered, it should be evident that because different individuals may have different own-production rates of return and because they may incur different, uncertain market-creation costs, there is no single, pure rate of interest in the market economy. Even if the rate of return paid to all lenders was identical, different individuals may earn different pure rates of interest. Thus the pure rates of interest are components of the rates of return paid to lenders, but this component may differ from one lender to the next. The rate paid to a lender also consists of an entrepreneurial component and a surplus that arises from the competition among borrowers.

Although part of the rate of return received by a lender is interest, the economist cannot tell how much the interest is. To tell this, she would have to know, among other things, how much of the return is profit or loss. She cannot know this because subjectivism demands that the economist regard the entrepreneur-lender as being in the best position to determine what part of her return is profit or loss. Even if the loan is fully guaranteed by a guarantor, the value of the guaranty may fall, thereby making it impossible for the lender to receive full repayment of the loans.

Interest is intimately related to the prices that exist in a market economy. An investigation of that relationship reveals the subtle ways that interest enters into the calculations that individuals make. In this part, it is shown how the interest rate is a part of goods' prices and factor prices. In addition, installment contracts are discussed.

Prices of Consumers' Goods

The price of a good in the market economy refers to a good that has already been produced. Such a price may be lower than or higher than that which is needed to reward those whose decisions caused the good to be produced and exchanged. This possibility reflects the fact that the price has an *entrepreneurial component*. This component can be divided into two parts. The first part might be called the market-creation component.[12] No good could have a price unless entrepreneurship was used to make and accept a proposal to exchange. The second part consists of the entrepreneurship that borrows the money to identify and hire the factors, makes the decision to produce the good, and bear all the uncertainty connected with these actions. For convenience, the following discussion ignores the market creation component. It treats the entrepreneurial component as if it consists entirely of the second part.[13]

The price of a consumers' good also contains an interest component. This is the additional amount that the entrepreneur must charge to allow her to pay pure interest.

That the price of a consumers' good contains these components can most easily be seen by considering the alternatives available to a consumer in a market economy. As opposed to purchasing an already-produced good, an individual could pay in advance for each good that he wants to consume at a later time, after it gets produced. For example, to satisfy his wants for eggs for the coming year, an individual may pay in advance each week for a carton to be received the following week. For convenience of exposition, assume that it takes exactly one week to produce an egg, once the production process is started. Then the advance price would be lower than the end-of-week price for two reasons. First, the act of paying in advance would cause some of the uncertainty involved in the egg business to be shifted from the producer and seller to the consumer. Specifically, the seller would no longer have to bear the uncertainty due to changes in the consumer's wants, abilities, and knowledge. Second, the advance payment could be used either by the producer to save on the loan costs involved in egg production or to earn income by making a week-long loan.

Contrast the image of a market economy in which consumers' goods are purchased after they are produced with an image in which payment for the goods is made by consumers in advance of production. In the latter image, many consumers' goods would not be produced because individuals acting the role of consumers would not be willing to bear the uncertainty connected with producing the goods for consumption. This problem could be partly alleviated by guaranty providers who would assure that the consumers receive either the goods they purchased or compensation. It seems likely, however, that the cost to a guarantor of providing guaranty on each separate consumer's advance payment would be substantially greater than the cost of providing guaranty to individuals who make large loans to producers. Thus the economy in which consumers always pay in advance seems to contain uncertainty-bearing arrangements that are less desirable to consumers, producers, and lenders.

Prices of Factors

Factors can be divided into two broad categories: capital and labor. Capital includes all recognized factors that are not human plus human capital. Labor includes all human contributions that are not produced. Consider each in turn.

The price of a capital good includes both an entrepreneurial and an interest component for the same reason that the price of a consumers' good does.[14] It must be produced in advance of its sale. The buyer of a capital good could pay a lower price if he was willing to finance and bear all the uncertainty connected with its production. But the buyer would not do so, since he is able to get a better deal by permitting the capital producer to arrange for financing and uncertainty-bearing.

The price of labor—wages—contains neither a pure interest component nor an entrepreneurial component.[14] When an employer pays labor in advance of the final sale of the product, she is in effect making her employees a loan. They get paid less because they are paid in advance; if they waited for their pay, the employer would not have to borrow so much (or forgo lending opportunities) in order to help finance the production project. In essence, the workers receive less than the wages for their contribution to the revenue of the firm because the employer makes them a loan, which is expected to be repaid with the results of their work.

By paying in advance, an employer shifts what would otherwise be her employees' uncertainties about the success of the production operation from them to herself. Thus, the wage does not include this type of entrepreneurial component either.

Installment Contracts

In an installment contract, the seller of a durable good may substitute a lower price for a higher loan rate and vice versa. Consider the extremes. The seller may offer to sell a very valuable good for the sum of $1, payable in installments for ten years. If the seller charges an interest rate of, say, 1,200,000 percent per year, the monthly payments are approximately $10,000. Of course, he cannot permit the borrower to pay off the loan until the tenth year. At the other extreme, the seller may offer to sell the good at a very high price to be paid in installments, but charge a zero loan rate. For example, the price may be $100,000 to be paid in equal installments of $10,000 over a period of ten years. When installment contracts are used the interest rate component of the price is concealed to an even greater extent than otherwise.

NOTES

1. The theorist who is interested in how individuals react when they suddenly lose confidence in their ability to correctly appraise the promises of bankers and other financial intermediaries would want to construct an image of an economy in which individuals had the option of saving privately. Such a loss in confidence is a likely consequence of government regulation of banking and other financial institutions. Since money and banking are beyond the concern of this book, private saving is disregarded.

2. It corresponds to the rate of return that is earned in the evenly rotating economy. But this is of no significance here.

3. The terminology used here differs from that of Mises. Mises (1966, chaps. 19 and 20) used the term "gross rate of interest" to refer to interest earned in the market economy. He defined it as consisting of "originary interest," an entrepreneurial component, and a price premium. Mises's originary interest in the market economy corresponds to what is called interest in this book.

4. See Mises (1966, 541–45). Modern economists might refer to this as an "inflationary expectations premium."

5. Note that the same effect could be achieved if C borrowed the money from B, using his (C's) property as collateral for the loan. He would then relend the money to A. This shows that collateral is a form of guaranty.

6. Writers on the employment relation often fail to realize that under the conditions specified by the definition of the market economy, everyone who contributes to a team production project has a right to a share of the proceeds unless they voluntarily trade their rights away.

7. This discussion shows that although it is true that every complete production-consumption action in a market economy entails uncertainty, it is not true that every individual who participates in such an action must bear uncertainty. The employee may completely avoid the uncertainty of the production-consumption action to which he contributes. The employee cannot, of course, avoid the uncertainty connected with his decision to become an employee in a particular production project as opposed to some alternative.

8. It is also possible that a saver would directly lend to a worker with the understanding that repayment of the loan depends on the amount of pay received from the worker's employer. The amount of pay, in turn, might depend upon the profitability of the team project.

9. The problem is even more severe (a) when guarantors are not held responsible for their judgments, and (b) when a national monetary policy and monopoly banking combine to cause systematic malinvestment. On malinvestment, see Mises, (1966, chap. 20).

10. Beyond this, there is the question of whether such a policy could be effectively implemented and enforced and, if it could, what the costs of the implementation and enforcement would be.

11. On page 532 of *Human Action,* Mises speaks of the rate of interest in a "market economy in which the assumptions of the evenly rotating economy are present." The rate of interest in such an economy is equivalent in the author's terminology to the rate in the image of fully integrated entrepreneurs. Also see his discussion on page 536.

12. Market-creation may entail a separate effort by a buyer and seller. For example, a seller might incur the expense of renting a space to retail his product and of advertising his product in the newspaper. A buyer might use his time and energy to search for newspaper ads and to travel to "the market." In this event, the price of the product would include the market-creation component of the seller, since he would not incur the costs if he did not expect to get reimbursed by the sales revenue. But the price would not include the buyer's market-creation costs. To make the buyer's action worthwhile, the price would have to be sufficiently lower than the buyer's evaluation of the good to compensate him for market-creation costs.

13. Some capital, in particular human capital, may not be priced in the market. The discussion here is confined for simplicity to capital that has a market price.

14. Keep in mind that market-creation is being disregarded here. All prices, including wages, have an entrepreneurial component due to the fact that prices must be announced and accepted.

Chapter 9

The Method of Contrasting
Images of Functions (6):
Profit and Loss

The concepts of profit and loss are derived from the economist's image of the entrepreneurial role's appraisals under the conditions specified in the definition of the market economy. If an individual acting in the entrepreneurial role appraises a factor at a higher (lower) money value than the estimated market price, he is said to anticipate a profit (loss) from employing it. Profit and loss are significant because they are the motivation to act entrepreneurially. If no one anticipated profit, there could be no entrepreneurship and the economic functions would not be performed. There could be no economy, as conceived in economic theory.

In economic theory, profit and loss are subjective. This has two immediate implications. The first and most important is that each individual in a market economy has a unique ability as an appraiser. Because of this, he is in the best position to know whether to anticipate profit or loss from a particular undertaking. He is also in the best position to know about the intersubjective uncertainty he faces. An outsider, including an economist, can only make hypotheses from afar, as it were. This implication reflects the economist's assumption that each individual in a market economy may be able to understand the actions and understandings of others as well as or better than the economist can.

The second implication is that the satisfaction obtainable with the money earned by one individual cannot be compared with the satisfac-

137

tion obtainable with the same amount of money earned by another individual. This second implication is not directly associated with the entrepreneurial role, since the goal of the entrepreneurial role is money, not satisfaction. Nevertheless, the implication cannot be avoided in a description of economic interaction in the market economy. Human beings in a market economy ultimately perform entrepreneurial acts in order to obtain satisfaction.

Unfortunately, economic theorists have seldom adopted the subjectivist definition of profit. Mainstream economists typically define profit as an objective magnitude that is sought after. Even more unfortunately, although Mises clearly recognized both implications and readily applied the second one, his descriptions of economic interaction in a market economy neglected the first one. This is so in spite of the fact that his methodological writings indicate that he knew the importance of placing the economic subjects and the economist in the same life world. This neglect gives his discussions of profit and loss a non-subjectivist tone.[1]

The purpose of this chapter is to explore the first implication of the subjectivity of profit and loss. Part 1 elucidates the process through which existing entrepreneurial knowledge gets acquired, communicated, and used. It constructs rigorous definitions of anticipated and realized profit and describes what a realized profit signifies to entrepreneurship. Then it shows how entrepreneurship can cause realized profit to be transformed into intersubjective economic rent. Parts 2 and 3 further clarify the subjectivity of profit and loss. Part 2 distinguishes profit from income due to the luck connected with risk-bearing and from income due to incorrectly appraised scientific knowledge. Part 3 discusses several related issues, including the relationship between profit and wealth, the concept of economic prosperity, and efforts to define profit statistically.

1. APPRAISEMENT AND PROFIT

In order to acquire an understanding of the meaning of profit and loss, the economist must consider the appraiser as a fully integrated entrepreneur whose goal is to make money. Then she must view the appraiser from two perspectives at the same time. First, the appraiser must be viewed as an entrepreneur who hopes to gain from his act of appraising. Second, he must be viewed as a prospective object of appraisal by other appraisers.[2] The discussion of profit and loss begins by considering the first perspective in isolation. It assumes that appraisers themselves are not appraised.

The Appraising Entrepreneur as a Subject

Mises provided a useful means of considering the appraising entrepreneur as a subject but not as an object when he constructed an image of an economy comprised of fully integrated, or pure, entrepreneurs.

> We may construct the image of an economy in which the conditions required for the establishment of futures markets are realized for all kinds of goods and services. In such an imaginary construction the entrepreneurial function is fully separated from all other functions. There emerges a class of pure entrepreneurs. The prices determined on the futures markets direct the whole apparatus of production. The dealers in futures alone make profits and suffer losses. All other people are insured, as it were, against the possible adverse effects of the uncertainty of the future. They enjoy security in this regard. The heads of the various business units are virtually employees, as it were, with a fixed income.[3]

In this image of interaction, profit and loss are made only by the dealers in futures, who Mises calls pure entrepreneurs.[4] Factor suppliers, including hired enterprisers, earn rent or wages; savers earn interest. Risk-bearers earn a gambling gain or loss, depending on their luck.

Fully integrated entrepreneurs are the ultimate appraisers, undertakers, and uncertainty-bearers. Taken as a group, they appraise all factors. Considered separately, each entrepreneur studies the price offers made by other entrepreneurs. Having completed her studies, the individual entrepreneur bids for the rights to the income resulting from a particular set of undertaking decisions. After buying a right to income, a fully integrated entrepreneur "activates" the undertaking by commanding hired managers (Mises's heads of business units) to perform the various actions that cause a good to be produced and sold.

Suppose that the entrepreneurs are $A, B, C \ldots N$. They appraise the rights to income streams due to the hiring of managers $1, 2, 3 \ldots M$. Then they bid to hire those managers and the other factors required to complete a production project. An entrepreneur who wins a bid pays with borrowed savings for which she also must bid. Entrepreneurs personally guarantee the repayment of their borrowing plus interest with their own money.

The image of fully integrated entrepreneurs can be compared with the FIREE introduced in chapter seven. In the FIREE, the economist specifies the profit-maximizing behavior of the robo-ents. In the image of fully integrated entrepreneurs, it will be shown, the economist specifies only that the entrepreneurs perform the three categories of entrepreneurial action.

Anticipated and realized profit. In the image of fully integrated entrepreneurs, it is easy to define profit. *Anticipated profit* is the difference between the highest bid that a fully integrated entrepreneur would be willing to make (i.e., her appraisal) and the price that she believes must actually be paid in order to bid the right to an income stream away from other fully integrated entrepreneurs. *Realized profit* is that part of the income stream that a fully integrated entrepreneur, in retrospect, attributes to her superior appraising ability.[5]

Anticipated profit and the belief in one's superiority. Anticipated profit is inextricably connected with a subjective feeling of superiority. The entrepreneur anticipates profit and is willing to bid higher prices for factors only because she believes that her appraisals reflect the true money-earning potential of the manager and other factors more correctly than the prices bid by others. Since prices are the bids of other entrepreneurs, each entrepreneur who acquires the right to an income stream must believe that her appraisals are superior to the revealed appraisals of the others. By definition, an individual could not anticipate profit if she did not believe that her appraisals were superior.[6]

It is evident that a person's belief about the superiority of his or her appraisal is subjective. This piece of intuition implies that profit is also subjective. To know the share of a person's total earnings that should be called profit, the economist would have to know the sum of money that the person attributes to what she believes to be her superior appraising ability.

What realized profit and loss signify to the fully integrated entrepreneur. To the fully integrated entrepreneur, the realization of the amount of profit that was predicted signifies that her appraisals of factors were correct. If realized profit differs from anticipated profit, the entrepreneur *learns* that her appraisals were incorrect. The importance of her learning depends upon future options. Suppose that the entrepreneur realizes a loss. If she must make the same type of appraisals again, she will revise her previous appraisals. The result will be a decision to carry out some other undertaking or not to undertake at all.

It may be helpful to make a physical analogy. Realized profit and loss may be regarded as analogous to the consequences of aiming at a target. If a bull's-eye is hit and conditions do not change, a competent marksman will shoot again in the same way. If the target is missed, he will either change his aim or quit shooting, unless conditions change.

Physical analogies can never fully describe human processes. The defect of this analogy is that it suggests that anyone could observe whether the appraiser had realized a profit. Because profit is subjective, the fully integrated appraiser would ordinarily be in the best and perhaps the only position to know whether he hit the target. In a market economy, the individual actor is ordinarily in the best position to know the share of his earnings that are due to the superiority of his appraisals. He knows that the rest are due to supplying factors, saving, and risk-bearing. Outsiders, including the economist, can only speculate on this.

The analogy is not misleading only if it is used to refer to how a person views his own action. As a normal human being, you know what it means to revise a prediction about how other individuals will act after finding out that an earlier prediction under similar circumstances was wrong. Because of this, you know the significance of determining the difference between the anticipated reactions by others to your action and the realized reactions. Your ability to know this gives you an intuitive basis for also knowing the significance of anticipated and realized profit and loss to a fully integrated entrepreneur.

The Appraiser as an Object

Up to this point, it has beem assumed that the appraising abilities of the entrepreneurs are not themselves appraised. Assume now that fully integrated entrepreneurs can bid for the rights to the income streams that result from each others' decisions to hire managers. In conjunction with this, assume they can appraise their own respective abilities as appraisers. In this event, each prospective entrepreneur would have to make a decision whether to be a self-employed appraiser or to hire herself out as an appraiser-employee to some other entrepreneur. If she decided on self-employment, she would have to make a second decision of whether to hire others.

Subjective profit vs. intersubjective rent. These assumptions allow one to identify a relationship between profit and rent. Consider a fully integrated entrepreneur who has enjoyed prolonged success. So long as no one else appraises his appraising ability and offers him employment as an appraiser-employee, the income due to his superior appraising ability is profit (although an outsider may not be able to identify it). Suppose now that other entrepreneurs, who observe the income received by the first, come to bid for him as an appraiser-employee. Under these circumstances, whether he would continue to anticipate profit from self-employment would depend upon whether the money that he would regard as profit if there were no bids for his employment was greater than the amount that is bid. If it were greater, he would still anticipate profit but the anticipated profit would not be as high as it would have been if no bidding had occurred. If the money he would anticipate as profit is less than the bids, he would anticipate a loss from remaining self-employed. He would earn higher income by choosing to be employed by other entrepreneurs.

An important conclusion follows from this discussion: As one's personally known superior appraising ability becomes evident to others, anticipated subjective profit gets incorporated into intersubjective economic rent. The dollar value of the appraising ability comes to be represented more fully by its price.

Superior Undertaking Ability Is Not a Source of Anticipated Profit and Loss

Undertaking consists only of the decision making that ultimately causes factors or goods to be produced and exchanged. It is included as part of entrepreneurship because no income can be earned unless goods are produced and exchanged. In the abstract, the decision making associated with undertaking need consist of nothing more than an act of will. The entrepreneur may simply command that her hired managers cause the production and exchange to occur. More specific production and exchange decisions can be delegated to the managers.

Although the act of will must be performed before profit or loss can be realized, the anticipation of profit or loss is not due in any significant way to this act. Instead, the act of will is a consequence of the anticipation of profit.

Individuals may differ in their abilities to make complex decisions regarding the use of factors. In other words, they may possess different undertaking abilities. However, it would be wrong to say that profit is due to superior undertaking ability. If an appraising entrepreneur does not recognize superior decision-making ability, that ability cannot be a source of anticipated profit. And if she does not recognize it, any income that can be attributed to it would be either rent (if others recognize it also) or profit due to her superior ability to identify her ability (which is a factor).

Suppose that an entrepreneur possesses superior decision-making ability that neither she nor anyone else recognizes. Then her production decisions will enable her to earn more income than she had anticipated. As she reviews these results, she may recognize her superior ability and upwardly revise her appraisal of it. If she regards her revised appraisal as superior to the appraisals of others, she may come to anticipate even greater profit from self-employment. In this event, the source of her additional anticipated profit is her belief that she has made a superior appraisal; it is not her superior decision-making.

In a market economy, an individual may believe that she has decision-making ability that remains unrecognized by prospective employers. In this event, she would have to become her own boss in order to earn a profit. Nevertheless, the anticipated profit, which provides the motivation to act entrepreneurially, is not due to the self-employed individual's superior decision-making ability. It is due to her belief that she is making a superior appraisal of her decision-making ability. The other prospective employers are, in the individual's eyes, inferior appraisers.

2. GAMBLING AND THE APPRAISEMENT OF SCIENTIFIC KNOWLEDGE

The concept of entrepreneurship is necessarily linked to one particular type of uncertainty—intersubjective uncertainty. In everyday life and in the market economy, other types of uncertainty are also present. However, the other types are not essential in identifying the role of the entrepreneur. The failure of economists to stress the necessity of intersubjective uncertainty in delimiting the entrepreneurial role has resulted in their mistakenly regarding risk-bearing and the possession of scientific knowledge as possible sources of profit and loss. This part first shows that entrepreneurship is necessarily linked to intersubjective uncertainty and not to other types. Then it uses this demonstration as a basis for distinguishing profit and loss from gambling gains and losses and from gains and losses due to superior scientific knowledge.

Entrepreneurial Uncertainty and Other Types

The type of uncertainty that is relevant to entrepreneurship in economic theory is narrow. It is the intersubjective uncertainty that one knows from intuition and experience would be borne of the hypothetical, fully integrated entrepreneur. This is uncertainty about the wants of consumer-savers and about the abilities, knowledge, and labor disutilities of factor-suppliers. In everyday life and also in the economist's image of the market economy, intersubjective uncertainty is mixed with other types. The other types can be divided into three categories. First, there is uncertainty associated with known scientific probabilities. Second, there is uncertainty associated with the fact that scientific knowledge is incomplete. Third, an individual may be uncertain about his own future wants, knowledge, and abilities.[7] Each is discussed in turn.

Uncertainty associated with known scientific probabilities. The first type of uncertainty refers to a situation in which it is known that if X occurs, Y will follow sometimes but not always.[8] The probability that Y will follow (or the probability distribution) is known. It might be said that science reveals that it is certain that Y will follow X with a given probability. If scientific facts of this type are known by everyone, they are relevant to economic theory only if different individuals are assumed to have different willingness and abilities to bear risk. Only then can there be differences in entrepreneurial appraisals of factors on this account. Differences in propensities to bear risk make it profitable for entrepreneurship to identify the differences and to create markets in which individuals who are more risk-averse can be insured by those who are less risk-averse and in which risks can be pooled.

It is important to recognize that differences in risk preferences do not, by themselves, prompt entrepreneurial action. It is the entrepreneur's recognition of these differences, along with his recognition of a method of profiting by intermediating in an exchange or by providing insurance, that gives an incentive for action. In other words, entrepreneurial action is prompted by an entrepreneur's knowledge of individuals' preferences regarding scientifically uncertain outcomes, not by the fact that differences in preferences exist or that outcomes are scientifically uncertain.

Suppose that it is absolutely certain that Y would follow X, but that everyone erroneously believes there is a given probability less than one that Y will follow X. Suppose further that they have different propensities to bear risk. Assuming further that entrepreneurs recognize the differences, they would still be prompted to intermediate in an exchange or to provide insurance.

Uncertainty due to incomplete scientific knowledge. The second type of uncertainty refers to the absence of scientific knowledge. There are many instances in which no scientist knows whether Y will follow X. It is believed, or hypothesized, however, that it will. Estimates, or guesses, may even be made of the probability that Y will follow X. The heart of the matter, however, is that no scientist currently knows the exact probability.

This situation in itself cannot, in any useful sense, prompt entrepreneurial action. It is the entrepreneur's task to appraise whatever scientific knowledge exists. The fact that some knowledge does not exist merely implies that there is nothing to appraise. Of course, it is the role of the entrepreneur to appraise what is proposed as new scientific knowledge. Thus an entrepreneur who fails to account for the prospect of new knowledge or who fails to appraise such knowledge as well as another entrepreneur may not realize the profit she anticipates. But the uncertainty that is relevant here is not the uncertainty due to incomplete scientific knowledge, rather it is the uncertainty about whether proposed new scientific knowledge is correct.

In delimiting the role of the entrepreneur, the subjectivist economist artificially separates scientific knowledge from intersubjective knowledge. He attributes the former to the factor-suppliers and the latter to the entrepreneur. Intuition and experience suggest, however, that an individual acting in the entrepreneurial role in the market economy would have to possess scientific knowledge in order to appraise the scientific knowledge of others. Still, it is not the scientific knowledge that is crucial to entrepreneurship. It is the ability to appraise that knowledge and the willingness and ability to bet that one's appraisals are correct that is the essence of entrepreneurship.

Intrasubjective uncertainty. Individuals in a market economy are uncertain about their own wants, abilities, and knowledge. If they had to pay in advance for goods not yet produced, many would be unwilling to buy. To avoid the uncertainty that their wants or abilities may change, they are willing to pay a higher price for a good that has already been produced. Still, some consumers are willing to provide the guaranty or to pay in advance. In addition, most people buy durable goods even though, in doing so, they are taking a chance that a change in their wants, abilities, or knowledge may render the goods less valuable to them. Thus, consumers in the market economy do bear intrasubjective uncertainty.

The personal actions that individuals perform in order to deal with intrasubjective uncertainty are of interest to economic theory only insofar as they interface with exchanges that occur in order to shift the uncertainty. Where such shifting occurs, it is not due to the fact that individuals face intrasubjective uncertainty but to their differences in beliefs about how the wants, abilities, or knowledge will change or to a difference in the willingness and abilities of individuals to bet that their beliefs are superior.

Conclusion. The essential phenomenon of a market economy is the entrepreneurial interaction that occurs when individuals differ in their appraisals and, most importantly, in their willingness or abilities to bet on their appraisals. In their interaction, individuals may make use of their knowledge of scientific probabilities, their estimates based on incomplete scientific knowledge, their intrasubjective knowledge, and their intersubjective understandings. However, this fact does not make it permissible for the economist to lump all of these together under the category of uncertainty. A proper understanding of the entrepreneurial role indicates that it is not the fact that an individual is a risk-taker or that he possesses superior scientific knowledge that leads him to undertake a production project; it is his belief that he has more correctly appraised his scientific knowledge. Only if he has such a belief is it correct to say that he anticipates profit. And only if he later comes to believe that his income was due to such a belief is it correct to say that his anticipated profit was realized. It is the uncertainty that gets manifested in different beliefs by entrepreneurs about the superiority of their appraisals that is fundamentally relevant to economics. In the author's view, only such uncertainty should be labelled as such by economists.

Improper Meaning of Profit and Loss

When applied economists associate profit and loss with risk-taking and scientific knowledge, they demote the entrepreneurial role. In this subsection, the confusion between entrepreneurial profit and loss and gambling gains and losses is considered first. Then the confusion involving returns to scientific knowledge is discussed. Finally, the concept of entrepreneurial luck is identified.

Entrepreneurial profit and loss vs. gambling gains and losses. Gambling is the act of betting on the outcome of an action when the actor knows the probability that any particular outcome will occur. An example is the role of a die. The kind of knowledge that enables the actor to know such probabilities is scientific knowledge. Suppose that a businessperson anticipates a profit of $100 from what she believes is a set of superior appraisals. On the basis of the best scientific knowledge available, she knows that specific unpreventable and unavoidable events may occur that would make her proceeds either higher or lower. If such an event occurs, yet everything else goes as anticipated, the businessperson will attribute whatever difference exists between her proceeds and the $100 she anticipated to luck. She will regard it as a gambling gain or loss and not as part of realized economic profit or loss.

If knowledge of her gamble was widely held, the businessperson could shift her risk by paying a fee to a risk-bearer. However, conditions may exist in a market economy that make it impossible for the businessperson to undertake a production project unless she also bears the risk. Specifically, no one else besides the businessperson may possess the scientific knowledge that reveals the true probabilities. And no one may have appraised the businessperson's knowledge accurately. Yet such knowledge is needed to determine the expected return of the gamble. Under these conditions, no risk-bearer would accept the risk. The businessperson would have to bear uncertainty and risk together.

The fact that the businessperson has unique scientific knowledge of probabilities is, by itself, unimportant. The important fact from the economist's viewpoint is that the businessperson appraises her knowledge of probabilities higher than others and that she is willing and able to bet that her appraisal is superior. For this reason and this reason alone, with the exception of possible gambling gains or losses, the total proceeds in such a case can be classified as profit or loss. To claim that profit or loss is due to risk-taking would demote the entrepreneurial role and threaten to undermine the new subjectivist revolution.

Profit and scientific errors. Suppose that, according to the businessperson's best scientific prediction about natural events (e.g., weather conditions), the profit and proceeds of an undertaking will be $100. She decides to undertake the project. Afterwards, however, she discovers that her proceeds are minus $50. Later, she learns that her prediction was wrong entirely because of her inferior scientific knowledge. If she had relied on the prediction of a competent scientist, she would have anticipated the $50 loss and declined to undertake the project. It might be thought that this outcome could be expressed by saying that, as a result of her error, the businessperson had realized a profit of $100 and a wage as a scientist of -$150, for net earnings of

-$50. This is incorrect. If the businessperson reaches the conclusion that her previous scientific knowledge was incorrect, she must, at the same time, reach the conclusion that her previous appraisal of her scientific knowledge was incorrect. She thought her knowledge was worth $150 more than it turned out to be. Upon reaching this conclusion, she would realize that she made an error as an appraiser. She was not a superior appraiser, as she thought. As a result, she realized a loss of $50 and earned $150 less profit than she anticipated.

It is part of the role of the entrepreneur to appraise factors, including her own scientific knowledge. If the businessperson had appraised her scientific knowledge correctly, she would not have made the undertaking decision in the first place because anticipated profit would have been negative. The proper conclusion is that the businessperson's inferior appraisal of her own scientific knowledge led to the negative proceeds.[9]

The concept of entrepreneurial luck. In order to appraise factors, the fully integrated entrepreneur must predict changes in the wants, abilities, and knowledge of others. Although entrepreneurs differ in ability, no entrepreneur can expect to predict changes in wants, and so on, exactly. From the entrepreneur's point of view, whether he earns more or less appears to depend on chance. He will regard himself as lucky if he earns more and unlucky if he earns less.

To a businessperson in a market economy who must also bear risk, there may be little difference between this concept of luck and a concept that is derived from the "certain" knowledge of natural science that there is only a given probability that a particular event in a class will occur. A choice to engage in a production project may appear as a gamble on both accounts. He may attribute the outcome in both cases to luck. The same is true of luck related to incomplete scientific knowledge.

The economist's definition of entrepreneurial luck must be different from this. In using the method of contrasting images of functions to construct the language of economic theory, the economic theorist assigns the entrepreneurial role to individuals who attempt to predict future wants, abilities, and knowledge. She assigns the economic function of risk-bearing to a robot. Thus, the entrepreneurial role cannot be that of a risk-bearer, by definition. The role must, however, bear intersubjective uncertainty.

It might be said that there are two concepts of luck that pertain to the businessperson in a market economy: gambling luck and entrepreneurial luck. Gambling luck refers to luck that is related either to scientifically determined probabilities or to one's having guessed more correctly than incorrectly about a scientific hypothesis. Entrepreneurial luck refers to luck related to having more correctly guessed about future wants, abilities, and knowledge. A guess in this case is a choice of one alternative over another when the subject does not have a reason for choosing an alternative that he can personally defend. Whether a choice constitutes a guess can only be determined subjectively. Thus, only the entrepreneur can truly judge whether some of his proceeds were due to entrepreneurial luck.[10]

3. RELATED ISSUES

This section considers three issues that are related to the concepts of profit and entrepreneurship. First, the relationship between profit and wealth is discussed. This is followed by a discussion of the relationship between entrepreneurship and "prosperity." Finally, statistical measures of profit are discussed.

Profit and Wealth

Production in a market economy requires entrepreneurship to bear the uncertainty connected with the loans needed to pay factors prior to the end of the production period. The set of individuals who adopt the entrepreneurial role with respect to a given project cannot afford to bear the uncertainty unless they possess enough wealth to fall back on in the event of a loss. Consider an enterprising individual who identifies a project that requires financing of $1 million. If he has the money and is willing to risk losing it, he will finance the project and become an entrepreneur. If not, then he must attempt to borrow the million. Yet no lender will lend him the money unless (a) he also appraises the factors, or (b) someone else provides guaranty for the loan. And no one would provide guaranty unless he first appraises the factors. Thus, the would-be enterpriser is faced with the task of convincing the lender or guarantor that his appraisals are correct.

However, communication of a prospective profit opportunity is costly and possibly destructive of the potential gain. In many cases, such communication would require the enterpriser to reveal the bases for his appraisals. This, in turn, may reduce the value to him of the ability that enabled him to make the appraisal in the first place. Specifically, after the lender or guarantor acquires the knowledge needed to make more accurate appraisals, she may proceed to undertake the project herself. Alternatively, she may offer to provide guaranty to another enterpriser at a higher guaranty fee. Unless one of the factors that is crucial to the plan is owned exclusively by the initial enterpriser, he may simply lose whatever gain he anticipated from obtaining the loan.

It may not even be possible for an enterpriser to convince a lender that his appraisals are superior. In this event, he would be unable to raise the funds necessary to provide guaranty for his project. Unless he has the wealth to finance the project himself or to provide guaranty for loans (and if he does have it he must be willing to use it), the project will not be carried out and the profit will not be earned.

Given these considerations, it is easy to see the basis for the proposition that the amount of profit an individual can earn is related to the amount of wealth he has. Possession of a sizable amount of wealth increases the potential for making profit in two ways. First, if an individual discovers that his appraisals of factors are higher than the factor prices, he can take advantage of his discovery immediately without borrowing. Second, a wealthy person who announces his desire to be a lender or guarantor will be showered with offers from enterprisers who are willing to communicate the bases for their beliefs that their appraisals are superior to the appraisals of others. In other words, wealth puts a person in a position to receive a relatively free education, which may increase his own entrepreneurial ability.[11]

Because of the many opportunities to profit in a market economy, the fact that an individual lacks substantial wealth does not exclude him from using his entrepreneurship. However, it does restrict the range of projects he can carry out. A person who lacks wealth may have no incentive at all to produce or use appraisement ability with respect to some projects, since his limited wealth gives him no opportunity to profit from carrying out those projects. To some degree, this limitation is moderated by the incentives that wealthy individuals have to discover and accurately appraise the appraisement abilities of those who are less wealthy. The limitation, however, still exists.

Entrepreneurship and "Prosperity"

It is improper for the economic theorist to claim that entrepreneurship in the market economy causes economic development or promotes economic growth. Terms like development and growth, or prosperity, ordinarily ignore the particular satisfactions of different individuals. Since the satisfactions of different individuals at different points in time cannot legitimately be compared, the use of such terms is improper.

The economist who wishes to claim that individuals benefit from entrepreneurial interaction must appeal to intuition and experience. She begins by asserting that whether someone believes she will earn an economic profit depends upon how correctly she believes she has appraised factors relative to other appraisers. Then she asserts that individuals who believe that their appraisals are superior are more likely to undertake, other things being equal. Finally, she asks whether, other things being equal, such undertakers are likely to be correct. In each case, the economist appeals to her readers' intuitions and experience. If the reader agrees with the assertions and answers yes to the question, then it can be deduced that correct appraisals will tend to be made more frequently than incorrect ones.

Next the economist can try to show that the making of correct appraisals benefits not only the entrepreneur but also others. She can do this by making an analogy with a simple exchange. She can show that if a prospective trader correctly estimates his trading partner's wants, abilities, and knowledge, he will benefit both parties to a greater extent, other things being equal, than he will if he makes incorrect estimates.[12] However, the economist can only reason by analogy, since the effects of any particular entrepreneurial action are too complex to fully describe.

Beyond this, the economist can create the image of interacting fully integrated entrepreneurs in order to isolate the categories of entrepreneurial action that, under the conditions specified in the image, would cause factors to be identified, relative costs to be estimated, and factors to be allocated among different uses. In addition, she can meticulously describe characteristics of the market economy. Finally, she can describe the coordinating and synchronizing actions of individuals acting in the entrepreneurial role. Each description may serve to eludicate the process whereby correct appraisals by entrepreneurship in a market economy yield benefits to specific individuals. In doing these things, the economist is elucidating the effects of entrepreneurship under the conditions specified in a market economy. However, it is improper for her to generalize from this by concluding that "the society is better off," or that "the society is more developed."

Statistical Measures of Profit

Many modern economists suggest that deductions about the presence of profit can be made on the basis of "evidence" of money holdings or money transfers that can be observed in everyday life. To what extent are they correct? The money holdings and transfers that occur in everyday life are not only economic phenomena. They are also political, legal, cultural, psychological, biological, and non-market phenomena. To determine what part of such holdings or transfers are economic requires the economist to engage in historical speculation.

Even if the money holding or transfer is evidence of an economic phenomenon, it may not be evidence of profit. It may be a reward for puppet-like behavior instead of a reward for appraisement, undertaking, and uncertainty-bearing. In order to determine whether it is profit, the statistician would have to use her ability to understand the plans and understandings of the individuals involved in the transfers. She would have to look into their minds, as it were.

Statistical economists who do not employ the method of contrasting images of functions cannot help but confuse profit with other income. They must use definitions that are at best typifications (see chapter six). Such definitions refer to definite categories that can be observed and distinguished objectively according to agree-upon, or authoritative, criteria; but their relationship to true economic categories is not established.

Notes

1. An example of Mises's (1966) lack of subjectivism in his discussion of profit and loss is that he associated profit with an objective sum of money. He says: "It is possible to ascertain in terms of money how much an individual has profited or lost. . . . [These profits or losses] reflect his fellow men's evaluation of his contribution to social cooperation" (p. 289). On the other hand, in some of his discussions of profit and loss, Mises seems to clearly recognize the subjectivity of these terms. On page 533, Mises says that "[o]nly the excess of proceeds over the costs so calculated is *in his eyes* entrepreneurial profit" (italics added). Similarly, in his 1980 essay "Profit and Loss," he points out that profit ultimately originates as a "mental act." It is a "product of the mind." The author's view is that Mises's statements about profit and loss, taken as a whole, reflect either a contradiction or an incomplete working out of the concepts of profit and loss in economic theory. With few exceptions, when he uses the concepts of profit and loss, he seems to have in mind an image of the FIREE. Yet he does not acknowledge using the image of the FIREE but instead speaks as if he is discussing the market economy.

2. This approach is adopted by Alchian and Allen (1983, 188–90). Also see Gurzynski (1976, 11).

3. Mises (1966, 256).

4. This concept of the pure entrepreneur should not be confused with Kirzner's representation of Mises's pure entrepreneur (Kirzner 1973, 39–40, 47). In Kirzner's conception, the pure entrepreneur owns no property whatever. In his 1979 book, Kirzner attaches the label of *capitalist* to Mises's conception of the pure entrepreneur. Compare Mises's description of the pure entrepreneur in the quotation in this chapter with the following description of capitalists made by Kirzner:

> If capitalists have, every one of them, failed to assess correctly the profitability of an idea advanced by a penniless entrepreneur because they have underestimated the competence or the integrity of its promoter, this creates, for capitalist-entrepreneurs, an opportunity for profit. Unless capital is monopolistically owned, capitalists will tend to compete among themselves with respect to the true measure of the competence and integrity of penniless, unknown would-be entrepreneurs (1979, 103).

In order to avoid confusion, the term "fully integrated" is used in this book in place of the term "pure."

5. Appraising by itself cannot result in profit or loss. The appraiser must also anticipate making an entrepreneurial decision. Thus, it is implicit in this discussion that the pure appraiser will perform the act of will (i.e., the undertaking act) that causes the purchased factors to be employed in a specific way.

6. This appears to be part of what Knight meant when he said that "[t]he

presence of true profit . . . depends on an absolute uncertainty in the estimation of the value of judgment . . ." (1921, 285). Later in his book he points out that

> . . . [t]he receipt of profit in a particular case may be argued to be the result of superior judgment. But it is judgment of judgment, especially one's own judgment . . . . If [the capacities of men to jduge other men in relation to the problems they are to deal with] are known, the compensation for exercising them can only be competitively imputed and is a wage; only, in so far as they are unknown or known only to the possessor himself, do they give rise to a profit. (p. 311)

7. In Chapter Three, this was called intrasubjective uncertainty.

8. Mises referred to this type of uncertainty as an instance of class probability. See Appendix 4.

9. Mises' discussion of this situation indicates both the ambiguity in his use of the term "entrepreneur" and his failure to identify the real source of entrepreneurial profit and loss. He says:

> . . . [T]he fact that not every process of production succeeds technologically in bringing about the product expected [does not] influence the specific entrepreneurial profit or loss. Such failures are either avoidable or unavoidable. In the first case they are due to the technologically inefficient conduct of affairs. Then the losses resulting are to be debited to the entrepreneur's personal insufficiency, i.e., to his lack of technological ability or to his lack of ability to hire adequate helpers. In the second case the failures are due to the fact that the present state of technological knowledge prevents us from controlling fully some of the known conditions. The price of the factors takes into account this unsatisfactory state of our knowledge and technological power. (1966, 291)

Presumably, the specific entrepreneurial profit and loss refer to what profit and loss are supposed to mean. For this reason, the discussion in this paragraph is not incorrect. However, it confuses matters to say that the "losses resulting are debited to the entrepreneur's personal insufficiency." Rather than use the term "entrepreneur" here, Mises should have substituted the term "businessperson." More importantly, Mises's failure to attribute the businessperson's losses to an incorrect appraisement of his technological ability or of the abilities of helpers shows that he failed to recognize the significance of the bet that the entrepreneur must make on his appraisement ability.

10. Knight clearly reconizes this distinction:

> The only risk which leads to a profit is a unique uncertainty resulting from an exercise of ultimate responsibility which in its very nature cannot be insured nor capitalized nor salaried. Profit arises out of the . . . sheer brute fact that the results of human activity cannot be anticipated and then only in so far as even a probability calculation in regard to them is impossible and meaningless. (1921, 310–11)
>
> The receipt of profit in a particular case may be argued to be the result of superior judgment. But it is judgment of judgment, especially one's own judgment and in an individual case there is no way of telling good judgment from good luck, and a succession of cases sufficient to evaluate the judgment or determine its probable value transforms the profit into a wage.

11. A shortcoming of *Human Action* is Mises's failure to identify the importance of guaranty. This shortcoming is in evidence when he criticizes what he called the general assertion that there is a correlation between the inequality of wealth and the satisfaction of wants for the remoter future. This assertion, he claims, is based on the idea that if an individual is more amply supplied in the near future, he will save more for the remoter future. A logical extension of this idea is that wealthier people are likely to save proportionately more than poor people. Mises did not deny this assertion but pointed out that it was based on psychological facts and thus was not a phenomenon of economic theory in a strict sense (p. 533).

If Mises had accounted for guaranty, he might have recognized a more substantial basis for the assertion. Because enterprising ideas are not perfectly matched with the wealth needed to finance them or to provide guaranty for loans, an important factor in determining whether wants for the remoter future are satisfied is the cost of knowledge transmission. Suppose that wealth is equally distributed. Then an enterpriser who wants to raise funds for a large project would have to transmit his knowledge about profitability to a number of different individuals. If wealth was unequally distributed, the number would be lower. Thus, the cost of transmitting knowledge between knowledgeable prospective enterprisers and initially ignorant owners of wealth is lower if the wealth is unequally distributed. Interpreted in this way, the assertion is not based on psychological facts. Indeed, it is not an assertion at all. It is a deduction based on an assumption about the costs of transmitting knowledge in order to deal with the problem of intersubjective uncertainty. Since knowledge transmission is a fundamental characteristic of the market economy, such a deduction is a good candidate for inclusion in economic theory.

12. The economist must, of course, also account for the prospect of externalities. She should also point out that one of the trading partners may not be a normal human being (e.g., a child or mentally deficient adult) or that he may not understand money and/or property.

Chapter 10

The Method of Contrasting Images of Functions (7): Entrepreneurship in the Market Economy

The consumer-saver robots of the ERE cannot deliberate over their choices among consumers' goods. They cannot evaluate their wants or think about alternative ways to satisfy their wants. Nor can they think about the future. Their consuming and saving behavior is entirely automatic. Similarly, the factor-supplying robots cannot appraise factors, search for alternatives, or attempt to negotiate a more favorable price. Neither the consumer-saver nor the factor-supplier faces uncertainty. These robots merely perform behavior according to algorithms specified by the economic theorist. Consumer-savers spend and save; factor-suppliers supply factors and receive income.

In the ERE, these behavioral roles are distinct and limited. The robot factor-supplier earns income but it does not spend. It cannot save its factor for later use. Nor can it get different degrees of satisfaction or dissatisfaction from different types of work. The robot consumer-saver, on the other hand, has no way to earn income. Nevertheless, it is assumed to receive a regular stream of money to spend. It owns no property; consequently, it cannot set property aside or delay its consumption of goods until a future time. It does save money but it cannot vary its saving.

As opposed to the imaginary robots in the ERE, the human beings who populate the market economy are assumed to be real people. They cannot survive without consuming goods and they cannot consume goods unless they earn income. In making their everyday choices to earn income and consume, they consider time and bear the uncertainty connected with their decisions. They do not behave according to specifiable algorithms; they are unique, original, alert, adaptive, and creative.

The purpose of this chapter is to show how entrepreneurship comes to be performed under the conditions specified in the definition of the market economy. To accomplish this, the chapter combines the image of the robotic roles of the ERE with the author's intuition about how entrepreneurial actions would be carried out by real, normal people who live under the conditions specified in the definition of the market economy. The aim is an image of a market economy that is populated by types of people. Such types are used to refer to the specialized individuals who are known in everyday life to consume, save, supply factors, produce goods, and act entrepreneurially.

The chapter begins by showing the entrepreneurship entailed in the performance of the economic functions. Part 1 shows how consumers in the market economy act entrepreneurially. Part 2 describes the entrepreneurship involved in saving. In Part 3, the entrepreneurship associated with supplying factors is described. In Part 4, the discussion turns to the entrepreneurial interaction and specialization entailed in appraisement, undertaking, and uncertainty-bearing.

Demonstrating how entrepreneurship gets manifested in the market economy is the last step in using the method of contrasting images of functions. It is also the most tenuous. As mentioned earlier, the market economy is so complex that the best the economist can hope for is to identify some of its most important characteristics. One can judge from intuition and experience whether she is on the right track. However, the lone judgment of a single economist can never generate the same confidence as a reasoned favorable critique by peers. Thus, although this chapter provides only a rough sketch of entrepreneurship in the market economy, it is the most venturesome of the text.

1. ENTREPRENEURSHIP ASSOCIATED WITH CONSUMING GOODS IN THE MARKET ECONOMY

In the following, it is convenient to use the term *consumption goods* to refer to goods that are purchased by consumers in the market economy. Consumption goods are goods that a consumer ultimately plans to consume, at least in part. There are many types and most are partly durable and partly storable. Durable and storable consumption goods may be resold. Some consumption goods are used as factors of production to produce other consumption goods and their intended use may change after they are bought.

Consumption goods can be contrasted with the consumers' goods that are bought by ERE consumers. Consumers' goods are used up completely when they are bought. Because of the versatility of many consumption goods, consumers in the market economy appraise, undertake, and bear uncertainty. This part of the text shows how consumers perform these categories of action.

Appraisement and Undertaking in the Purchase of Durable Consumption Goods

Consumption goods can be divided into classes based on their duration of serviceableness. Goods with longer durations of serviceableness are more durable. Consumption goods can also be differentiated according to whether the duration of serviceableness depends upon when they are used. To take an extreme, one type of consumption good may be capable of providing service for the first ten days after its purchase but not later, while another may be capable of providing service for any ten days during the indefinite future. The duration of serviceableness may differ with the way a good is used. If good A is used to complement good B, its duration of serviceableness may be greater or its serviceableness may occur for a different time period than if it is used to complement good C. Besides duration of serviceableness, the satisfaction from a good may be greater or less depending on the particular time period during which it is used, the place where it is located, or the other goods with which it is used.

When a consumer buys durable consumption goods, he uses his knowledge of these properties in conjunction with his knowledge of his projected wants, abilities, and knowledge. By deciding which consumption goods will be used in which combination and when they will be used, he directs the goods to be employed so that they can best satisfy his wants. In doing this he treats the consumption goods as robot entrepreneurs would treat factors in the image of an economy composed of fully integrated robot entrepreneurs. In other words, the consumer appraises and undertakes.

Consumer appraisals of consumption goods in a market economy occur for another reason. In a market economy, consumers recognize the prospect for reselling durable consumption goods at some future date. As a result, they consider the possible profit they might earn from resale, the interest they must forego when they purchase the good, and whether the good might be used as guaranty. Thus, consumers are involved in appraising their own consumption goods by speculating on future demand and supply conditions. The best example of this is housing. A home buyer not only considers his own wants for housing; he also considers the wants of others. If he expects a house to have a low resale value, he will pay only a low price for it. He takes account of the interest his money could earn if it was loaned out instead of being tied up in the house. And he thinks of the possibility of using his house as collateral or guaranty.

Uncertainty-Bearing in the Purchase of Durable Consumption Goods

Buyers of durable consumption goods in the market economy can be said to face two kinds of uncertainty: intrasubjective and intersubjective. Intrasubjective uncertainty exists because the consumer's wants, personal abilities to work, or knowledge of alternative means of satisfying her wants may change. A change in her wants means that the good would yield more or less satisfaction over its duration of serviceableness than she expected. A change in personal abilities— perhaps as a result of injury or sickness—affects her ability to earn income. A change in her knowledge may cause her to recognize other goods that are more efficient in satisfying her wants than the ones she bought.

Another form of intersubjective uncertainty that the consumer bears is that a consumption good will not turn out to be what it physically seems to be when it is purchased. The good may not yield the expected satisfaction, it may not last as long as expected, or it may be less safe than expected.

A consumer in a market economy faces intersubjective uncertainty because she has the option of buying and selling her goods in markets and because her income-earning power depends upon the demand for the various services she can supply. Changes in others' demands for and supplies of consumption goods of the same type as those purchased by the consumer affect a good's resale price. Changes in demands for and supplies of the factors supplied by the consumer cause changes in her money income. Either an unanticipated rise or an unanticipated fall in money income may cause a consumer to regret that she purchased a particular consumption good. The consumer must bear the uncertainty of the loss associated with such a prospect for regret. Another source of regret is the possibility that a good that is paid for in advance will not be delivered.

To avoid the worst effects of such changes, consumers in the market economy may purchase or otherwise acquire information about future product availabilities and prices, about future income-earning possibilities, and about how wants change as human beings grow old. Alternatively, they may set aside a sum of money or goods to be used in the case of an emergency. This money or goods is personal guaranty.[1]

A consumer can often avoid bearing the uncertainty that a consumption good will not turn out to be what it physically seems to be by purchasing only those goods that have guarantees, warranties, and even buy-back assurances. Thus, participation in a market economy enables a consumer to shift some of his uncertainty-bearing to others. Still, she may decide not to pay the additional money cost that must typically be paid for these.

A consumer can often obtain lower prices for goods by agreeing to pay for them in advance. In this way, she comes to bear some of the uncertainty that would otherwise be borne by producers, lenders, and/ or employers.

2. ENTREPRENEURSHIP ASSOCIATED WITH SAVING IN THE MARKET ECONOMY

Saving in the ERE means merely that factors that could be devoted to producing consumption goods are devoted to maintaining capital. It might be said that such saving is motivated by the desire not to consume less in the future than is consumed in the present. In order to avoid a fall in consumption over time, capital in the ERE is maintained. A different way to say this is that saving in the ERE consists entirely of capitalist saving.[2] In the ERE, the robot consumer-saver is restricted to consuming the same goods again and again. It saves only to avoid a reduction in income.

In a market economy, saving consists of both capitalist saving and plain saving. To the consumer-saver in the market economy, capitalist saving means that he can earn a return on his saving. It is motivated by a desire to earn income or to keep one's income from falling too low. Plain saving means that the saver may decide to consume more or less goods of different kinds in the distant future than in the near future. He need not consume the same amounts of goods during each period of time.[3]

Because consumption goods in a market economy are durable and storable, every decision to buy or keep a consumption good is also a decision to save. The consumer decides which consumption goods to buy or sell on the basis of his desire not only for immediate satisfaction but also for satisfaction in the future. Since the purchase of consumption goods has already been considered, the discussion in this part will focus on money saving and dis-saving.

Consumer-Savers as Lenders

Due to financial markets, savers of money in a market economy are confronted with a wide array of prospects. At one extreme, they can choose among the highly secure savings accounts at insured financial institutions. At the other extreme, they can buy shares of stock in speculative corporations such as mineral exploration firms. In the first case, they expect to earn a small but relatively secure return. In the second, they expect either to lose much of their savings or to gain a large return. To select the most suitable form of saving, the saver must use her appraisement ability. Suppose that the saver opts to purchase stocks. She may personally appraise the boards of directors and the management of different corporations, she may choose to follow the advice of others who she believes are dependable, she may choose according to a previously developed strategy, or she may act on a hunch.

Because of the decision-making structure of a corporation, a saver who buys stocks contributes partly to the undertaking that occurs. By exercising her voting rights, she influences the selection of the board of directors. Even if she does not plan to attend stockholders' meetings or to respond to proxy requests, her decision to purchase a share of stock gives the other owners an additional source of funds for their undertakings. At the same time, her decision denies such funds to owners of other corporations.

The saver who saves her money with an insured intermediary bears less uncertainty than the saver who buys stocks. In this case, she takes advantage of an opportunity to shift some uncertainty to the intermediary and the insurer. Still, she contributes to undertaking. Her saving helps make it profitable for the bankers and insurers to operate as specialized appraisers, uncertainty-bearers, diversifiers of uncertainty, and poolers of risk. When the intermediaries decide to make loans to businesses or to buy stocks, they contribute to the undertaking of businesses.

A saver who opts for less uncertainty is not indifferent to the insured intermediary she chooses. She chooses the intermediary that offers what she believes is the combination of high rates of return and security that she wants. There is never complete certainty in the market economy. Even savings held by an insured intermediary are in some measure insecure, since the intermediary's insurer can go bankrupt. Since a saver's choice of one intermediary over another helps determine how much money different intermediaries will be able to lend to businesses, the saver indirectly helps to decide the types of undertaking that borrowers from intermediaries can carry out.

Consumer-Savers as Guarantors

Consumer-savers in a market economy have another opportunity to earn income that is not available either to the individual operating alone or to consumer-savers in the ERE: It is to use the wealth that they own in the form of durable consumption goods, money, or promises as guaranty for loans made by others. If a consumer-saver is a wise guarantor, he may be able to earn income on his consumption goods and have use of them as well. Or he may be able to earn a high profit on his money.

Consumer-Savers as Borrowers

Consumer-savers in a market economy can finance their purchases of consumption goods by borrowing. In doing this, a consumer-saver acts like an entrepreneur in the follwoing sense. She bets that her appraisal of her labor, human capital, and other income sources is not so inaccurate that repaying the loan will require a substantial unanticipated reduction in her satisfaction at some future time. A consumer-saver may also provide guaranty for her loan. If property is pledged, then the guaranty consists of that property, which she may have to forfeit. If future labor or human capital income is pledged, the guaranty consists of the promise to earn and turn over such income. By pledging to forfeit collateral or future income, a consumer-saver shifts to herself some of what would otherwise be a lender's uncertainty.

3. ENTREPRENEURSHIP ASSOCIATED WITH SUPPLYING FACTORS IN THE MARKET ECONOMY

In discussing the factor-suppliers in the market economy, it is convenient to distinguish between suppliers of nonhuman factors (land and physical capital) and suppliers of human factors (labor and human capital). Each type is discussed in turn.

Suppliers of Nonhuman Factors

An individual who owns an item that he believes is regarded by others as nonhuman capital or land typically tries to earn the money income that he believes will yield the highest valued stream of satisfaction over time. In order to earn as much as he can, he appraises his capital or land. He tries to discover demand and supply conditions for products that can be produced with his factor and acquires information about the prices offered by producers. After making his appraisals, he considers the prospect of self-employment but rejects it. Instead, he decides whether to rent or sell his rights for what he regards as the best price offer. However, he cannot be certain that his appraisal is correct. After he accepts an offer, he may become aware of a more attractive one. Thus, he must bear the uncertainty connected with his decision to rent or sell the factor at any given time.

Owners of all factors often have the option of bearing more or less uncertainty. By agreeing to wait for their pay until after revenue is received by the employer of their factors, they can bear uncertainty regarding future market conditions. By not waiting, they shift their uncertainty to others.

Capital- and land-owners may have the option of maintaining or improving their factors. In deciding how profitable it will be to maintain or improve, they appraise the factors used for maintenance or improvement. If they choose this option, they become producers with respect to their own factors.

A distinguishing feature of some capital is its potential specificity. Considering the range of possible employments of a factor, its producer can try to make it more or less transferrable from one employment to another. If he has this option, he must bear the uncertainty connected with the alternative he chooses. He can reduce his uncertainty by producing a less specific factor. When he produces a more specific factor, he may face the prospect of becoming more dependent on the actions of others. He may avoid some uncertainty and also some appraisement by obtaining an advance commitment from a prospective buyer of the factor.

Suppliers of nonhuman factors may contribute to undertaking in two ways. First, they may become undertakers themselves by producing, improving, or maintaining their own factors. Second, by offering their factors for sale, they enable the ultimate buyers or renters of the factors to undertake the production projects that employ the factors.

Suppliers of Labor and Human Capital

Individuals who own what is regarded as labor and human capital must similarly choose among alternative renters or buyers of their factors. In making such choices, they act as appraisers and uncertainty-bearers and they contribute to undertaking. Owners of labor and human capital must also decide whether to use some types of labor and human capital to maintain, improve, or otherwise alter other types. They may even purchase training or education to help them decide. When such individuals use their other factors to maintain, improve, or otherwise alter their skills, they are acting as producers.

Selling v. renting. One way to avoid the uncertainty connected with owning a factor is to sell it. Strictly speaking, the laws that help to define the market economy do not prevent the sale of one's future labor or human capital. As a result, an individual can reduce her uncertainty about difficult-to-predict future demand and supply conditions for her services by agreeing to be an indentured servant. In modern capitalist economies, however, this option is precluded. Thus, the owner of labor or human capital cannot take advantage of what she may judge to be superior ways of reducing uncertainty.

The employment agreement.[4] A special relationship that forms as a result of the exchange of human factors is the employment agreement. An employer pays his employees a specified wage in exchange for their agreement to aid in his production. The wage is paid regardless of whether the higher income the employer anticipates is realized.

It should be obvious why an employer agrees to make an employment agreement. He has in mind an opportunity to profit by using an employee in a production process. The interesting question is why the employee would make the agreement. Typically, the employee believes that the employer has knowledge the employee does not have about the value of the employee's work when it is combined with other factors. The employee may believe that she could acquire the knowledge to become an employer but she may choose not to do so because of the costs to her. Or she may lack the ability or insight to acquire the necessary knowledge. An employment agreement that arises in cases like these economizes on the acquisition and transmission of entrepreneurial knowledge.

The employment agreement may also be a means of shifting uncertainty. The employee may be unwilling or unable to bear the uncertainty that would be present if she became a partner. Even though she has the same knowledge as the employer, she may not want to bet that her knowledge is superior to that of others. The employee may differ from the employer only in the fact that she is not able to borrow the money needed to finance production. She may be regarded as a less trustworthy borrower by prospective lenders and/or she may be unable to provide guaranty or to get others to provide it for her.

There are other reasons unrelated to entrepreneurship why an individual might choose to be an employee. She may have a personal preference either to be an employee in general or more specifically to do a particular job with particular workmates. Also, she may want to have money before a production project is complete, yet she may be unable to obtain a loan. The fact that an employer is willing to pay her before the proceeds from her contribution are forthcoming may give her an opportunity to get money sooner than other alternatives.

The division of individuals into the categories of employer and employee results in a situation in which the entrepreneurship exhibited by some individuals is more important or relevant to the interests of economists than that exhibited by others. As the main appraisers and uncertainty-bearers, the employers, more than the employees, are responsible for the goods that are produced in a market economy. When the applied economist uses the word "producer," he is referring to the individuals whose entrepreneurship is more important or relevant to him.

4. ENTREPRENEURIAL INTERACTION

Entrepreneurial interaction refers to intersubjective appraisement, undertaking, and uncertainty-bearing, the results of which are the prices of goods and factors (including incomes), the distribution of factors among various employments, and the satisfaction of wants. These results are determined simultaneously, as it were. In this part, interaction in each of the entrepreneurial categories is discussed in turn.

Appraisement

The exchange of factors is mainly the result of a difference in appraisals. The buyer appraises the factor at a higher value than the seller. Believing that his appraisal differs from that of a prospective trading partner, an individual announces his willingness to buy or sell. Given that individuals use money as the common denominator for making announcements, the result of appraisal differences and price announcements are factor prices.

Because production entails the use of complementary factors, the appraisals of all the factors used in a production process are interdependent. When an individual appraises any single factor, he is aided greatly by price announcements for the other factors. It is reasonable for him to predict that he will be able to buy other factors approximately at their announced prices. Because of the price announcements, an individual can more accurately appraise factors that do not have prices. To do so, he simply calculates the difference between the anticipated sales revenue and the sum of the announced prices of the other factors.

It is often said that the entrepreneur makes a profit calculation based on his anticipations of revenues and costs. Since costs refers to factor prices, this means that the entrepreneur uses his knowledge of anticipated revenue and the announced prices of some factors to appraise other factors.

If an entrepreneur did not know the offer prices of any of the factors he planned to use, he would have to create markets for each factor. His task of economic calculation would be multiplied substantially. When he is told that a factor-owner is interested in selling his factor, the entrepreneur would have to personally estimate the prices he would have to pay for each complementary factor.

This interaction among appraisers is not a cooperative endeavor. In other words, the appraisers do not agree to announce prices so that they can help each other make appraisals. Factor-owners announce selling prices because they want to earn income for themselves. Nevertheless, although the supplier of each type of factor acts in his own private interest, he makes it easier for producers to appraise the other prospective factors that complement his factor. In this indirect way he helps to create a market not only for his own factor but also for what become the factors owned by others.

The price of a factor depends upon a combination of the seller's estimate of the buyer's appraisal and the buyer's estimate of the seller's appraisal. These estimates are used as a basis for negotiating a price. Since the profitability of a production project depends upon the height of factor prices, other things being equal, an appraiser who can get a favorable price is more likely to earn profit.

Negotiations between sellers and buyers of factors depend in some measure on competition. A seller who faces competition cannot gain as much from negotiation, other things being equal. The same is true of a buyer who faces competition. A seller who sells to many buyers and a buyer who buys from many sellers may find it profitable to establish a take-it-or-leave-it posture. The profit due to such a posture comes from savings in transaction costs. Such a posture makes it less profitable for the buyers (or sellers) to attempt to negotiate.

Specialization. Appraisement and reappraisement are not the province of a special class of individuals. Everyone participates in making appraisals. As Mises emphasized, different individuals differ in their reactions to changes in conditions.[5] Such differences may be of a general nature in the sense that some individuals may naturally have an absolute advantage over others no matter what types of appraisals they want to make. Alternatively, the differences may be specialized. Some individuals may have a comparative advantage in appraising some types of factors or in appraising factors for some types of employments, while other individuals have advantages elsewhere.

Mises focused on natural differences. Regardless of natural differences, the prospect for profit is likely to lead to the development of differences simply because of the limitations of the human mind. A single human mind is capable of assimilating only a small part of the total actions that must be understood to make all the appraisals that are made in a market economy. As a result, individuals seek to occupy specialized niches where they anticipate that their appraisals will lead to greater profit, other things being equal, than other niches.[6]

In seeking a particular niche, individuals try to identify complementarities between their appraisement of different factors in different employments. In addition, they consider the prospect that an appraisement ability that is acquired with respect to one type of factor or employment can be transferred to another type of factor or employment in the future.

Human beings are capable of improving their appraisement abilities. They can prepare themselves to occupy different niches by producing human capital that they anticipate will be suitable for such niches.

As noted in chapter nine, a particularly significant type of appraisal consists of the appraisement of appraisement ability itself. If an individual appraises another person's appraisement ability at a higher value than the appraiser herself, the former may be able to profit by employing the latter. Alternatively, she may be able to gain by copying the latter's appraising behavior. Many stock market experts are specialists in appraising the appraisement abilities of other experts and of hired managers. Some are sufficiently competent to make good decisions about when to copy.

Undertaking

The most well known interaction among undertakers is their competition for the money spent by consumers. This competition was described in chapter seven. Here, the discussion of undertaker interaction will be extended to interaction among undertakers at different stages in the structure of production and among undertakers who produce complementary goods.

Interaction among undertakers at different stages of production. The output of some undertakings are factors of production in other undertakings. In other words, individuals produce goods of different stages, or orders, in the structure of production. Interaction among undertakers between two adjacent orders in the structure (for example, between undertakers at the second and third order with respect to a given consumer good) may be necessary before the good of the lower order (the second-order good) can be produced. Thus, an undertaker who produces a good of the second order may have to buy a good of the third order, which is produced by another undertaker. Similarly, the undertaker who produces a good of the third order may require a good of the fourth order. And so on.

Because of these relationships, the decision to produce and sell a lower-order good contributes to undertaking prospects with respect to the higher-order good. By the same token, the decision to produce a higher-order good contributes to undertaking prospects with respect to the lower-order good. Thus the interaction is reciprocal.

When the undertaker of a higher-order good sells her output to the undertaker of a lower-order good, she automatically gives up her right to determine the good's employment. At the same time, the buyer of the higher-order good depends upon the seller. The buyer's undertaking is determined by the availability of the higher-order good. Thus, the reciprocity entails both mutual benefits and mutual dependence. An undertaker can reduce her dependence by integrating the production of the higher- and lower-order goods under her own authority.

However, integration may be sufficiently costly that she would rather engage in the reciprocal interaction.

Interaction among undertakers who produce complementary goods. Suppose that the outputs of two different undertakers are complements. Then a buyer of the two goods will plan to deal with at least two different undertakers. The deal he gets from one will affect the deal that he offers the other. Two or more different sets of transactions may have to be coordinated and synchronized for the buyer to be satisfied. The buyer and sellers are related not bilaterally but multilaterally. In this case, coordination and synchronization by means of commitments become relevant. Coordination and synchronization are discussed extensively in chapter twelve.

Uncertainty-Bearing

Every undertaking entails uncertainty-bearing. Consider the act of buying a set of nonhuman factors and renting labor and human capital in order to produce a saleable good. The uncertainty consists of the prospect that the selling price of the good will be less than the prices of the factors, given the appropriate discounting.[7] Someone must bear the uncertainty connected with the potential for incurring losses.

There are many types of intereaction that may arise as individuals deal with the problem of uncertainty-bearing in this general circumstance. To see this, one can begin by considering the fully integrated entrepreneur as the principal appraiser and undertaker. He bears all the uncertainty. Beginning with this extreme, consider the variety of possibilities for sharing the uncertainty. First, a group of wealthy individuals may act as partners and share the uncertainty. Second, factors may be purchased on credit. Whether the bills for the factors get paid when they are due (or what proportion of the bills are paid) may be made to depend on the profitability of the undertaking. In this event, the factor-suppliers bear part of the uncertainty. Third, buyers of the product may be required to pay in advance and thereby bear the uncertainty that their wants will change during the period of production. Alternatively, they may bear the uncertainty that the product will not be available at the expected time. Fourth, the money needed to pay factors may be totally or partially borrowed from a saver. Whether the saver gets repaid may depend upon the profitability of the undertaking. In this event, the saver bears part of the uncertainty. Fifth, the money may be borrowed from a financial intermediary who, in turn, borrows from savers. The loan from the intermediary may be one of a group of loans to different undertakers that is arranged according to a plan that the intermediary believes to be optimal in dealing with the uncertainty. Finally, in any of these cases, one or more people may provide guaranty for the loans.

Financial markets are essentially markets in which the distribution of uncertainty and guaranty provision are decided by mutual agreement. The specialists in such markets give advice on saving prospects, they act as agents in the transfer of guaranty, and they pool different guaranty obligations in order to diversify, thereby reducing the overall uncertainty-bearing and guaranty requirements.

NOTES

1. Consumers may also insure themselves against risk. Because of this, the money set aside as guaranty may be difficult to distinguish from the money set aside as insurance.

2. Mises (1966, 530–31).

3. See chapter five, Part 1, of this text.

4. The employment agreement is the essence of the *firm*. For further discussion of it, see the section on theory of the firm in chapter thirteen of this text.

5. . . . [V]arious individuals do not react to a change in conditions with the same quickness and in the same way. The inequality of men, which is due to differences both in their inborn qualities and in the vicissitudes of their lives, manifests itself in this way too. There are in the market pacemakers and others who only imitate the procedures of their more agile fellow citizens. The phenomenon of leadership is no less real on the market than in any other branch of human activitites. (Mises 1966, 254–55)

6. In other words, appraisers appraise their own potential appraisement abilities in order to determine the expected profit and uncertainty-bearing associated with occupying different niches.

7. If there is some doubt about whether technical knowledge is correct, there may also be uncertainty about whether the good will actually result from the production process. This possibility is ignored here for simplicity.

Chapter 11

The Method of Economic Teleology (1): Conceptualizing Individual Action

1. INTRODUCTION

The classical and neoclassical economists sought to describe economic interaction in a market economy. To accomplish their goal, they had to employ the method of contrasting images of functions. One of Mises's most important contributions to economics was to recognize this. Even if Mises had done nothing else, this would be enough to put him in the hall of fame of economic methodologists, if such a place existed.

The Method of Economic Teleology

Mises made a second and in some ways more important contribution to economic methodology. It was to recognize that classicals and neoclassicals also used what the author has called the *method of economic teleology*. The method of economic teleology is a way to form an image of economic interaction. To form the image, the economist conceives of potentially observable behavior. The behavior is regarded as an *endpoint*. It is assumed to be the result of the *joint* selections of many separate robots. The selections are then contrasted with the economist's intuitive and experientially based understanding of how human beings would cause such behavior to occur under the assumed circumstances.

The method of economic teleology is derived from the simpler and more obvious method of teleology, which the student of action uses to help her understand and describe the action of a single individual. According to the method, the student of action first constructs a model of behavior. In this model, the behavior is performed mechanically, as it would be performed by a robot. The model consists of two parts: (1) directly observable behavior, and (2) an indirectly observable algorithm. The behavior is regarded as an endpoint that is reached "by means of" the algorithm. The algorithm is then contrasted with what the modeller can know by intuition and experience about how a human actor would cause the same directly observable behavior to occur. The method directs the student's attention to the preselection deliberation of an actor, which is aimed at reaching the endpoint.

The usefulness of economic teleology in helping to understand economic interaction is less obvious and even hazardous. To apply the method, the economist must conceive of a macroeconomic endpoint. This is an endpoint in which the behavior of many separate robots is coordinated or synchronized.[1] The robots are assumed to perform the essential economic functions. The endpoint is assumed to result from a multitude of different preselection algorithms, which are followed by the different robots. The algorithms are then contrasted with what the economist knows by intuition and experience to be the way that real human actors would cause the behavior to be performed under the assumed circumstances. The contrast directs the economist's attention to the methods that economic actors use to coordinate and synchronize their actions.

The method of contrasting images of functions enables the economist to identify the wide range of complementary entrepreneurial actions that are performed by many different specialized individuals under the conditions specified in the definition of the market economy. The method of economic teleology helps the economist identify different types of economic behavior and the entrepreneurial actions that must coordinate and synchronize them.

Coordination and Synchronization

The economist uses the method of economic teleology to help him make connections between entrepreneurial action and its effects. The method consists of working backward, as it were. Beginning with an endpoint like the ERE and an image of a noncoordinated or nonsynchronized beginning point, the economist tries to identify types of entrepreneurial actions that have the effect of coordinating and synchronizing.

Logically, there are two types of entrepreneurial actions that coordinate and synchronize: *independent adjustment* and *commitment making*. Consider an individual who wants to work with others in order to help satisfy her own wants. She can independently adjust to the others' actions. Or she can try to arrange a deal in which the others make commitments to behave in a given way in the future. Independent adjustment entails *positioning*. For example, an individual may independently produce human capital that she believes will command a premium from some future employer. Commitments help bring about coordination and synchronization by enabling people to more correctly anticipate each others' future actions.

The Analogy with Individual Action

The method of economic teleology, like the method of contrasting images of functions, is grounded in an analogy with how one reasons about an isolated individual action. The imagined result of an isolated individual's action is a greater coordination and synchronization between the individual's wants and his actions. Analogously, the imagined result of entrepreneurial action is a greater coordination and synchronization between the wants of a number of individuals and their actions. An obvious difference is that an isolated individual's action is aimed at satisfying his wants directly while the actions of an individual in a market economy are aimed at satisfying his wants indirectly. In order to earn the money to satisfy his own wants, the individual in the market economy must first entice others to pay him. Others will pay him only if he contributes to the satisfaction of their wants.

Macroeconomic and Microeconomic
Views of Economic Interaction

When the economist wants to describe economic interaction from a macroeconomic point of view, she employs the methods of contrasting images of functions and economic teleology together. She uses the former as a means of keeping in mind the fact that the economic functions and the three categories of appraisement, undertaking, and uncertainty-bearing must be present in every logically complete discussion of synchronization. The method of economic teleology can also be used to describe economic interaction from the *microeconomic* point of view. This view may consider only one of the economic functions or only parts of the fully integrated entrepreneurial action. For example, a simple two-person exchange can be regarded as an endpoint that is reached as a result of the appraisement and undertaking actions of prospective traders. It can be considered in isolation of the other entrepreneurial actions that each trading party may have in mind at the time of the exchange. Similarly, a *firm* can be regarded as an endpoint that is reached as a result of the entrepreneurial actions of a prospective employer and prospective employees. It can be regarded as such even though the economist knows that the firm is only a means to a more distant end of satisfying the wants of consumers.

The purpose of the microeconomic view is to enhance the macroeconomic image. The economist accomplishes this by first isolating some parts of the totality of economic functions and/or some part of the fully integrated entrepreneurial actions for further analysis. Then, after using the method of economic teleology to elucidate that part, she reintegrates it with the other functions and entrepreneurial actions.

The Method of Economic Teleology in *Human Action*

It is clear that Mises used the evenly rotating economy as an endpoint of economic interaction. If individuals interacted under a set of given conditions, he said, the result, or endpoint, can be imagined to be the ERE.[2] Unfortunately, he did not use the method of economic teleology to help identify the making of commitments. Indeed, there is virtually no discussion of commitments in *Human Action*. One can only speculate about the reason for this omission. In any event, the discussion of commitment making in the next two chapters is intended to fill this gap.

Purpose and Plan of the Chapter

This chapter describes the method of teleology as it is used in elucidating the action of a single individual. Its purpose is to set the stage for a description of the method of economic teleology in chapter twelve. The discussion begins in Part 2 by describing the problem of forming an image of isolated action. Then it identifies three essential characteristics of such an image. Part 3 shows how to construct a model of a particular choice. Part 4 examines the concept of equilibrium in a model of a particular choice. Part 5 contrasts the logical meaning of equilibrium with the mathematical meaning and with the concept of equilibrium in natural science. Part 6 develops a distinction between different forms of reasoning: mathematical, logical, and prax-eological. This leads, in turn, to a more adequate definition of praxe-ology.

2. THE INITIAL IMAGE OF INDIVIDUAL ACTION IN THE NEW SUBJECTIVISM

A person cannot construct a complete image of action. Nevertheless, he can gain an understanding of action. To do this, he begins by constructing an initial image of a particular action by trying to concep-tually separate a particular action from other actions and from the milieu of reflexes and conditioned behavior that he performs in every-day life. After he constructs the initial image of action, he constructs a model of choice. Then he contrasts the two. This part shows how to construct the initial image of a particular action.

Impossibility of Forming a Complete Image of Action

It is beyond human capacity to form a complete image of action. This assertion can be supported by referring to two types of experi-ences. First, it seems evident that action precedes reflection. A human being acts first; only later can she reflect on her action. Action must begin at some time during a normal human being's lifetime. But the human mind seems to conceal this beginning point. Thus, a complete image of action cannot be formed because an actor cannot identify the beginning point.

Second, it seems correct to say that, at any point in time, a human being is alert to an indefinite set of characteristics of herself and her environment. She knows that changes in these characteristics, or changes in some combination of them, may turn out to be relevant to a choice she can make. Another way to describe this alertness is to say that a normal human being is in a continuous state of deliberation with respect to an indefinite number of choices that she might make. Thus there is "a lot of action" continuously, even if no particular choice is made (other than the choice to remain alert). Because it is impossible to enumerate all the characteristics to which an individual is alert, it is beyond human capacity to form a complete image of action.

Characteristics of the Initial Image of a Particular Action

In constructing an image of a particular action, one is naturally—and it seems inevitably—led to employ three concepts. These are (1) decision making, (2) an endpoint of action, and (3) a motivation to act. Each is considered in turn.

Decision making. The performance of a particular action implies decision making. A decision is made as to when deliberation stops and behavior begins. The actor thinks: "I stopped deliberating and started behaving." Decision making constitutes the act of will that causes behavior to be performed. Decision making in action necessarily is cognizant of uncertainty.

Deliberation involves the mental projection of the consequences of at least two alternative behaviors. This projection may be based on previous experiments. That is, the chooser may have previously chosen a behavior at least partly in order to acquire knowledge that would assist in his later choice. If so, the earlier experiment is part of the deliberation exercise.

If one wanted to focus specifically on experimentation, he could regard an experiment as an action of itself. Ordinarily, however, the focus is on a later action, which is based partly on the knowledge acquired as a result of the experiment.

During deliberation, an actor uses his inventiveness and creativity. He considers the results of previous actions of a similar type, he takes account of the conditions under which a behavior will be performed, and he makes a prediction. Human beings will presumably never be able to fully understand this process, since action must precede reflection and is indefinitely complex. In any event, it would be improper for the subjectivist to assume that she knows the process.

An endpoint of a particular action. It is impossible to conceive of action in which the passage of time is not implied. One who forms an image of a particular action takes it for granted that there is (1) a time when creativity, inventiveness, and deliberation stop; (2) a time when the behavior that is chosen begins to occur; and (3) a time when the effects are to be felt.

In forming an image of a particular action, one says that the endpoint of action occurs at a time when deliberation stops, yet the behavior that is decided upon has not begun to occur. The time of the endpoint can be contrasted with the time that precedes it, during which the deliberation occurred. It is possible to imagine a point in time before deliberation began but it is also possible to imagine that there is no definite beginning point of deliberation. What is crucial is that there is an endpoint, which follows a duration of time, which may or may not be definite.

The motivation to act. If a choice of one behavior over another is caused by a decision, what causes the decision? In other words, what is the motivation to act? The answer is the prospect for removing uneasiness, which is equivalent to the prospect for gaining utility. Utility means:

> the causal relevance for the removal of felt uneasiness. Acting man believes that the services a thing can render are apt to improve his own well-being, and calls this the utility of the thing concerned. . . . (T)he term utility is [equivalent to the] importance attached to a thing on account of the belief that it can remove uneasiness.[3]

What then, it might be asked, causes "acting man" to perceive a prospect for gaining utility? The answer is that there is no cause. It is the human being's nature to perceive such a prospect. The praxeologist knows this a priori.

3. CONSTRUCTING A MODEL OF A PARTICULAR CHOICE

Intuition reveals that the beginning point of even a particular action cannot be identified with certainty and that the connection between any particular action and action in general is indefinite. Nevertheless, there is no way to identify the creative, inventive, and deliberative aspects of action other than to try to form an image of a particular action. The procedure for doing so should be obvious: It is to contrast one's initial image of the particular action with a model of a particular choice. The purpose of this part is to show how to construct a model of a particular choice.

To construct such a model, one thinks of a maximizing robot, which selects behavior according to an algorithm. The algorithm is assumed to take time to complete. The robot is then used as a reference for launching a discussion of the creativity, inventiveness, and deliberation that intuition reveals can be associated with a real choice. The discussion here focuses on the model-construction process and it begins by showing why such a model is necessary.

A Model of Choice

A model of a particular choice contains an algorithm that takes time to complete and an endpoint that signifies the behavior that is to be performed. The algorithm simulates the reasoning behind a choice. In the simplest model, the algorithm consists of a simple process of identifying which among a number of alternatives will yield the highest utility.

In a model of choice, the robot has no capacity to choose in the full sense of the term. The robot is a creature of the modeller. How the robot selects is not decided by it; it is decided by the modeller.[4]

Every human being, as this term was defined earlier, knows from introspection (i.e., he knows a priori) that a real choice entails an iterative, indefinite, subjective deliberation process for which the beginning point may not be identifiable. He knows that he is not merely a robot but also a creator, innovator, and planner. The modeller of choice can model the deliberation process in part by specifying a deliberation algorithm. However, no matter how elaborate a model he builds, he knows that he could build a more elaborate one. For the telling example, the modeller could build a model in which the subject deliberates over whether to employ the model that the modeller had built for him. Because of this (i.e., because of subjectivism as defined in chapter two), and also because there are so many factors involved in an individual's deliberations and choosing, the sensible modeller abandons the thought of attempting to completely model a particular action.

Real Choices and Hypothetical Choices

The ultimate goal of constructing a model of a particular choice is to capture the aspects of action that, for one reason or another, are of interest.[5] A model is meant to describe a hypothetical choice, the characteristics of which are thought to be relevant to the particular historical facts one wishes to understand or to the particular predictions one wants to make.[6]

A hypothetical choice should not be confused with an unrealistic choice. A good model captures as distinctly and fully as possible the reality of some aspect(s) of action. There is no contradiction in saying that one wants a model that is both hypothetical and realistic. Action is so complex that all the facets of a particular action cannot possibly be represented.[7]

Whether a hypothetical choice contains relevant and realistic characteristics can be determined by consensus. A modeller can ask her colleagues and the chooser herself whether her model of choice is relevant and whether it does indeed capture real features of action. They can answer her referring to their own personal experiences. If the remarks of colleagues and the chooser indicate consensus, the modeller has verified, to the extent that she can, the claim that her model is realistic.

Deeper Models of Choice

There is virtually no limit to the depth of a model of individual choice. The undisputed leader in the construction of deeper models for economics is G. L. S. Shackle.[8] To engage in exercises such as Shackle has done ought to be required of all serious students of human action. It is only by attempting to construct deeper and deeper models of choice that one can come to recognize both the multiple facets or dimensions of action and the ultimate need to settle on some model in order to answer the questions that led to the exercise in the first place. To grapple with the task of attempting to construct a complete image of action is frustrating but worthwhile. It leads the modeller to recognize that, because of the complexity of action, he must be content to select out the aspects of action that are most relevant to his goal.

4. THE CONCEPT OF EQUILIBRIUM IN A MODEL OF CHOICE

In the economics classroom, the term equilibrium in a model of choice is used to refer to the state that exists when the time required by the algorithm has passed and a behavior is selected. So long as one keeps in mind that she is using the method of economic teleology, there is no danger in using this term.[9] Different concepts of equilibrium are discussed in Part 5 of this chapter.

Equilibrium Analysis

The term equilibrium analysis can also be employed. Equilibrium analysis consists of three specifications: (1) an initial, non-equilibrium state; (2) a second, equilibrium state; and (3) the algorithm that is assumed to precede the change from the non-equilibrium state to the equilibrium state. To describe deliberation, the analyst uses intuition and experience to judge (a) how a real actor would act in the assumed initial, non-equilibrium state, and (b) whether a real actor would be in that assumed state and only in that state.

Repeatable and Nonrepeatable Choice Situations

Equilibrium can be defined with respect to a nonrepeatable or repeatable choice situation. For a nonrepeatable situation, it refers only to the condition that is present at the time the robot chooser selects its behavior. The modeller of choice may not be interested in situations in which an individual's behavior results in the utility that he expects. In particular, the modeller may wish to model an erroneous choice. For a repeatable choice situation, equilibrium refers to a condition in which the robot chooser selects behavior to be performed throughout the indefinite future. The same behavior is repeated again and again. The modeller of a repeatable choice situation may have the aim of elucidating the process that an actor uses to correct errors that he believes were made in previous iterations.

Necessity of the Concept of Equilibrium

In everyday life, deliberations about one set of alternatives seldom if ever occur in a form where they are isolated from other deliberations and other actions. Individuals are practically always deliberating about an indefinite number of actions. In addition, the deliberations change as individuals become aware of changes in their wants, abilities, and knowledge. Given these facts, it is obvious that an actor can seldom if ever identify distinct endpoints of her actions in everyday life.

Nevertheless, the endpoint, which the concept of equilibrium represents, is an absolutely necessary part of the process of forming an image of action. One who tries to form an image of action must have in mind some selection or set of selections that a subject will ultimately carry out. The equilibrium is not intended to describe an observable state (i.e., a human chooser having reached equilibrium). Instead, it is a tool that helps one understand action. It is a necessary part of economic teleology.

5. OTHER CONCEPTS OF EQUILIBRIUM

In *Human Action*, Mises distinguished his definitions from mathematical and scientistic definitions. He called his definitions *logical*. Logical definitions or meanings refer to those that are derived from a priori reasoning through the methods of the new subjectivism. In this part, the logical meaning of equilibrium is distinguished from the mathematical meaning and from the meaning in natural science.

The Mathematical vs. the Logical Meaning of Equilibrium

Consider the mathematical model of a single consumer's budget choice that is found in all of the mainstream intermediate microeconomic textbooks. The consumer's preferences (indifference map) and her opportunities to satisfy them (budget line) are specified. Then an equilibrium set of quantities is "deduced." The model is sometimes represented by a set of simultaneous equations. This is the *mathematical* meaning of choice.

Without any restrictions, a set of simultaneous equations could as easily represent the idea that the quantities purchased and the assumed opportunities cause a particular range of preferences as it could the idea that the quantities are caused by the preferences and the opportunities. In the classroom, economists do not emphasize (or even mention) the former interpretation because such a possibility is not meaningful. The teacher implicitly assumes that such an interpretation is inconsistent with everyone's personal knowledge of the causes and effects connected with their own actions.

When the classroom economist says that a particular behavior is caused by a choice, he is saying that the choice *causes* an equilibrium. He is implicitly inserting an actor's will, which he assumes to exist a priori, into his model.

The logical meaning of equilibrium goes a step further. It interprets choice in terms of the a priori conception of action. When the applied praxeologist (i.e., the historian) uses the concept of equilibrium in her descriptions of chosen phenomena, she always includes in her descriptions the indefinite concepts of reason, deliberation, will, time, and uncertainty. To the praxeologist, the assumption that an individual has particular preferences and faces particular opportunities means that the applied praxeologist has chosen a particular question to answer. To answer that question, she has drawn on her intuitive understanding of action in general in order to identify a reason for some particular action. That reason is partly, but only partly, represented by the assumed preferences and opportunities in her model of choice.

In short, the logical meaning of equilibrium consists of the idea that equilibrium has meaning only when a choice whose endpoint is the equilibrium in a model of choice is contrasted with the image of action. Because the image of action itself is indefinite, the logical meaning of equilibrium is also indefinite. Equilibrium, in the logical sense, is a signal of what the praxeologist must do next if she wishes to describe chosen behavior. It is not only a state of being in a model of choice.[10]

The Scientific vs. the Logical Meaning of Equilibrium

In natural science, equilibrium is part of a model of physical change. The concept is used to help the scientist describe or hypothesize relatively unchanging patterns or relationships among physical objects or forces. It refers to an imagined state of rest toward which a set of non-choosing entities is assumed to be tending. The equilibrium state, as well as a sequence of different states at different objective times, can be expressed mathematically. It is often useful and seldom misleading to do so because the patterns of natural science are relatively unchanging. Such a mathematical model describes the operation of a relationship between exogenous and endogenous variables through time.

Equilibrium to the praxeologist refers to an endpoint with respect to which the preselection characteristics of action are defined. The notion that an individual deliberates with the intent of eventually making a choice has no equivalent or good analog in the natural sciences, since physical objects and forces do not, so far as is known, deliberate. It is true that the robot chooser in the model of choice adheres to an algorithm, just as the adjustment to a change in natural science is assumed to be in accord with an algorithm. Moreover, both algorithms can be expressed mathematically. However, the aims of identifying and using an algorithm in the two cases are quite different. For this reason, it must be concluded that the concept of equilibrium in natural science is not like or even the analog to the concept of equilibrium in a choice.

Modern economists often write as though the models of choice they construct are analogous to models in the natural sciences. Such a claim is misleading and hazardous if one's goal is to understand economic interaction. That physical analogies can be misleading is evident first from the fact that physical objects and forces cannot deliberate. Besides deliberation, there are two other differences between human action and the motion of physical objects that make the use of such analogies hazardous. First, the time that is relevant to action differs from the time that is relevant to the motion of physical objects. Time in an individual action is, most importantly, subjective time. Deliberation and decision-making time differs from one human actor to another and from one action to another for the same actor. Second, the environment of action refers to unknown and partly unknowable changes in wants, abilities, and knowledge. The environment of physical motion refers to changes that the natural scientist knows or assumes he can come to know. It often refers to changes that he knows as a consequence of repeated experiments. The economist assumes that wants, abilities, and knowledge can never be fully known.

In the logic of human action, equilibrium refers to an endpoint in the model of choice, which is a necessary part of the economic theorist's effort to construct an image of action. In the theory of physical motion, equilibrium is a word used by the scientist to refer to his perception of the uniform, or near-constant, way that different objects or forces are related.

6. MATHEMATICAL, LOGICAL, AND PRAXEOLOGICAL REASONING

Praxeology is the use of logical reasoning to make deductions about human action and interaction. It begins with the identification of the a priori categories. Then it combines the a priori categories with subsidiary assumptions in order to logically construct indefinite images of particular actions. An image of a particular action is a combination of a model of choice and an image of action in general, given an assumed set of circumstances.

Praxeological reasoning can be contrasted with other forms of reasoning. *Mathematical reasoning* is about relationships that lack an element of causality. *Logical reasoning* is about cause and effect relationships. Both mathematical and logical reasoning are deductive systems.

When mathematical and logical reasoning are applied to physical and not human events, they yield identical results. They are merely different modes of expression. Mathematical reasoning employs symbols that refer to relationships among objects or forces, while logical reasoning employs words that refer to causes and effects. In this framework, the words are the equivalent of exogenous and endogenous variables. When the two forms of reasoning are applied to human action, however, they yield vastly different results. The difference is due to the fact that logical reasoning starts with the a priori categories—which refer to cause and effect in their teleological sense, and which cannot in any useful way be represented by mathematical formulae and can only partly be represented by logic.

Mathematical formulae are specifically applicable to relationships that remain constant, or nearly so. In human action, although a person may change slowly at times, her changes are so rapid in relation to the changes in physical phenomena that mathematical reasoning is inappropriate. Besides this, a person has some personal control over the magnitude, direction, and character of his changes. Logical reasoning is the only appropriate method for conceptualizing action and communicating one's images of action.

When logical reasoning is applied to human action, it is called *praxeological reasoning*. The usefulness of praxeological and economic reasoning lies in the fact that they can elucidate some aspects of reality. They can do this in two distinct ways: (1) by demonstrating how the categories of action would operate in different hypothetical circumstances, and (2) by contrasting a model in which an a priori category is not present with an image based upon what one can know about reality by recognizing that the a priori category (or categories) is present.[11]

NOTES

1. Synchronization, as the term is used here, refers to coordination through time.

2. To a careful reader of *Human Action*, these remarks may appear incorrect. The author's interpretation is defended in Appendix 7.

3. Mises (1966, 120).

4. This point was perhaps best expressed by Alfred Schuetz (1943). Schuetz says that a social scientist as such must meet three requirements. First, as an observer, he "replaces the human beings he observes as actors on the social stage by puppets created by himself and manipulated by himself" (p. 143). "The [puppet] is but a model of a conscious mind without the faculty of spontaneity and without a will of its own. . . . [The puppet's] destiny is regulated and determined beforehand by his creator, the social scientist" (p. 144). But a puppet is always constructed with reference to a particular problem to be solved. It must be relevant. "We cannot speak simply of a [puppet] as such; we must indicate the reference scheme within which this [puppet] may be utilized, that is, the problem for the sake of which the [puppet] has been constructed" (p. 145). Schuetz calls this the *principle of relevance*. The second and third requirements are described in Appendix 2 in this text, where they are called postulates of subjective interpretation. (It is these postulates that distinguish the [puppets] from a role, as described in Appendix 6. Schuetz actually uses the term "ideal type" in place of the term puppet in some of his discussion. In the author's view, the term puppet is more appropriate.)

In a market economy, puppets have such labels as entrepreneur, promoter, speculator, household, resource supplier, financier, financial intermediary, investment advisor, guarantor, insurer, statistician, enumerator, accountant, and so forth. The economist would construct puppet roles for each relevant problem to be solved. Also see Schuetz (1953) and Stonier and Bode (1937).

5. Mises (1966, 236–37).

6. On the concept of relevance, see Mises (1966, 57–58) and footnote 4 of this chapter.

7. The argument is sometimes made that the goal of economic analysis should be realism. This, of course, is true. But the argument typically does not address the fact that reality is so complex that a decision must be made concerning which aspects of reality to study.

It has often been stated that the decision to study one aspect instead of another implies a "value judgment." This is true if one chooses to call every criterion used by a praxeologist to make a choice regarding relevance a value judgment. What is not true is that one can avoid making value judgments in this sense by studying reality. The phenomena are too complex. The phrase "to study reality" is meaningless unless it is accompanied by a judgment of relevance.

8. See Shackle (1966, 1969, 1970, 1972). Regarding Shackle's work, one

must question the exclusive use of introspection. Introspection is not only a window to self-knowledge and to knowledge of others, it is also a lens that has the potential to distort images and lead to self-deception. The only way to check one's bearings is to attempt to grasp the knowledge and choice making of others. This has traditionally been the task of epistemology and particularly of cognitive development in psychology. It would seem that the best lens is one that is made of a mixture of introspection (a priori knowledge) and systematic observation of the cognitive development of other human beings in similar situations, the contents of this mixture being periodically checked through interaction among those with similar interests.

9. Mises did not like to use the term equilibrium. The reason is that he associated it with natural science. He believed that the term had led many economists to mistakenly view economic interaction like natural scientists view the relationships involving physical objects and forces in nature. Nevertheless, it is clear from Mises's discussion that his evenly rotating economy is similar to the equilibrium conceived by such neoclassical writers as J. B. Clarke, Wicksteed, Schumpeter, and Knight.

10. Mises did not discuss the mathematical model of individual choice. That he would have agreed with the statements here can be deduced from his discussion of the evenly rotating economy. See his distinction between the logical and mathematical method (1966, 250). Also see pages 353–57 and his distinction between logical and mathematical catallactics beginning on page 350. For an interpretation that is similar although less fully developed than the one presented here, see Lachmann (1977).

11. These views correspond to those of Mises:

> . . . Praxeology is a theoretical and systematic, not a historical science. Its scope is human action as such, irrespective of all environmental, accidental, and individual circumstances of the concrete acts. Its cognition is purely formal and general without reference to the material content and the particular features of the actual case. It aims at knowledge valid for all instances in which the conditions exactly correspond to those implied in its assumptions and inferences. Its statements and propositions are not derived from experience. They are, like those of logic and mathematics, a priori. They are not subject to verification or falsification on the ground of experience and facts. (1966, 32)

> Aprioristic reasoning is purely conceptual and deductive. It cannot produce anything else but tautologies and analytic judgments. . . . The significant task of aprioristic reasoning is on the one hand to bring into relief all that is implied in the categories, concepts, and premises and, on the other hand, to show what they do not imply. It is its vocation to render manifest and obvious what was hidden and unknown before. (1966, 38)

Both Hayek and Kirzner have characterized Mises as presenting a "pure logic of choice." A pure logic of choice presumably refers to a set of deductions made on the basis of assumptions about particular wants, abilities, and knowledge. It should be clear from this discussion that a more appropriate term for Mises's economic theory is *pure logic of action*. In a pure logic of action, deductions are contingent on understanding and acceptance of the a priori categories. Even though the a priori categories are evident to every normal human being who directs her attention to them, they cannot be fully described. There are no words to correspond to them. There is only the human ability to understand.

It follows that to say, as Hayek does, that Mises employs a pure logic of choice is misleading. To go on and say that "[i]t is only by [the assertion that there is a tendency toward equilibrium] that economics ceases to be an exercise in pure logic and becomes an empirical science" cannot refer to Mises. (See Hayek 1937, 44; and Kirzner 1979, chap. 2).

Chapter 12

The Method of Economic Teleology (2): Conceptualizing Entrepreneurship

1. INTRODUCTION

According to the method of economic teleology, it is possible to elucidate entrepreneurship in a way that is analogous to the way the method of teleology was used in chapter eleven to elucidate individual action. It was pointed out that individual action can only be understood by constructing an image of a particular action. To construct an image of a particular action, one contrasts a model of choice with her intuitive and experience-based understanding of how a real human actor would cause the behavior that is specified as the endpoint to occur. In the model of choice, the modeller must make reference to a beginning point, an endpoint, and an algorithm that is used in selecting a particular set of behaviors. A specific endpoint is probably never achieved in a person's everyday action. Nevertheless, it is impossible to conceptualize action without employing the notion of an endpoint. The endpoint can be called an equilibrium.

Analogously, economic interaction in general can only be understood by constructing an image of a particular economic interaction. The economist accomplishes this by contrasting a model of robot choices with her intuitive and experience-based understanding of how real economic actors would cause a set of individual behaviors that is regarded as an endpoint. The model has a beginning point, an endpoint, and an intervening period during which the algorithms of the robot entrepreneurs are put into operation.

Robots consist of two general types: (*a*) robot consumer-savers and factor-suppliers that perform the economic functions, and (b) robot entrepreneurs that coordinate and synchronize the behavior of the function-performing robots. The function-performing robots merely select the lowest prices for goods, the highest loan rates, and the highest factor prices that are available to them. Their aim is to maximize utility or earnings. The prices, loan rates, and rates of pay are proposed by the robot entrepreneurs. Unlike the function-performing robots, the robot entrepreneurs have expectations about the effects of their undertakings that may be disappointed. Disappointed expectations mean that expected robo-profit is not realized. Their algorithms specify how they are to adjust their behavior if this occurs. After a period of time and adjustment, each robo-ent reaches a point at which its behavior has precisely the consequences it expected. This is the endpoint, or equilibrium. A specific endpoint is never achieved in economic interaction under the conditions specified in the definition of the market economy. Nevertheless, the idea of an endpoint is a necessary part of the model of robot choices.

The economist elucidates coordination and synchronization by putting herself in the positions of robo-ents. Then she constructs the algorithms she assumes they follow with what she knows from intuition and experience to be the entrepreneurial actions of real entrepreneurs under the conditions the model is intended to simulate.

The categories of entrepreneurial action have already been identified as appraisement, undertaking, and uncertainty-bearing. The method of economic teleology cannot help the economist identify more categories. Instead, it helps her identify and describe two forms of action that lead to coordination and synchronization: positioning and mutual commitment.

Part 2 of this chapter describes two models of entrepreneurial interaction based on the two forms of coordinating and synchronizing actions: the model of independent actors and the model of simultaneous commitments. Parts 3 and 4 are devoted to an investigation of the merits and limitations of the teleological method in economics. Part 3 makes a number of methodological points by comparing economic equilibrium with an endpoint in individual action. Part 4 presents an assessment of the analogy between economic equilibrium and equilibrium in individual action, and points to its limitations.

2. TWO MODELS OF COORDINATION AND SYNCHRONIZATION

Individuals in the market economy can take account of each others' behavior in two extreme ways. In the first, each can adjust independently to the others. In the second, they can reach a set of agreements, or commitments. When the economist constructs a model of robo-ents, he wants his robot behavior to simulate these two extremes.

A Model of Independently Acting Robo-ents

The model of independently acting robo-ents can be described as follows. At the beginning point, each robo-ent is assumed to possess less than correct initial expectations about whether its offer of goods, goods' prices, loan rates, and factor prices will be acceptable to the function-performing robots. Nevertheless, the robo-ents select behavior that, according to their respective initial expectations, is optimal. When the initial expectations are disappointed, each robo-ent responds according to how its algorithm specifies it should respond under the circumstances. The response algorithms are designed to simulate learning. As each robo-ent adjusts its behavior in accordance with the algorithms that simulate learning, the time eventually arrives when all robo-ents' expectations are realized. At that time each one makes a selection of behavior that, given the selections made by the other robo-ents, is the best it can make, given its now correct expectations. At that time, each selects a behavioral routine to perform again and again.

The imagined point in time at which each robo-ent selects a repeating behavior is the economic equilibrium. The behavior of each robo-ent becomes fully coordinated and synchronized with the behavior of the others. A good name for this model is the *model of independent robo-ents* (MIRE).

Usefulness. The equilibrium in the MIRE is analogous to the equilibrium in a model of individual choice in the case of repeated selections. It exists when the conditions that trigger the operations of the robo-ent algorithms are no longer present because, from the standpoint of each robo-ent, the behavior expected by others actually occurs. At this point, each robo-ent would make a once-and-for-all decision to perform some optimal behavior routine throughout the indefinite future.

The MIRE enables the economist to identify categories of entrepreneurial behavior that involve *positioning*. Positioning refers to the action of independently changing one's behavior in order to increase the benefits or to reduce the harm due to the prospective actions of others. A fully integrated entrepreneurial act entails positioning when an individual independently appraises and bears uncertainty with the aim of undertaking a profitable production project at the optimal time and place. In the market economy, examples of positioning include making new exchange offers, accepting newly made exchange offers from others, avoiding the harmful effects of others' actions, and copying the successful actions of others.

Entrepreneurship. Entrepreneurship with respect to the MIRE is conceived as a type of mutual trial-and-error process in which each robo-ent monitors others' behavior and their responses to experiments. An experiment consists of borrowing money, purchasing factors, producing a good, and then offering it for sale. The economist may build a simple or complex model of the experiment and of the process that follows it. In whatever model is used, the robo-ent must have expectations about the rate it will pay for loans, the prices it will pay for factors, and the price at which it will sell its output. Given these expectations, it makes simulated initial appraisals of factors on the basis of its robo-profit expectations. If it expects a robo-profit, it borrows money, uses it to buy factors, produces a good, and offers it for sale at the expected price. In doing this, the robo-ent "tests its hypotheses" about consumers' reactions to its offers.

The initial expectations are assumed to be incorrect. In light of this, the robot is assumed to revise its robo-profit expectations and its simulated appraisals. Given its revisions, it "chooses" to produce less or more of the same good in the future or to shift to another industry. It also "chooses" to buy more or less of a given factor in relation to its substitutes. It is assumed that, over time, as robo-ents revise their initial selections, their expectations come closer and closer to reality. Eventually, each "learns" enough to be able to predict exactly what the others will do in response to all of the possible behaviors it can perform. It "knows" which of its alternatives will maximize its robo-profit. In the model, knowing is equivalent to getting into a position in which all expectations are realized. When all robo-ents reach this point, each selects a behavioral routine that it will perform again and again throughout the indefinite future. This is the equilibrium.

A Model of Simultaneous Commitments

In the second model, robo-ents are assumed to deal with the prospect that their expectations will be disappointed by seeking out and making commitments. In a mutual commitment, two or more individuals make an agreement in which at least one promises the other that he will perform some specified behavior. This enables the promisee(s) to make more profitable appraisals or undertakings, it reduces uncertainty, or it leads to a more mutually satisfactory, more desirable means of uncertainty-bearing.

In a market economy, an individual might ask for a commitment if he is uncertain about how others will respond to some action he might perform yet he believes it is too costly or impossible to conduct an experiment to find out how others would respond. If he expects that he can gain when others perform some behavior, he may propose to pay them for their promises to perform it. If he expects to lose from their behavior, he may pay them for their promises not to perform the behavior.

In the model, an economic equilibrium is conceived by assuming that each robo-ent makes promises or commitments to every other relevant robo-ent such that no further exchanges of promises or commitments would be jointly agreed to. As in the equilibrium of independent actors, the behavior of each robo-ent becomes fully coordinated and synchronized with the behavior of the others.

The equilibrium is a mutual commitment by all robo-ents to select specific behaviors. This is analogous to the model of individual choice, in which the selection of a specific set of behaviors is the equilibrium. A good name for this model is the model of simultaneous commitments (MSC).

The property that no further exchanges of promises could achieve joint agreement has a number of implications that have become part of the tradition in mainstream economics. First, the commitments specify the shares of total output of each good that each function-performing robot will receive. Second, the commitments specify approximately equal marginal rates of substitution for each function-performing robot.[1] Third, each good has a price in terms of other goods that approximate the ratio of the marginal rates of substitution between that good and the other goods. Fourth, if risk is ignored, marginal rates of transformation are approximately equal for each robot entrepreneur. Fifth, the prices of products must approximate the sum of the prices of the factors that are used to produce them. Sixth, if the periods of provision for all goods are assumed to be the same, there would have to be a single loan rate that corresponds to the ratio of the price of each good in the present to the price of the same good in the future. Seventh, the net loan rate would equal each robo-ent's ratio of the current marginal evaluation of each expected future good to each present good of the same type, minus one. Unless these characteristics were present, there would be further gains from recontracting. The prospect for such gains would prompt further deliberation and changes in the mutual commitment.

Usefulness. It is obviously beyond the capacities of individuals in a market economy to make all the commitments needed to reach an equilibrium. Changes in wants, abilities, and knowledge are continuously occurring and being identified. In addition, there are substantial differences in individuals' knowledge of the future, in their abilities to learn about different aspects of the future, and in their abilities to acquire abilities to learn. These factors preclude not only the reaching of agreements but in many cases even the prospect that an agreement would be meaningful to all the parties who would have to agree to it. Even if these differences were not so great, subjects would recognize that the production of some types of commitments entails such high costs that positioning is more sensible.

Under the conditions specified in the definition of the market economy, individuals would often not incur the cost of obtaining commitments. They would either not get the satisfaction that would be possible if commitment making were costless or they would try to avoid the uncertainty in other ways. In particular, they would often rely on custom, precedent, their knowledge of habits, their abilities to understand others' plans, and natural science in order to form their expectations about the others' future behavior.

Nevertheless, individuals do make rather elaborate contracts and take other precautions precisely in order to avoid some of the uncertainty associated with the outcomes of the future actions of others. The MSC provides a means of comprehending the more elaborate commitments that individuals make. By constructing a model of economic choices that culminate in a mutually acceptable structure of simultaneous commitments, the economic theorist can illustrate the idea that real human actors would seek commitments in order to facilitate performance of the economic functions. Thus, the theorist can use this framework as a means of identifying important entrepreneurial behavior relating to commitment seeking and commitment making.

Entrepreneurship. Entrepreneurship in the MSC consists of the making, buying, and selling of commitments. Each robo-ent makes simulated appraisals of factors and announces a willingness to trade its commitments for the commitments of others. But no robo-ent actually begins a production project. Tentative commitments are made but they are revocable if a seller is able to command a higher price from another buyer or if the buyer is able to obtain a lower price for an identical commitment from another seller. As robo-ents revise their respective expectations about each others' willingness to buy and sell commitments, they eventually reach a point where each "knows" that it is getting the highest possible prices for the commitments it buys. When each robo-ent reaches this point, a set of agreements that involves everyone is consummated and each proceeds to carry out the terms of its commitment to others.

The identification of and making of commitments cause the ownership of rights to change. When A makes a commitment to B, B acquires the legal right to force A to perform the behavior that is specified in the commitment. In chapter thirteen, it will be shown that the exchange of rights can contribute in a variety of ways to the satisfaction of wants in an economy. It enables prospective undertakers who have no funds to obtain them from savers. It permits uncertainty-bearing and risk-bearing to be shifted. And it makes it possible to take advantage of production techniques that require inputs that complement each other through time. For the time being, it is sufficient to recognize that the making of commitments, or the exchange of rights, is one possible consequence of entrepreneurship.

Entrepreneurship in the Market Economy vs. Robot Entrepreneurs in the Models

In these models of entrepreneurship, the robo-ents are assumed to learn enough about wants, abilities, and knowledge that their expectations about others' responses to their behavior will be realized. As a result of this learning, it is said that there is a tendency towards equilibrium. Such learning and the corresponding tendency towards equilibrium is not a characteristic of the market economy because the assumptions necessary for its presence are not a part of the market economy. Consumer wants, including wants through time, are continually changing in the market economy, whereas they are fixed in the MIRE and MSC. Perhaps more importantly, the idea that individuals acting in the role of entrepreneurs could come to know enough about how everyone else would react to their independent behavior or about what commitments others would accept is incomprehensible. First, each one's knowledge is continually changing. Second, the knowledge that each may possess at any particular time can be so complex that others could not comprehend it. Finally, there are a large number of individuals whose knowledge can be learned about.

It is the role of entrepreneurship to learn and to try to avoid losses associated with the prospect that others will act differently than expected. A teleological model of learning helps the economist describe these two types of actions. However, the robo-ents of the model should never be confused with entrepreneurship in the market economy.

3. METHODOLOGICAL ISSUES

To understand economic interaction, an economist must contrast her intuitive image of the market economy with a model of a particular fully coordinated and synchronized set of individuals' choices. The endpoint of the model is an equilibrium. In this part, we describe the model and equilibrium from the standpoint of methodology.

The Model of Coordinated and Synchronized Economic Choices

When she constructs a model of coordinated and synchronized choices, the economist has in mind some economic problem that she believes an image of economic interaction will help her solve. In view of this goal, she constructs a model of robots. Next she specifies the forms of coordinating behavior that cause the economic equilibrium: positioning or commitment making. She attributes this behavior to the robo-ents, then specifies the equilibrium.

Although there is a sense in which the model contains entrepreneurship, it is clear that whatever entrepreneurial choices or abilities the economist identifies and models, there are others that she could have modelled and still others that could never be modelled.[2] The way to identify these additional entrepreneurial choices is to contrast the model of coordinated and synchronized, choices with one's intuitive understanding of how individuals would act under the conditions specified in the definition of the market economy. In part at least, entrepreneurship is regarded as the creative or programming aspect of action. It stands in contrast to behavior, which can be fully modelled.

The Concept of Equilibrium

Real vs. hypothetical equilibrium. As is the case with equilibrium in individual action, there is no pretence that economic equilibrium can ever be or would ever be achieved for any set of interacting individuals in a market economy. Two distinct reasons can be given for this. First, even a single individual's action does not have an endpoint. The praxeologist must construct an image of a particular action but action in general is indefinite. Second, even if every actor's action had an endpoint, it would be a miracle if all the endpoints were to occur at the same time. Thus, economic equilibrium is a hypothetical set of selections and is not intended to represent real selections.

Necessity of the equilibrium concept. Although economic equilibrium cannot represent the result of economic interaction in a market economy, the fullest comprehension of economic interaction is not possible without the concept. Suppose that there was a complete absence of coordination and synchronization. Then there could be no interaction in any meaningful sense. The concept of economic interaction implies some degree of coordination and synchronization, yet the notion of "some degree" of coordination and synchronization cannot be rendered intelligible without an image of complete coordination and synchronization. The ERE, MIRE, and MSC are such images.

A tendency toward equilibrium? It is no more correct to say that economic interaction is tending toward equilibrium than it is to say that an individual is tending toward equilibrium in individual action. It is meaningful, however, to say that entrepreneurship is performed with the intention of enabling individuals to earn profit. Similarly, it is meaningful to use equilibrium as a contrasting image and to say that if there were no further changes in wants, abilities, and technical knowledge; if individuals could learn all there is to know about others' actions and/or willingness to make commitments; and if entrepreneurship was not itself always a source of unanticipated change, profit-seeking actions would reduce the prospects for earning profit until none were left. The equilibrium in this sense is simply a makeshift device that is used to delineate a particular set of entrepreneurship effects.[3]

Another point can be made regarding the MSC. For this equilibrium, the oft-heard question of whether equilibrium would ever be reached refers not to whether the effects of the behavior or joint agreement will occur as anticipated. It refers rather to whether the mutual agreement to perform the behavior will be made in the first place.

Deeper Models of Entrepreneurship

Just as it is always possible to construct deeper models of choosing by more thoroughly describing the deliberation process, it is also always possible to construct deeper models of the network of exchanges by more thoroughly describing behavior that may aid entrepreneurship. Such models may contain more behavior, behavior of different dimensions (orders), and behavior with respect to a broader range of wants and factors.

4. ASSESSMENT OF THE ANALOGY WITH INDIVIDUAL ACTION

There is an obvious objection to the analogy that is drawn in this chapter between individual action and economic interaction. It is based on methodological individualism. The objection acknowledges that every normal human being can understand the meaning of an endpoint in an individual action. It allows that whenever one analyzes his own action, he identifies an endpoint (or endpoints). It rejects, however, the idea that everyone can understand what it means for there to be an endpoint in economic interaction. Indeed, it points out that no one can understand what this means. As a result, the objection holds, the use of the analogy may be a source of misunderstanding and erroneous thinking. Its use may obfuscate rather than elucidate.

This is a serious objection. It must be answered in two parts. First, one must consider the alternatives. It is easy to show that the analogy with individual action is more appropriate than other analogies that have been used. Second, one must identify the dangers of miscommunication and erroneous thinking so that he can avoid exposing himself to them. Each part of the answer is considered in turn. Afterwards, there is a brief discussion of what it means to compare methodologies.

Three Analogies

One who wants to conceptualize or describe a modern economy can adopt one of three different analogies. The first is an analogy with nonhuman life. This analogy may be called the *organic* analogy. In the organic analogy, the economic system is viewed as a changing, perhaps growing, composite that is analogous to animal or plant systems. According to this analogy, the "system of markets and prices" is an ecological system. If this analogy were employed, the language for describing human action would have to be borrowed from biology. Mises had little to say about this first analogy, and this text is not concerned with it either.

The second analogy is with relationships among nonliving objects. This may be called the *scientistic* analogy. The system of markets and prices is viewed as a set of constant or near-constant patterns that can be represented by mathematical equations. This viewpoint is associated with a mathematical meaning of economic interaction and equilibrium. The scientistic analogy must be rejected because there are no near-constant patterns among the phenomena that the new subjectivist defines as fundamentally relevant to economic theory.

The third analogy views the interdependence in an economy as a consequence of prior choices. The analogy is between (1) the hypothetical perceptions by entrepreneurs of ways to gain from exchange and the network of exchange agreements that result, and (2) the hypothetical perception by an individual of opportunities to gain from taking a particular action and the behavior that results. Using this analogy, the system of markets and prices is said to be caused by entrepreneurship. This may be called the *logical* analogy. When the price and market system is related to the choices that cause it, logical meanings of the economic interaction and equilibrium are being constructed.

Use of the logical analogy is the only means of identifying and describing economic interaction that is consistent with the new subjectivism, as it was described in chapter two. Mises used the logical analogy and the logical meaning of economic interactions specifically in order to separate the entrepreneurial aspects from physical, biological, psychological, and legal aspects. He wanted to focus on the subjective, entrepreneurial aspects of economic interaction.[4]

Dangers of Using the Logical Analogy

The dangers of using the logical image of economic equilibrium as an endpoint that is analogous to an endpoint in individual action can be said to exist at two levels: theoretical and applied. Each is discussed in turn.

Economic theory. The theoretical danger lies with the possibility that the theorist will not follow the proper procedure in interpreting the economic equilibrium. The proper procedure consists of: (1) identifying a priori categories of action; (2) transforming these categories into functions to be performed in economic interaction; (3) specifying functional behavior that is performed by robots in the equilibrium; (4) constructing a model of coordinated and synchronized economic choices; and (5) contrasting the model of coordinated and synchronized choices so constructed with the independent adjustments and commitment-seeking entrepreneurship that one knows intuitively and by experience to occur in a market economy. The economic theorist can go wrong if she fails to properly identify a priori categories; if transformations of the categories into behavior-performing robots is not logical; if the robots do not perform all of the functions and only the functions; if she neglects to account for individual diversity in entrepreneurial interaction; and if she fails to recognize the open-endedness of the entrepreneur concept.

Applied economics. The dangers are much greater for the applied economist. The applied economist cannot identify an economic phenomenon in a market economy without having knowledge of natural science, culture, and law. His problem in this regard is to obtain correct knowledge. Incorrect knowledge can lead him to use or construct models and images that are inappropriate for describing the phenomena in which he is interested.

A second danger is that the applied economist will attribute particular wants, abilities, and knowledge to his subjects that do not reflect reality. He may choose his assumptions on the basis of his own goals, while ignoring the true wants, abilities, and knowledge of actors. This is particularly easy to do when the same word is used in the formal language of economics to define a role as is used in everyday speech to describe a typification.[5]

To avoid these dangers, the applied economist must be able to defend his judgments that the phenomena he identifies are economic. To do this, he must refer to his knowledge of natural science, culture, and law. Second, he must be able to defend the relevance of his assumptions about individuals' wants, abilities, and knowledge. The important thing here is that his descriptions and predictions be stated in such a way that they can be assessed by someone who might have different views. Of special importance is that he describes the problem he is attempting to solve.

Contemporary Economics vs. the New Subjectivism

Contemporary economists typically define economic phenomena to include all market behavior, including that which is not chosen. This is in sharp contrast to the definition of economic phenomena in the new subjectivism, which does not include non-chosen behavior. Because of this difference, it is not surprising that contemporary economists and subjectivists often talk past each other. In this subsection, two disputes are considered from this perspective: (1) the dispute over the use of mathematical and statistical models, and (2) the dispute over methodology.

Mathematical and statistical models. Mathematical models and statistical techniques of prediction are designed specifically for a world of constant or near-constant relations. Some market behavior may appear, at least for a time, as if it is a near-constant relation. Everyday businesspeople operate within a relatively constant (i.e., predictable) physical world, within a social world in which much behavior is customary or habitual, and in a legal world that limits the exercise of their creativity and use of their abilities. As a result, the student of business may find it useful to model some behavioral relations by using mathematics and to attempt to predict future behavior on the basis of statistical extrapolation techniques. For example, pricing patterns due to seasonal changes in agriculture, to religious customs, and to the government regulations of business can be handled effectively in this way.

Contemporary economists differ from new subjectivists. The former regard all market behavior as economic phenomena. The latter define economic phenomena as consisting only of entrepreneurial interaction and the resulting performance of the economic functions. Because subjectivists limit their definition of economic phenomena, they believe that mathematical models and statistical methods of prediction are inappropriate. Subjectivists point out that entrepreneurship refers precisely to those causes of human behavior that can only be understood by putting oneself in the positions of the individuals who are assumed to act entrepreneurially.

Even in applied economics, the logically prior task, as the subjectivist sees it, is to construct economic theory. In constructing economic theory, one assumes that economic interaction takes place under the widest range of assumptions about the physical environment and customs. Given the absence of a specific physical environment, custom, or law; given the diversity of possible wants, abilities, and knowledge; and given the variety of ways that independent action, coordination, and synchronization may be carried out, it is easy to see why it is useless to try to represent the abstract phenomena of economic theory by means of mathematical models.

The subjectivist economist does not deny the existence of near-constant patterns in business. Nor does she deny that patterns can be shown to exist by means of statistical techniques and represented effectively by mathematical models. She recognizes that these patterns are the result of a relatively predictable physical world, and relatively predictable customs, habits, and laws. The patterns must be taken into account by applied economists in making descriptions of economic interaction in everyday life. However, they are not in any specific sense relevant to the construction of economic theory.

Mises periodically levelled harsh criticism at economists who use mathematical concepts of equilibrium.[6] He would presumably not deny the usefulness of mathematical models in describing market *behavior*. But market behavior is not the same as economic phenomena, as it is defined in the new subjectivism.

Methodology. One who uses the concept of methodology has in mind a comparison of at least two ways of accomplishing a goal. Mises claimed that there was only one way (praxeology) to study economic phenomena, as he defined them. If Mises was correct, as the author claims he was, someone who uses the term methodology to refer to the new subjectivism is hinting that Mises was wrong. That is, the use of the phrase "methodology of the new subjectivism" suggests that there is more than one way to study economic phenomena, as Mises defined them. One who says that Misesian methodology is incomplete or suspect must have in mind some alternative way of studying subjectivist economic phenomena.

In fact, no one has disputed Mises's claim as it applies to subjectively defined economic phenomena. A recent purported critique of Misesian methodology contrasted the new subjectivism with positivism.[7] Unfortunately, the critique failed to recognize that economic phenomena are defined differently by subjectivists than by so-called positivists. A comparison of a method that is suggested for studying phenomena that are not defined subjectively with the new subjectivism, which is specifically intended to study subjectively defined phenomena, is not a comparison of methodologies. It is a comparison of different methods of doing different things.

NOTES

1. The term "approximately equal" is used in order to imply that trading does not entail the mere transfer of infinitesimal amounts of goods. Goods exist in discrete sizes and their exchange with different individuals entails different transportation costs. In addition, complementarity exists among goods of various orders.

2. A more convenient way to look as this point for some readers may be through the lens suggested by the marginal productivity theory of value and distribution. As soon as the actions that might at one time be called entrepreneurial are modelled, a portion of the value of the product can be attributed to them. At that point, the modelled actions no longer correspond to entrepreneurship in the strictest sense because entrepreneurship in the strictest sense refers to actions that create the conditions for production, exchange, and distribution but that are not themselves part of the conditions.

3. The author must admit that he cannot explain what Mises had in mind when he spoke of there being a tendency toward the evenly rotating economy prevailing in every action (see Appendix 7). There are two ultimate reasons why there cannot be a tendency toward equilibrium. The first is that it is impossible to imagine a process that is both consistent with human action and through which the knowledge required for economic equilibrium could be acquired. The second is that equilibrium assumes a compatibility of wills that is unimaginable even if everyone is assumed to possess the knowledge necessary for economic equilibrium to exist.

4. Mises (1966, 355–56). It is interesting to note that the history of economic thought contains examples of economists who have used the other two analogies. Those who have used the first analogy view human beings as animals in a distinct stage of species evolution. The particular interaction that occurs at a particular time is regarded as the inevitable next step in the stages of evolution. Partial examples of this point of view can be found in the work of Marx and Simon Patten. The second analogy is used implicitly, at least by the modern positivists. They regard economics as fundamentally an objective science in the sense expressed in Pareto's 1900 and 1901 papers. These economists do not study economic interaction. Instead, they study the observable results of both economic interaction and whatever else may influence the empirical facts they observe.

5. See Appendix 6.

6. See Mises's distinction between the logical and mathematical method (1966, 250), and his distinction between logical catallactics and mathematical catallactics (1966, 350–57).

7. See Caldwell, 1982.

Chapter 13

The Method of Economic Teleology (3): Creating Markets and Rights in the Market Economy

To follow the implicit directive of the first postulate of subjective interpretation, the economist must allow the subjects he studies to possess the ability to create the economic conditions that he assumes to exist in his models of economic interaction.[1] He can accomplish this by defining entrepreneurship such that it has the capacity to create such conditions. Of particular interest in this chapter, he can replace the assumption that markets and rights exist with the assumption that markets and rights are created by individuals acting in the entrepreneurial role. The method of economic teleology is particularly suited to the task of identifying and defining such creative entrepreneurial acts. In it, the economist regards a market or right as the endpoint of an action. Then he tries to construct explanations, on the basis of intuition and experience, of how the market or right gets created.

Such explanations are essentially preliminary images of entrepreneurship. To elucidate the market- and rights-creating actions further, one can construct a model of robot entrepreneurs in order to define specific behavior that leads the endpoint to emerge. Then he can contrast his model with what he knows from intuition and experience to be how real economic actors would act under the circumstances that the model is intended to elucidate.[2]

The method of economic teleology as applied to economic phenomena from the microeconomic view was probably discovered by Menger. Along with marginalism, Menger is probably best known for his theory of imputation. The theory of imputation maintains that because goods and factors are linked in markets, the market value of each factor of production can ultimately be attributed to the market value of the final consumers' (first-order) good it is intended or expected to help produce. When economists give examples of this theory, they ordinarily refer to tangible factors. In fact, Menger applied the theory to any thing or action that contributes in one way or another to the ultimate production and sale of a consumers' good. So far as Menger was concerned, if the creation of the market or a right facilitates the ultimate production and exchange, the value of that market- or rights-creating action could be imputed from the value of the consumers' good. Thus it is from Menger and not Mises that the author's inspiration for this chapter is drawn.[3]

The creation of a specific market and a specific right is a distinctly microeconomic phenomenon. Thus in this chapter, the author abandons the macroeconomic perspective that has been used throughout the rest of the book.

This chapter provides a number of initial images of market- and rights-creating actions. No effort is made to elucidate these actions further by constructing a model. Instead, the discussion of markets- and rights-creation is used as a basis for constructing a definition of the firm. Part 1 describes market-creating actions and Part 2 describes rights-creating actions. Part 3 describes the combination of market- and rights-creating actions that result in the formation of the economic firm. Part 4 discusses the difference between the microeconomic view of entrepreneurship developed in this chapter and the macroeconomic view described in earlier chapters.

1. MARKET-CREATING ACTIONS

In those societies that contain a substantial element of freedom of enterprise, human beings are born into a world in which specialization and exchange already exist. As children, they learn about markets that have already been created, they learn where the markets are located and when they can be used, and they learn how to promote exchanges. In light of this, it is understandable that economists, including Mises, construct their images of a market economy on the assumption that markets already exist. Nevertheless, it is evident that a deeper understanding of entrepreneurship can be acquired by taking account of the prospect for creating new markets.

Entrepreneurship is continually discovering new products and new methods of production, new wants or combinations of wants, and previously unknown human abilities. These discoveries occur simultaneously with the creation of new markets, each helping to create further incentives for individuals to cause the other. This part first describes some market-creating actions that one person can perform in order to promote an exchange with another. Then it describes some market-creating actions in a many-person situation. In each case, the agreement to exchange is regarded as the endpoint of the economic interaction. The beginning point is the pre-exchange situation in which only one individual anticipates a gain from exchange. The task faced by the economist is to identify the actions an individual can perform to enable the endpoint to be reached when only that individual initially believes that there is a gain from exchange. The assumption that one person recognizes the potential benefits from exchange before the other(s) is a logical extension of the assumption that a market economy is characterized by specialization and the division of labor.

Market-Creating Actions in a Simple Two-Person Exchange

The means an individual can use to promote an exchange may be as simple as *A* making *B* an offer that *B* did not expect. Or it may be as complex as *A* teaching *B* how to use a good in order to show her its benefits. In either case, *A* may have to position herself at an opportune place and time in order to get *B*'s attention. If *A* wants to promote the exchange of a good that is not yet produced, she may have to first produce the good in order to demonstrate its want-satisfying capacity. In short, an individual can promote a two-person exchange by making an unexpected offer to trade an existing good, by teaching, by positioning, and by producing a good to be later offered for sale.

These actions may occur separately. But they may also occur in combined form. The economist can imagine a case where a promoter of exchange must first produce the good, position herself where she can make an offer to teach a prospective trading partner how to use it, and then make an offer to sell it. Experience suggests that such a combination may be the ordinary way that individuals promote a two-person exchange involving a new product.

Market-Creating Actions in a Many-Person Situation

The main difference between a two-person and a many-person case is that an individual can promote an exchange in which he is neither the owner (or producer) of a good nor the prospective buyer. Examples that come readily to mind are: middleman activity, brokerage, construction of a marketplace like a shopping center or stock exchange, publication of newspapers and trade journals, and provision of communication and transportation facilities. In a many-person situation, a promoter can also take advantage of mass advertising and he can often rely on both formal and informal markets for information to carry the message about his product or price to otherwise uninformed consumers.

2. RIGHTS-CREATING ACTIONS

The purpose of this part is to show how rights-creation helps individuals shift uncertainty and risk. The discussion begins by citing three ways in which rights-creation may be relevant to economics. Following this, it is shown how rights-creation enables individuals to shift uncertainty and risk, respectively.

The Relevance of Rights-Creating Actions

Rights-creating actions are relevant to economics in several ways. First, the existence of rights to the property one produces helps to give prospective producers an incentive to produce. Second, rights-creating actions help resolve the problem of external costs. Third, such actions help individuals achieve an allocation of uncertainty and risk that is more desirable to them. Each of these is considered in turn.

Rights and the incentive to produce new goods. First, a proper definition of the conditions of the market economy requires that rights exist in all goods. This raises a problem, however, for goods that have not yet been produced. Consider a person who believes that he can produce a good that can be sold for more than the costs of producing it, including interest. Once the good is produced, economics assumes that the right to it exists. However, economics does not specify who owns the right. If the law specifies that the right to a good is owned by its producer, the producer can expect to reap all of the profit due to a good's production and sale. Under these conditions, a prospective producer has an incentive to identify profit-making situations. If he determines that it is profitable to produce a new good, then he has an incentive to produce it, since he has the exclusive right to the revenue he earns from selling it. Suppose, however, that the right is owned by someone else. Then the producer would have to negotiate a deal before he could informatively decide how much profit to expect from producing the good. Ordinarily, such a transfer would be possible, since the right has no value until a good is produced.[4] However, the owner of the right may have personal reasons for not transferring it. Indeed, it is the systematic denial of rights to produce that is the hallmark of social systems dominated by class and status considerations. Even if the owner of the right has no non-financial reasons not to sell and even if monopoly is not relevant, the prior transfer of right entails an extra and costly step in the production process. Before a good gets produced, the prospective producer must negotiate the transfer of the right. By itself, this would deter the production of some goods.

This problem is easily solved by expanding the definition of the market economy. The market economy can be defined in such a way that the right to every new good is owned by its producer. If the producer uses factors that are initially owned by others, then there is joint ownership of the good, unless the factor-suppliers agree to give the producer what would otherwise be their rights.

Rights and the problem of external costs. Rights-creating actions are relevant to economics in a second way. The problem of external costs can be said to arise because rights to avoid the harmful actions of others do not exist or are imprecisely defined. Efforts to reduce conflicts due to external costs can be framed in terms of figuring out a way to define previously nonexistent property rights or to define existing rights more precisely.[5]

Outside of economics, the theory of conflict can be couched in these terms. In particular, the evolution of law can be understood in terms of a theory of the resolution of the problems of external costs that arise when property rights are not initially defined or not defined precisely enough.

Rights, uncertainty, and risk. Rights-creation is also a means of shifting uncertainty and risk-bearing. A good takes time to produce. In a market economy, someone must bear the uncertainty that the consumer for whom the good is intended will experience a change in wants, that the technology for producing the good will change, that the anticipated availability of means of production may not be realized, and that other means of satisfying the consumer's wants will change. In addition, the prospect for accidents of nature mean that someone must bear risk. The rights that are implicit in the definition of the market economy make the producer (or producers in the case of a good produced jointly by several factor-suppliers) responsible for the uncertainty and risk-bearing. When the producer(s) trades away her responsibility, it can be said that new rights are created. Thus, the creation of rights enables individuals to shift uncertainty and risk.

Rights-Creation to Deal with Uncertainty

One way to avoid uncertainty is to make an independent adjustment. Such an adjustment may be made with or without an attempt to predict the other's behavior. Consider a case in which one attempts to make a prediction before he adjusts. To predict B's behavior, A may study B's past behavior under similar circumstances, and he may try to understand B's plans and understandings. On the basis of his prediction, A may modify or adjust his own action in order to avoid all or some of the effects of B's behavior.

In attempting to predict B's action, A may employ specialists. He may hire a consultant whom he regards as more knowledgeable, he may hire an agent to make decisions for him, or he may contract with someone to teach him how to better predict the future. Although independent adjustment entails the creation of rights in connection with the employment of specialists, it does not ccause uncertainty to be shifted. Thus, it is not relevant to the topic that is of interest here. The concern of this part is with (1) how rights-creation can cause uncertainty to be shifted, and (2) how the joint creation of rights by A and B can reduce A's uncertainty about B's future actions. Each is discussed in turn.

Creation of rights to shift uncertainty-bearing. Suppose that A is considering whether to perform an action. After some deliberation, she concludes that it is a profitable action so long as B does not act in a particular way. She predicts, however, that B will indeed act in that way. Accordingly, left to make her choice in isolation, A would choose not to perform the action.

Given the same circumstances, now suppose that A consults with C. Upon being made aware of A's predicament, C also deliberates over the consequences of A's action. As it turns out, C makes a completely different prediction about B's behavior. C believes that B will behave differently and that A will be able to achieve the gain in satisfaction from her action. This difference in judgment cannot be resolved through discussion and argument.

Given this difference, a prospective profit can be earned by means of rights-creation. Suppose that C offers A the following deal. C offers to pay A a sum of money if B acts in the second way in exchange for

A's promise to pay *C* a smaller sum of money in the event that *B* behaves in the first way. The sum offered by *C* is large enough to compensate *A* for whatever harm *A* expects if *B* behaves in the second way. Moreover, the sum paid by *A* is small enough that *A* would still be able to gain if *B* behaved in the first way.

Such an agreement would create the right of *A* to collect from *C* or of *C* to collect from *A*, depending on the behavior that *B* performs. The creation of the right would enable a prospective gain to exist and it would result in *A*'s decision to perform the action.

The proper way to interpret this case is to recognize that it entails shifting uncertainty-bearing from *A* to *C*. *A*'s appraisal of her personal knowledge of the situation leads her to be unwilling to perform the action if she has to bear the uncertainty. *C*'s appraisal of his personal knowledge makes him willing to bear the uncertainty. The rights-creating act causes uncertainty to be shifted and, in the process, provides an incentive to *A* to perform the act with respect to which the uncertainty exists.

It is clear that if *A* is wrong and *C* is right about *B*'s behavior, then the rights-creating act enables an action to occur that *A* believes will yield satisfaction. In this sense, it raises *A*'s opportunities. It is also clear that *C* would gain also because he wins his bet on his own knowledge. The outcome turns out as he predicted. It is equally clear that if *A* is right and *C* is wrong, the anticipated gain to *A* comes at the expense of a loss by *C*.[6]

The attentive reader will recognize that such shifting of uncertainty-bearing is precisely what happens among entrepreneurs in a market economy, as described in chapter nine. Individuals who believe they are superior appraisers bid the highest prices for factors and then bear the uncertainty connected with the decision to use the factors to produce and sell. Similarly, in this case *C* believes that he has superior knowledge of the outcome of the interaction between *A* and *B*. Therefore, he bids the highest price for the right to cause *A* to perform the action.

This similarity is not a coincidence. Uncertainty-bearing of this first type is the simplest type of uncertainty-bearing for which one can demonstrate the incentive for those who believe they have made superior appraisals to agree to bear the uncertainty of actions that would otherwise not be performed. Thus, the simple case discussed in this subsection provides the basis for the conclusion reached in chapter nine.

In a market economy, some individuals may specialize in uncertainty-bearing. In particular, they may evaluate the characteristics of different uncertainty-bearing situations with an eye toward discovering production projects in which a change in economic conditions will affect each project's profit in opposite directions. For example, a specialist may judge that an increase in the popularity of one type of automobile is likely to be accompanied by a decrease in the popularity of a different competing type. If so, he might believe that he could reduce his overall uncertainty by agreeing to provide guaranty for the production and sale of both types of cars.

Creation of rights to reduce opportunism. Uncertainty due to opportunism can be illustrated by the following simple example. Assume that *A* is considering whether she will produce a good (or factor) that she knows she will be able to trade with *B*. The good takes time to produce and the costs of production must be incurred now. *A* knows that *B* would be willing to pay her a sum of money that is greater than the costs of producing the good, including the interest cost. *A* would not choose to produce the good for her own personal use and no one else would be willing to pay a price that is high enough to cover her costs. Under these conditions the prospect arises that once *A* produces the good, *B* would not be willing to pay her enough to cover her costs. The reason is that *B* recognizes that once the costs of production have already been incurred, *A*'s bargaining position is significantly weakened.

If *A* fails to anticipate this prospect, the result is merely that *A* will be disappointed. The good will still be produced. The disappointment of *A* due to her error would be offset, in money terms, by the increase in satisfaction to *B*. The significant case is when *A* anticipate's *B*'s opportunistic action. In this case, *A* would be unwilling to produce the good in the first place unless she received an advance commitment from *B* to pay her an amount that exceeds her anticipated costs.

The special characteristic of uncertainty due to opportunism is that individuals can use their abilities to understand the plans and understandings of others to make reliable predictions about when it will occur. *A* may be confident that *B* is likely to engage in opportunistic action if he gets in a position to do so.

Rights-creation provides a solution to this dilemma. Because *A* can predict that *B* will be opportunistic, she can seek a preproduction commitment to pay a given price for the good once it is produced. Such a commitment would benefit both parties, since *A* would not agree to produce the good for *B* unless such a commitment was made.

In everyday life, the creation of rights in order to deal with uncertainty due to opportunism manifests itself in many ways. Home improvement businesses require customers to sign contracts. Buyers demand warranties on durable goods. Businesses borrow money from savers by issuing bonds, which give lenders legal claims to the assets of the business if the money is not repaid. Banks and other lenders require an agreement by the borrower to forfeit collateral if a loan is not repaid. Manufacturers sometimes require advance payment before they agree to produce goods for retailers. And retailers often require deposits from consumers for special orders from manufacturers. An especially interesting case from the perspective of the history of economic thought is the decision by prospective members of a production team to give up their rights to shift to another employer in order to provide an incentive for an individual to form the team. This case is discussed in Part 3.

Creation of Rights to Shift Risk

A simple example can be used to illustrate how the creation of rights can enable individuals to shift risk. Suppose that A can produce a good that will yield high returns nine out of ten times. Because of risk, however, he will incur a high gambling loss one-tenth of the time. The outcome of any particular trial is not known in advance. Because he is unwilling to bear this risk, A decides not to take the gamble. If B is less averse to taking risk than A, a right can be created that will enable both A and B to gain and that will make it profitable to produce the good. B would propose to pay A a fixed sum of money and to bear whatever gambling losses are incurred in exchange for the right to take all the gains.

A similar result can be achieved by means of insurance. In this case, A agrees to pay B a small fixed amount in exchange for the right to collect a larger sum of money from B in the event that gambling losses are incurred. In a market economy, insurers can gain by pooling the risks of many customers. Insurance, as popularly understood, may also emerge because of a difference between the insurer and the insured in their appraisals of their respective scientific knowledge.

Interaction of Market-Creating and Rights-Creating Actions

A contract is an exchange of a promise for a good, a factor, or another promise. Because it is an exchange, market-creating actions may facilitate rights-creating actions. Individuals may teach, learn, position themselves, and produce goods with an eye on the future benefits from an exchange of commitments.

Rights-creating actions may also facilitate market-creating actions. An individual may be unwilling to incur the costs of acquiring a specialization, or of learning, teaching, or positioning unless he is guaranteed that he will not be subject to opportunistic action by a prospective trading partner. It is seen then that market-creating actions and rights-creating actions may be mutually reinforcing.

3. THE FIRM

Rights-creating actions (commitments) have now been considered from two perspectives: the macroeconomic perspective, which makes use of the MIRE and MSC, and the microeconomic perspective, which uses the image of two-person production and exchange.[7] In between are three-person images, four-person images, and so on. The task of the applied economist is to determine which images are relevant. A highly relevant microeconomic image is the *firm*. In this part, it is shown how the method of economic teleology can be used to construct an image of the choices that result in the firm.

The firm, as it is defined in modern economic theory, is a team of complementary human inputs (i.e., a team of different individuals who supply labor and human capital), possibly combined with other non-human inputs, the purpose of which is to produce goods in order to exchange them for money. A firm contains an uncertainty-bearing agreement concerning how the proceeds are to be allocated. It is useful to call these proceeds the firm's accounting profit or accounting loss. The agreement specifies the rights of different team members to the firm's accounting profit and their obligation to make good on debts or other liabilities if there is an accounting loss.[8] A firm also contains a governance or decision-making structure, which defines the role that each human input plays in directing the factors to do this or that.[9] In the simplest case a single individual receives all the residual accounting profit and is personally responsible for paying debts in the event of an accounting loss. She is also the firm's manager and, as such, directs the human factors, to whom she pays a fixed wage. In short, she is a fully integrated entrepreneur, as described in chapter six. This book is exclusively concerned with this simplest and most fundamental case.

The simplest firm is a contract between an entrepreneur who undertakes and bears uncertainty and the owners of other human factors that complement her. The contract specifies that the entrepreneur has the right to any residual accounting profit as well as the obligation to pay liabilities in the event of an accounting loss. The role of the entrepreneur who has these rights and obligations can be called the *employer*.

In this simple case, the employer ordinarily turns out to be the owner of a ***strongly strategic*** factor of production. This is a factor that (1) is one of a class of factors, any of which could be used to complement members of other classes of factors; and (2) is believed by the employer to be worth more in its contribution to the firm's accounting profit relative to other members of its class than all of the other complementary factors combined, relative to other members of their respective classes.

The reason why the residual claimant is ordinarily the owner of the strongly strategic factor is complex. In forming a team, someone must do the preliminary calculations of profitability. Someone must create the markets for the factors that will ultimately comprise the team. Such a person may identify factors, estimate relative costs, teach prospective team members about the benefits of team production, and place herself in a position where she can achieve the most gain. She must use her own factors to perform these market-creating actions. This could be summarized by saying that someone must incur "startup" costs. The pivotal question is whether there will be an incentive for someone to incur these startup costs.

If there is one factor that is strongly strategic, such an incentive will exist. The owner of this factor will have an incentive to incur the startup costs because her position as owner of a more strategic factor effectively preempts the opportunities of other prospective team members to earn as much income on similar teams as they can earn by becoming members of the team that is run by the owner of the strategic factor. Suppose that the owner of the strategic factor incurs the startup costs, then offers employment to other prospective team members under the condition that they give her the sole right to be the employer. If, after the startup costs are incurred, any other factor-owner threatens to not join the team on the grounds that her wage is too low, the employer can replace her with a substitute at only a slightly higher cost than she had projected.

In short, only the owner of the strongly strategic factor is likely to succeed in recouping her startup costs. Thus, only she is likely to form a firm. Someone who does not own such a factor is likely to fail because of the opportunistic action of a strongly strategic factor-owner.

Suppose that no factor is strongly strategic. Indeed, suppose that they are all equally strategic. Then no one will be able to position herself well enough to recoup her startup costs. In this event, the team could not form unless a rights-creating interaction occurred first. Such interaction would give a single individual the sole right to be the employer.

To see this, suppose that one of the factor-owners mistakenly incurred the startup costs, thinking that she could recoup them by becoming the employer. As part of her market-creating actions, she would proceed to make employment offers to other prospective team members. Suppose that she sets her wage offers to prospective employees low enough to recoup her startup costs yet high enough to attract the factors away from their best alternatives. Now consider the scenario from the standpoint of one of the other prospective team members. Since he would hear the offers made by the individual who had incurred the startup costs, he could simply offer wages that were slightly higher. Prospective team members would be attracted by the higher wages to work for the copier. The copier could profit because he did not have to incur the startup costs.

The situation can be remedied by means of a *foreclosure contract*. In a foreclosure contract, the prospective members of the team would agree to give up their right to work with any team of the same type. An effective foreclosure contract would insure a prospective employer against the possibility that someone would gain by copying her price offers. It would enable a firm to form when it would otherwise be unprofitable for anyone to incur the startup costs.

It is possible that factors would differ in their relative strategicness yet no one would own a strongly strategic factor. In this event, the discussion would shift to the possibility of forming coalitions. There is no need at this point, however, to complicate the analysis by including this possibility.

Thus, the image of the firm that emerges from applying economic teleology is one in which suppliers of factors to a team production process face a problem of creating rights to the anticipated accounting profit. Without such rights, no one would be motivated to incur the startup costs. If there is a strongly strategic factor, its owner possesses de facto rights. She becomes the employer. In the absence of a strongly strategic factor, the exclusive right to the expected accounting profit must be created in order to provide an incentive for someone to incur the startup costs.[10]

4. THE MICROECONOMIC AND MACROECONOMIC VIEW OF ENTREPRENEURSHIP

The discussion of market-creation and rights-creation in this chapter has been based on what is essentially a microeconomic view of entrepreneurship. When one seeks to elucidate entrepreneurship from the microeconomic view, the endpoint is not a macroequilibrium, like the ERE, but a simple exchange or combination of production and exchange.

In using the microeconomic view, the economist asks first about the most proximate cause of a particular microeconomic interaction, such as an exchange. Having identified a set of choices that cause the exchange, he then asks how those choices could themselves have been caused by previous choices. In this way, he identifies a less proximate cause. Next he may ask about the causes of these less proximate choices in order to identify even less proximate causes. He proceeds in this fashion to the extent that he feels is relevant. At the end of his investigation, he is able to identify a chronology, or structure, of choices that he claims to be causes of the interaction. At the same time, he is aware of the fact that deeper causes may play a role and that if he were to carry his investigation further, he could discover the additional causes.

A variation of this procedure can be used to **define** a particular consequence of an interaction. In this case, the economist assumes that wants, abilities, and knowledge take a more-or-less specific form. Given that form, a particular set of choices are deduced. These choices lead to a joint outcome that is given a label. The outcome is thereby defined in terms of the assumptions about wants, abilities, and knowledge. The burden of such a procedure in economic theory is to select assumptions that are sufficiently general so that the outcomes would be regarded as important to colleagues who are also economic theorists.[11]

While the microeconomic view is indispensible for the purpose of elucidating market-creation, right-creation, and the firm, it would be a grave mistake to attempt to describe economic interaction without shifting views to the macroeconomic. Such a shift would require the economist to understand and specify particular markets, rights, and firms in relation to the performance of the economic functions and in relation to the categories of entrepreneurial action.

Mises seems to have not used the microeconomic view, as described here. Rather he used the macroeconomic view and in so doing was able to capture the essence of the method used by neoclassical writers like J. B. Clark, Wicksteed, Schumpeter, and Knight. Because of this, Mises was more capable of evaluating macroeconomic policy arguments than the above-named economists and their various successors, since these persons did not correctly identify the methodology they were using.[12] Considering the twists and turns that mainstream British and American economics took during this century, one cannot help but admire the accomplishments that Mises and some of his students were able to make simply by recognizing the method used by the founders of the macroeconomic view.

NOTES

1. See Appendix 2.

2. The method of economic teleology can also be used to describe the entrepreneurial actions entailed in creating a monetary system. In this text, the creation of a monetary system is disregarded. This is a significant omission. Nevertheless, it follows Mises, who did not seriously describe the monetary system creation process.

3. Menger discussed the idea that rights and markets are produced in his 1981 book (1981 [1871], 53–55, 288). See Appendix 8 for further discussion of Menger's contribution.

4. The right may be valuable to a prospective monopolist, who can use the right to restrict competition.

5. See Appendix 9 for a discussion of Mises's handling of the problem of external costs.

6. Since the act itself would not have been performed by A if she knew that B would behave in the second way and since a given sum of money is transferred from C to A, it can be said that there is a realized net loss from the transaction in terms of money, since C's loss of money is greater than A's gain of money minus the monetary value A would place on her loss due to her choice to perform the action that she otherwise would not have chosen to perform.

7. See chapter twelve.

8. Alchian and Demsetz (1972) stress this feature, which they call the employer's status as a "residual claimant." In modern economics, the profit- and loss-sharing agreement is also a risk-bearing agreement, since modern economic theorists do not make a distinction between intersubjective uncertainty, intrasubjective uncertainty, and risk. In this text, the risk-bearing nature of the agreement is ignored.

9. On governance structures, see Williamson (1985, chap. 3).

10. It is worth noting that the employer may be able to shift all or part of the uncertainty to someone who is more willing or able to bear it. Thus, the employer need not be an entrepreneur in the day-to-day operation of the firm. She must, however, be able to attain the right to sufficient revenue to enable her to get compensated for incurring the startup costs. She must bear whatever uncertainty there is that a foreclosure contract will not be made because conditions changed between the time when she began to incur the startup costs and the time when the foreclosure contract is negotiated.

11. This method is described more fully in Gunning (1986, 81–84) in his discussion of the "actual interpretation of economic events."

12. This fact was most evident in the disputes between Mises and Schumpeter and between Mises and Knight, which are mentioned in *Human Action*. (The dispute with Schumpeter is described on pp. 530–31; the dispute with Knight is described on p. 492 and 848.) It was also abundantly evident in the

debate between Hayek and Keynes. Although it is questionable whether Hayek ever fully appreciated the macroeconomic view, as described here, he was a competent user of it. As a result, he found it easy to expose the obvious fallacies in Keynes's earliest book in macroeconomics. (See Hayek 1931, 1932; for Hayek's retrospective look at his relationship with Keynes, see Hayek 1983.) Henry Hazlitt, an American who studied under Mises, presented a competent exposure of the fallacies in Keynes's more popular book. (See Hazlitt 1959.)

Chapter 14

Conclusion

The aim of this book has been to elucidate and extend Mises's contributions to economic theory (excepting his theory of money and credit). By far his most important contribution, in the author's view, was his recognition and explication of the methods used by the classical and early neoclassical economists to describe the market economy. Mises recognized that the problem of constructing an image of the market economy was a special case of the problem of "understanding," or *verstehen*. He discovered, partly through his study of Weber's works, that when normal human beings attempt to understand the actions and understandings of other normal human beings, they necessarily make a priori assumptions that individuals possess a subjective understanding of causality, teleology, time, and uncertainty. In *Human Action*, he used the method of imaginary constructions to prove that individuals possess these a priori categories. He showed that one could not conceive of a normal human being who did not possess them.

If the student of action, or praxeologist, must assume that individuals possess the a priori categories, it follows that her own personal understanding and descriptions of particular actions must be couched in terms of the a priori categories. The praxeologist must describe a particular action by referring to the particular ends, means, time frame, and uncertainty of the actor.

In light of the subjectivist revolution of the nineteenth century, a praxeological description must also acknowledge that the subjects described may have particular ends and means which the praxeologist cannot fully understand. This acknowledgment can be highlighted by making a contrast between (*a*) a robot behaver, whose ends and means can be fully specified, and (*b*) a unique and not fully specifiable human actor who is assumed to face the same circumstances as the behaver. The contrast brings into relief the truly human aspect of behavior.

Because economics is simply *verstehen* applied to the market economy, the economist must also use the a priori categories. The economist focuses on interaction, and a particular realm of it at that. Because he is concerned with consumption, production, and exchange in the market economy, he incorporates the a priori categories by expressing these market economy characteristics in terms of the intermediate end of earning money. He defines an integrated economic actor as one who uses a specialized factor (means) in a production process that is aimed at producing a good for consumption (end) through time in an environment of intersubjective uncertainty in order to earn money that can be used to buy consumption goods. The environment of intersubjective uncertainty reflects the subjectivist assumption that, like the economist, an economic actor cannot expect to fully understand the means and ends of other actors.

The great accomplishment of some of the later classical and early neoclassical economists is that they developed the marginal productivity theory of value and distribution, in which economic interaction is placed into functional categories. This procedure helps the economist construct an image of fully integrated economic interaction from the "macroeconomic" view. Mises recognized that the marginal productivity theory was the application of methodological apriorism and the old subjectivism to economic interaction under the conditions specified in the definition of the market economy. The particular characteristics of economics are represented by the functional categories of consuming, saving, producing, and supplying factors, which are associated with the roles of the consumer-saver, producer, and factor supplier. To show how these functions get performed by human actors—in other words, to incorporate the a priori categories of action into his images of the market economy—the economist defines consuming as the ultimate end and producing through the employment of factors as the means. He also assumes that all economic action occurs through time in an environment of intersubjective uncertainty. To demonstrate the subjectivity of economic analysis, he contrasts (*a*) an image of an economy in which robots who behave according to algorithms ("maximizers") occupy the roles of consumer, producer, and factor supplier, with (*b*) an image of a market economy, in which these behaviors are performed as a consequence of entrepreneurship. Entrepreneurship encompasses the role of making appraisals and, most importantly, of betting that one's appraisals are more correct than someone else's by bearing uncertainty. The image is built step-by-step by identifying more and more manifestations of entrepreneurship.

In short, the early economists succeeded in converting economics into the study of the abstract and only distinctly human activities entailed in a market economy: those activities that get personified in the image of the appraising, decision-making, and uncertainty-bearing entrepreneur. Following the marginal productivity theory, the study of economics became (or should have become) mainly the study of entrepreneurship and its various manifestations.

Mises's great accomplishment was to recognize how the method used by the early economists, which he dubbed the method of imaginary constructions, was related to the subjectivist revolution of the nineteenth century. It is this connection that makes it appropriate to call Mises's work the new subjectivism.

To distinguish the method used by economists from the method of imaginary constructions used by all students of human action, the author has rejected Mises's label in favor of a more descriptive one, namely the method of contrasting images of functions. In addition, the author showed how a related method—the method of economic teleology—was also used by Mises. In the latter method, entrepreneurship is said to causes the economic functions of consuming, producing, and factor-supplying to be performed.

Unfortunately, Mises did not succeed in convincing others of the significance of his discoveries. Most economists simply ignored him. Even those who claim to be his followers have apparently not incorporated the implications of his discoveries into their method of economics. To help rectify this, the present book has attempted to communicate the rationale for the methods of contrasting images of functions and economic teleology by making an analogy, at every step, with the method that one must use to study the action of an isolated individual. For example, chapter five showed how to use the method of imaginary constructions to derive the essential characteristics of action, while chapter six showed how to use the method of contrasting images of functions to derive the essential characteristics of an integrated economic action. Chapter eight showed the relationship between saving, uncertainty-bearing, and guaranty in a market economy by first showing the relationship between these characteristics in an image of an isolated actor. And chapter eleven showed how to use the method of economic teleology to help conceptualize individual interaction, while chapter twelve used the same method to help conceptualize economic interaction.

Most of this book has been devoted to elucidating ideas that can be directly attributed to Mises. These include his refutation of positivism; his treatment of the concepts of *verstehen* and ideal types; his illuminating presentation of a variety of other methodological issues; and his definitions of logic, methodological apriorisim, the a priori categories of action, theory, history, praxeology, economic theory, economic functions, entrepreneurship, the evenly rotating economy (equilibrium), saving, and interest. In addition, however, this book attempted to extend the new subjectivism in several ways. It revived the subjectivism of Alfred Schuetz in order to show that the new subjectivism is a revolution against elitism. It systematically derived the three essential characteristics of entrepreneurship and showed why they are inseparable. It took issue with Mises's labelling of entrepreneurship as a function. It identified the concept of guaranty, the importance of which Mises apparently failed to perceive. It systematically constructed the foundations for a definition of profit and loss that is more subjectivist than that provided by Mises. And it showed how the new subjectivism could be extended to deal with market-creation, rights-creation, and the theory of the firm.

The most obvious implication of this book is that to the extent that economists are interested in the distinctly human part of economic behavior, economics, including what has come to be known as Austrian economics, needs a nearly complete overhauling. It needs to be rebuilt on new subjectivist foundations. Mises was correct to believe that many of the classical and early neoclassical economists were subjectivist in their work. However, the fact that, broadly speaking, they did not recognize the deeper implications of subjectivism made it virtually impossible for them to leave a legacy that would enable young intellectuals to quickly and easily perceive the flaws of unfettered positivism. It is virtually impossible for the mind that is trained in modern schools to avoid entering a stage in which it conceives of experimentation and meticulous observation as a means of proving various hypotheses. Schools reinforce the child's natural confidence in experimentation and observation by teaching the discoveries made by noted physicists and chemists. As a result, one of the easiest transitions an aspiring economist or social scientist can make is to think that the same methods that succeeded in the physical sciences—experimentation, meticulous observation, and ingenuity of interpretation—can also succeed in economics. It is this easy transition with which economic teachers should be prepared to do battle at every turn. The most important lesson that economists can impart to young minds is that one cannot succeed in understanding economic interaction unless she supplements meticulous observation and clever interpretation at every step with a priori assumptions about individual ends and means and about individual perceptions of time and uncertainty. Such a task is essentially a negative one and this fact accounts for subjectivism's lack of penetration into modern academic institutions, where tolerance of criticism is weak.

The extensions of new subjectivism presented in this book contain two other important implications. The first is that the role of guaranty provision needs a more thorough analysis than it has achieved to date. It is the author's belief that the entire theory of money and credit needs to be rebuilt on a foundation of a subjectivist understanding of issues relating to guaranty. It is hoped that future work in this area will proceed with this in mind.

Second, the discussion of market- and rights-creation in chapter thirteen reinforces the idea that the economist needs to be continuously alert to the danger of elitism. The economist must construct models in which markets and rights are assumed to be defined so that she can contrast them with images that bring indefinite entrepreneurship into sharp relief. However, there is a persistent danger that her action of constructing models will lead her to lose perspective regarding her own role. The economist is not a supra human being. She lives in the same life world, to use Schuetz's phrase, as the subjects she describes. In light of this, subjectivism requires that the economist keep in mind the fact that the subjects she studies may be even more competent than she at the task of understanding the actions of others. Among other things, they may be able to create markets and rights that she is unable to imagine. Subjectivism prescribes a measure of humility to counter the economists' strong susceptibility to the disease of egotism.

Sometimes it seems as difficult for individuals who have travelled a road of consistent success in their schooling and peer interaction to achieve this humility as it is to pass the proverbial camel through the eye of a needle. If so, it is not surprising that economics, as it is defined in the modern world, is an elitist profession. The fact that students and new members of established social groups can succeed by copying the models of their teachers and superiors may also explain why subjectivism has not succeeded politically or socially. Still there may be hope that it will succeed intellectually. And, if it does, we will have to thank Mises for his critical contribution.

Appendix 1

Subjectivism and Positivism

In contrast to the new subjectivism, modern economists have adopted positivism—the very program of study that Mises intended for the new subjectivism to replace. Positivism defines economic phenomena to include all behavior that is related to production and exchange for money, as it takes place in a particular culture, in a particular physical environment, and under a particular set of laws. With its aim of predicting behavior, it treats human actors as robots without regard for what the subjectivist claims to be the truly human character of economic action.

From the standpoint of the economics of knowledge, it may seem strange that positivism would have succeeded in the field of economics. Even if we disregard Mises's attack on it, positivism appears untenable as an intellectual movement in economics. It is obvious that the relevance of positivist predictions must be confined to the particular cultures, physical environments, and laws in which the behavioral and/ or statistical data were collected. Moreover, the positivist predictions must ignore the human capacity to be creative and inventive. Thus, positivism cannot help one understand why individuals produce, consume, and supply factors. Nor can it help one understand how the laws that facilitate market interaction contribute to the satisfaction of wants. It also cannot help one understand why money is used, why people position themselves vis-à-vis others, or why people seek and make commitments. Yet it is precisely such questions as these that economists have always thought to be the proper subject matter of their field.

Economics yields an important insight about positivism: that the skills asssociated with positivist prediction can be appraised by entrepreneurs in the market economy. Because of this, the graduates of colleges and universities who have the ability to use statistical skills to make behavioral predictions can find employment in the private sector. As higher education has moved in the direction of education for the trades, so also has "economic education" moved in the direction of preparing its students to be competent employees.

The fact that positivists can command a wage in the private sector does not explain the success of positivism as an intellectual movement, however. To explain this, one must consider politics. The success of positivism as an intellectual movement is largely confined to the colleges and universities. There, three different factors have nurtured positivism. First, especially at the smaller state-supported colleges and universities, legislators have set rules that are interpreted by administrators in such a way that they come to expect faculty to please students by helping them to prepare for jobs or by catering to their particular predispositions. Since positivist skills can be appraised, teachers can succeed by teaching this skill. The modern emphasis on statistical and computer skills among economics majors is mainly political. In short, citizens and the bureaucrats in universities find that by teaching positivism in economics, they are better able to justify educational expenditures by state legislatures on their institutions. It is important to recognize that when public funds are used to support this education, it amounts to a subsidy to the students, the teachers, and the myriad other people who participate in or supply resources to the endeavor.

Second, positivist skills are cheaper to monitor than other cognitive skills. Monitoring positivist skills is a cheaper means for administrators to decide who should be promoted and receive special privileges than monitoring the understanding of economic phenomena, properly defined. Similarly, teachers find it cheaper to construct and grade examinations on positivist skills.

Third, the growth of government, combined with the desire to make officials and researchers accountable, has resulted in disproportionate funding for those college and university professors who do positivist analyses. This reinforces the job market for positivist graduates, creates opportunities for colleges and universities to increase their funds by employing and rewarding positivist faculty, and creates what appear to be legitimate evaluations of the intellectual abilities of faculty and students.

A final factor in explaining the success of positivism is the demand by politicians and other political opportunists. Politicians and government bureaucrats have discovered that when their arguments favoring the expropriation of wealth from the market economy are backed up by positivist "evidence," they are capable of generating greater public support. That people accept such arguments seems to be partly due to their unwillingness to consider or to understand more complex arguments.

Appendix 2

Two Postulates of Subjectivism

The author's definition of subjectivism is a composite of two of three "postulates for scientific model constructs of the social world" proposed by Alfred Schuetz. Following his participation in Mises's famous private seminars in Austria in the 1920s, Schuetz later achieved fame as an expositor of phenomenology in the social sciences. The first of the two postulates is the postulate of subjective interpretation. Schuetz described it as follows:

> . . . In order to explain human actions the scientist has to ask what model of an individual mind can be constructed and what typical contents must be attributed to it in order to explain the observed facts as the result of the activity of such a mind in an understandable relation. The compliance with this postulate warrants the possibility of referring all kinds of human action or their result to the subjective meaning such action or result of such action had for the actor.

This postulate complements a second, which Schuetz called the postulate of adequacy:

> . . . Each term in a scientific model of human action must be constructed in such a way that a human act performed within the life world by an individual actor in the way indicated by the typical construct would be [reasonable and] understandable for the actor himself as well as for his fellow-men. . . . Compliance with this postulate warrants the consistency of the constructs of the social scientist with the constructs of common-sense experience of the social reality. (Schuetz 1953, 34)

Also see Schuetz, 1943.

The difference between the old and the new definitions of subjectivism lies with their level of abstraction. It is of the utmost importance to understand this difference if one is to evaluate the argument made here that Mises ushered in the new subjectivist revolution. If one adopts subjectivism only in the sense of *verstehen*, she can proceed to interpret social events. But unless one adopts subjectivism in the revolutionary sense described in this text, she cannot understand the proper way to construct theory because she cannot evaluate the prospective consequences of adopting alternative theories, except by means of trial and error.

Mises recognized this point when, in criticizing the German historicists, he remarked: "They did not see that without recourse to propositions accepted as universally valid, even history cannot be understood and that the theory of human action is logical prior to history" (1981, 132). For more on Mises's recognition of this point see the full discussion in chapter four of his 1981 book and pp. 51–58 in his 1966 book.

Mises defended subjectivism in the "science of human action" in the following way:

> . . . it is in . . . subjectivism that the objectivity of our science lies. Because it is subjectivistic and takes the value judgments of acting man as ultimate data not open to any further critical examination, it is itself above all strife of parties and factions, it is indifferent to the conflicts of all schools of dogmatism and ethical doctrines, it is free from valuations and preconceived ideas and judgments, it is universally valid and absolutely and plainly human. (1966, 22)

Appendix 3

Verstehen and Understanding

In introducing the term understanding to the English-speaking audience, Mises (1966) pointed out that his meaning was identical to that of Henri Bergson's concept of *verstehen* (p. 49). Mises described understanding as follows:

> The **understanding** establishes the fact that an individual or a group of individuals have engaged in a definite action emanating from definite value judgments and choices and aiming at definite ends, and that they have applied for the attainment of these ends definite means suggested by definite technological, therapeutical, and praxeological doctrines. It furthermore tries to appreciate the effects and the intensity of the effects brought about by an action; it tries to assign to every action its relevance, i.e., its bearing upon the course of events. (p. 50, italics added)

Mises took great care to distinguish between understanding and a priori knowledge. A priori knowledge is, among other things, one's knowledge that individuals possess wants, abilities, and knowledge, a sense of causality and teleology, and a sense of time and uncertainty. A priori knowledge is not knowledge of the particular wants, and so on, that individuals possess. Knowledge of particulars belongs to the realm of understanding.

Although understanding is the method one uses in making sense of historical facts, one could not get very far without a method of sorting out the "infinite multiplicity of events." To do this, one constructs ideal types. "No historical problem can be treated without the aid of ideal types" (p. 60). Examples of ideal types are the business firm, an industry, the industry leader, and the bureaucrat. Whether a particular case (General Motors, shoe-producing firms, the middle-level supervisor) is an example of an ideal type is decided by the historian. This is because an ideal type is always created by the historian. It always refers to his understanding of the intentions and expectations of the acting individuals (p. 60).

Unfortunately, the word "understanding" has a variety of connotations in everyday speech. At least one of these promotes an impression that is just the opposite of what Mises intended. For example, it would be acceptable to say that the goal of a natural scientist is to understand relationships among material phenomena that cannot choose. Yet the concept of understanding, as used by Mises, is reserved exclusively for the study of human subjects. A careless reader of *Human Action* who used the concept to refer to nonhuman, material phenomena might mistakenly think that Mises was saying a human being could be treated as a material phenomenon. Besides the problem with terminology, Mises seems to have too often compromised lucidity of presentation in order to confront criticisms of which he was aware and in order to attack what he regarded as false doctrines.

In the author's view the problem of terminology has been the major reason why non-economist readers of *Human Action* have been unable to grasp Mises's methodological message. Mises's claim was actually quite simple: that the study of economics is the systematic application of "common sense" to economic matters. But a simple message is not always easy to communicate. To communicate this message, one must be able to speak of the common sense in terms that are familiar to readers at the most fundamental level, that is, with regard to readers' common childhood experiences upon which their conceptual schemes and language are built. There is no reason to expect that Mises, a native of Austria and latecomer to the United States, would know how to accomplish this for the American reader. Indeed, given the diversity of cultures in America, there is some question as to whether Mises's goal could be accomplished by anyone who had not delved deeper into the universals of cognitive development.

Appendix 4

Uncertainty and Probability in *Human Action*

Mises distinguished two extreme types of probability: "class probability (or frequency probability) and case probability (or the specific understanding of the sciences of human action)" (1966, 107). Class probability refers to situations in which, although the particular outcome of a choice is uncertain, the probabilities that it will be one or another are known for certain. Examples are games of chance.

He describes case probability as follows:

> Case probability means: We know, with regard to a particular event, some of the factors which determine its outcome; but there are other determining factors about which we know nothing. . . . Case probability has nothing in common with class probability but the incompleteness of (the subject's) knowledge. In every other regard the two are entirely different. (p. 110)

Most uncertainty in everyday life entails both types of probability. Accordingly, to identify the case probability aspect of an uncertain situation, one must imagine separating out the class probability:

> . . . Everything that outside the field of class probability is commonly implied in the term probability refers to the peculiar mode of reasoning involved in dealing with historical uniqueness or individuality, the specific understanding of the historical sciences. (p. 112)

Recognizing that these concepts are not easy to grasp in light of our everyday usage of language relating to chance and probability, Mises

237

attempted to clarify his distinction in four ways. First, he distinguished between two groups of predictors. The first group includes the scientist and the diagnostician. These people use class probability to tell the frequency with which (or probability that) a particular physical event will occur. The second are game prognosticators. One who attempts to predict an election or the outcome of a match among athletic teams uses case probability for the most part, since each case is unique. The prediction made by a game prognosticator depends upon the particular choices he expects individuals to make.

Second, Mises distinguished three different types of actors: the gambler, the engineer, and the speculator. The gambler, such as the roulette player, knows the frequency of a favorable particular outcome in a series of events and trusts that she will have good luck. She uses class probability. The engineer distinguishes between problems that can and those that cannot be solved under the present state of knowledge. He may try to render his knowledge more complete. "[I]t is his principle to operate only in the orbit of certainty." The engineer also uses class probability. The speculator differs from these in that his success or failure depends on his greater or lesser ability to understand others' future actions. This is because he must "adjust his actions to other people's actions" (p. 113).

Third, he translated four statements from everyday language into the class and case probability framework. Finally, he distinguished between a gambler and a bettor, the latter being one who attempts to account for the wants, abilities, and knowledge of the human participants in a game. The bettor employs her understanding of others' actions.

Appendix 5

Mises on the Three Categories of Entrepreneurial Action

The three categories of entrepreneurial action described here are derived from the new subjectivist approach to macroeconomics, as described by Mises. However, it would be incorrect to say that Mises derived them. It would be equally incorrect to say that he did not recognize their significance. Probably the most correct statement is that he did not regard a meticulous identification of the characteristics of entrepreneurship as a priority. He seemed more interested in describing the "processes" that are entailed in entrepreneurial interaction. Thus, he focused more on the process whereby individuals who are better at serving the interests of consumers than others get selected by being rewarded higher incomes for their services than their rivals. Similarly, he focused on the process whereby competition among entrepreneurs causes decreases in consumer prices that are initially "high" and increases in factor prices that are initially "low."

The purpose of this appendix is to defend the author's claim that the concepts of appraisement, undertaking, and uncertainty-bearing are implicit in the new subjectivism of Mises. Quotations and text references are provided for each case.

APPRAISEMENT

In introducing appraisement, Mises (1966) first applies it to his selective process. He says:

239

. . . the market that catallactics deals with is filled with people who are to different degrees aware of the changes in data and who, even if they have the same information, appraise it differently. The operation of the market reflects the fact that changes in the data are first perceived only by a few people and that different men draw different conclusions in appraising their effects. The more enterprising and brighter individuals take the lead, others follow later. The shrewder individuals appreciate conditions more correctly than the less intelligent and therefore succeed better in their actions. (p. 328)

He implies that appraisement, carried out by the "promoting and speculating entrepreneurs," is the driving force of the market economy:

The driving force of the market process is provided neither by the consumers nor by the owners of the means of production—land, capital goods, and labor—but by the promoting and speculating entrepreneurs. These are people intent upon profiting by taking advantage of differences in prices. Quicker of apprehension and farther-sighted than other men, they look around for sources of profit. They buy where and when they deem prices too low, and they sell where and when they deem prices too high. They approach the owners of the factors of production, and their competition sends the prices of these factors up to the limit corresponding to their anticipation of the future prices of products. They approach the consumers, and their competition forces prices of consumers' goods down to the point at which the whole supply can be sold. Profit-seeking speculation is the driving force of the market as it is the driving force of production. (p. 328)

UNDERTAKING

Regarding undertaking, Mises says: "The specific entrepreneurial function consists in determining the employment of factors of production" (pp. 290–91). Also, he says: "The function of the entrepreneur cannot be separated from the direction of the employment of factors of production for the accomplishment of definite tasks. The entrepreneur controls the factors of production . . ." (p. 306).

Finally, he says:

The entrepreneur determines alone, without any managerial interference, in what lines of business to employ capital and how much capital to employ. He determines the expansion and contraction of the size of the total business and its main sections. He determines the enterprise's financial structure. (p. 307)

It is obvious in these passages that Mises is speaking of the effects of the entrepreneur's decision making—or undertaking, to use the author's term.

UNCERTAINTY-BEARING

There is a long tradition in economics of relating the role of the entrepreneur to uncertainty. If there was no uncertainty, the future would be fully predictable by all actors. The only decision making that would have to be done would consist of selecting from among the known alternatives. There would be no need for experimentation or deliberation. In fact, there would be no need for action in the sense that the term has been used in this book. Mises follows this tradition of associating entrepreneurship with uncertainty. He says that the "term entrepreneur in [economic] theory means: acting man exclusively seen from the aspect of the uncertainty in every action" (p. 253).

Regarding uncertainty-bearing, it is sufficient to note two things. First, even though Mises points out that uncertainty is inherent in every action, he nevertheless goes to substantial lengths in an effort to isolate uncertainty-bearing from other entrepreneurial characteristics. He begins by trying to imagine a "propertyless entrepreneur." The propertyless entrepreneur proposes to a financier that, in exchange for a fixed fee, he will use the financier's money to produce a good and sell it. He offers to give the financier the rights to all of the residual income but requires that the financier accept the responsibility for making up, from her own funds, any loss that may occur. By this Mises means the "propertyless entrepreneur" becomes an employee of the financier, who herself comes to bear all the uncertainty and who is "also" an entrepreneur (Mises 1966, 253).

Following this, Mises focuses on the ownership rights and responsibilities regarding the residuals. He imagines that there are futures markets in all rights and responsibilities concerning business residuals. In this circumstance, only the dealers in futures would make profit and incur losses. Everyone else would be an employee. As shown in Part 2 of chapter 9, "[t]here emerges a class of pure entrepreneurs. The prices on the futures markets direct the whole apparatus of production.

. . . All other people are insured, as it were against the possible adverse effects of the uncertainty of the future" (p. 256).

The second thing to note about uncertainty-bearing is the nature of the uncertainty that is borne. It is essential to recognize that Mises uses a restricted definition of uncertainty. In the modern economics literature, the term has often been used to mean a lack of knowledge about any future event, regardless of the source. For example, the prospect of an earthquake, a technical error in calculation, or a change in the law is said to be a source of uncertainty. Uncertainty in subjectivist economic theory refers solely to the uncertainty that one individual has about the ends and means of other individuals. In no way does it refer to disturbances in the physical environment or to what in econometrics are called stochastic elements.

In speaking of uncertainty and the need, because of uncertainty, to speculate, Mises says:

> In the real world acting man is faced with the fact that there are fellow men acting on their own behalf as he himself acts. The necessity to adjust his actions to other people's actions makes him a speculator for whom success and failure depend on his greater or lesser ability to understand [in the sense of *verstehen*] the future. Every action is speculation. There is in the course of human events no stability and consequently no safety. (p. 113)

Regarding what it is that individuals are uncertain about, Mises says: "Future needs and valuations, the reaction of men to changes in conditions, future scientific and technical knowledge, future ideologies and policies can never be foretold with more than a greater or smaller degree of probability" (p. 106).

Mises discusses the relation between uncertainty and entrepreneurship on pages 251–56 of *Human Action*. In reading these pages it is important to recognize Mises's special definition of data. Data refers to

> . . . the bodily and psychological features of acting men, their desires and value judgments, and the theories, doctrines, and ideologies they develop in order to adjust themselves purposely to the conditions of their environment and thus to attain the ends they are aiming at. (p. 646)

Appendix 6

On Ideal Types

Mises points out that ideal types "are entirely different from [a priori] categories . . ." (1966, 59–60). Yet it is easy to confuse the two, since one often uses the same word to refer to both an a priori category and an ideal type. Mises demonstrates this by identifying two uses of the word entrepreneur. As an a priori category, entrepreneur means "acting man exclusively seen from the aspect of the uncertainty inherent in every action" (p. 253). In economic theory, it is used as a counterpoint to the concept of an economic system in which there is no uncertainty and, therefore, no entrepreneurship (p. 252). But the term "entrepreneur" is also used in describing historical events. In this application, it is an ideal type. It means, for example, "the American entrepreneur of the time of Jefferson, German heavy industries in the age of William II, New England textile manufacturing in the last decades preceding the first World War . . . and so on" (pp. 61–62).

This distinction can be clarified further by exploring the meaning of the term *homo economicus*. Homo economicus is an a priori human being whose actions are limited to the production, purchase, and sale of factors and goods in markets, and to consumption and saving. It is a combination of an a priori category and the economic theorist's definition of economic action. It is the embodiment of the economist's motives, ideas, aims, and means. The applied economist, or historian, may attribute specific motives, ideas, aims, and means to a particular individual in order to explain why she acted the way she did. For example, she may say that the owner of an assembly business watches over her workers carefully in order to avoid shirking and pilfering. The owner is an ideal type that is constructed on the basis of the applied economist's experienced-based understanding of "the motives, ideas, and aims of the [subjects studied by the economist] and of the means [those subjects] apply . . ." (p. 60).

A priori categories cannot be imagined away in the sense that without them there can be no image of human action. Without homo economicus, the economist could not represent economic action. Ideal types are composites of particular characteristics, like particular wants, abilities, opportunities, and so on. Any ideal type can be replaced by a different ideal type that has different particular characteristics. Thus, one can imagine defining the owner of an assembly line business as a person who does not watch over her employees or as one who watches over them for a different reason.

In constructing a conception of a market economy, the economic theorist mixes specific classes of wants, abilities, and knowledge that are based on the traditional definition of the subject matter of economics with a priori categories. The result is the roles of the producer, the consumer-saver, the factor-supplier, and the entrepreneur. A fully integrated economic action could not occur if these roles were not present.

Because the economist uses roles while the lay person uses typifications, confusion has been present from the very inception of economics as a distinct discipline. The layperson has erroneously interpreted the statements of economists to be about typifications, while they were really about functions. Professional economists themselves have used deductions concerning roles to make unsupportable generalizations about typifications. And opportunists have claimed support for their generalizations about typifications from the writings of economists about roles.

Appendix 7

Mises on the Evenly Rotating Economy as an Endpoint

A critic might claim that Mises did not use the term ERE to refer to an endpoint. Instead, the critic would say, he used the terms *final state of rest* and the *final price* to mean endpoint. He reserved the ERE to refer only to an actionless economy. The answer to this claim is that in his introductory discussions of the ERE, Mises does seem to confine his meaning of the ERE to the actionless economy. Later, however, he speaks of the ERE as an endpoint. Indeed he appears to use the terms final state of rest and ERE to mean the same thing. This fact suggests that his earlier discussion deserves a reinterpretation.

That Mises wanted to draw a distinction between the final state of rest and the ERE is clear from the following statement:

> The imaginary construction of the final state of rest is marked by paying full regard to change in the temporal succession of events. In this respect it differs from the imaginary construction of the *evenly rotating economy*, which is characterized by the elimination of change in the data and of the time element. (p. 246–47)

That he intended to use the final state of rest as an endpoint is evident in his introduction to the section entitled "The State of Rest and the Evenly Rotating Economy." Here he used the term in conjunction with a **plain state of rest** (a beginning point). He said:

> The only method of dealing with the problem of action is to conceive that action ultimately aims at bringing about a state of affairs in which there is no longer any further action, whether because all uneasiness has been

removed or because any further removal of felt uneasiness is out of the question. Action thus tends toward a state of rest, or absence of action. (p. 245)

After saying that the plain state of rest is a condition that exists in a market, he described it further in order to show its relation to the final state of rest:

In dealing with the plain state of rest, we look only at what is going on right now. We restrict out attention to what has happened momentarily and disregard what will happen later. We are dealing only with prices really paid in sales, i.e., with the prices of the immediate past. We do not ask whether or not future prices will equal these prices.

But now we go a step further. We pay attention to factors which are bound to bring about a tendency toward price changes. We try to find out to what goal [!] this tendency must lead before all its driving force is exhausted and a new state of rest emerges. The price corresponding to this future state of rest was called the *natural price* by older economists; nowadays the term *static price* is often used. In order to avoid misleading associations it is more expedient to call it the *final price* and accordingly, to speak of the *final state of rest*. (p. 246)

It is only after Mises described this use of the concept of the final state of rest that he introduced the ERE. Specifically, he briefly distinguished between the final state of rest and the ERE. Thus, at this point in *Human Action,* it seems that Mises did not intend the ERE to be used as an endpoint. Instead, he wanted it to be treated as an actionless economy in which behavior is repeated again and again, as it is when it is contrasted with what he calls the stationary economy (pp. 250–51).

Even at this early stage, however, he seemed to acknowledge the use of the ERE as an endpoint. Consider how he viewed the relationship between the final price and the evenly rotating economy. After defining the final price as the price toward which a market is always tending, and after saying that the "final price can only be defined by defining the conditions required for its emergence" (p. 246), Mises defined the evenly rotating economy as "a fictitious system in which the market prices of all goods and services coincide with the final prices" (p. 247). It is difficult to avoid concluding that the ERE also can be defined by defining the conditions required for its emergence, although Mises did not say this outright.

Return now to the relationship between the final state of rest and the

ERE. Later in his text, Mises's distinction between the final state of rest and the ERE becomes less clear. Consider the following lengthy description of the market economy.

> The tasks incumbent upon the theory of prices of factors of production are to be solved by the same methods which are employed for treatment of the prices of consumers' goods. We conceive the operation of the market of consumers' goods in a twofold way. We think on the one hand of a state of affairs which leads to acts of exchange: the situation is such that the uneasiness of various individuals can be removed to some extent because various people value the same goods in a different way. On the other hand, we think of a situation in which no further acts of exchange can happen because no actor expects any further improvement of his satisfaction by further acts of exchange. We proceed in the same way in comprehending the formation of the prices of factors of production. The operation of the market is actuated and kept in motion by the exertion of the promoting entrepreneurs, eager to profit from differences in the market prices of the factors of production and the expected prices of the products. The operation of this market would stop if a situation were ever to emerge in which the sum of the prices of the complementary factors of production—but for interest—equaled the prices of the products and nobody believed that further price changes were to be expected. Thus we have described the process adequately and completely by pointing out, positively, what actuates it and, negatively, what would suspend its motion. The main importance is to be attached to the positive description. The negative description resulting in the imaginary constructions of the *final price* and the *evenly rotating economy* is merely auxiliary. For the task is not the treatment of imaginary concepts, which never appear in life and action, but the treatment of the market prices at which the goods of higher orders are really bought and sold. (p. 334, italics added)

Mises went on to attribute the method to Gossen, Carl Menger, and Bohm Bawerk.

Consider also his discussion of short-run and long-run effects of an increase in saving.

> All these changes in the prices of factors of production begin immediately with the initiation of the entrepreneurial actions designed to adjust the processes of production to the new state of affairs. In dealing with this problem as with the other problem of changes in the market data, we must guard ourselves against the popular fallacy of drawing a sharp line between short-run and long-run effects. What happens in the short-run is precisely the first stages of the chain of successive transformations which

tend to bring about the long-run effects. The long-run effect is in our case the disappearance of entrepreneurial profits and losses. The short-run effects are the preliminary stages of this process of elimination which *finally, if not interrupted by a further change in the data, would result in the emergence of the evenly rotating economy.* (p. 296, italics added)

After seeing how Mises used the term ERE later in the text, one is prompted to return to his earlier discussion to see whether there is any hint of his later meaning. One discovers that indeed there is. Consider the following statement.

The imaginary construction of the evenly rotating system is a limiting notion. In its frame there is in fact no longer any action. Automatic reaction is substituted for the conscious striving of thinking man after the removal of uneasiness. (pp. 249–50)

Finally, the clinching evidence is Mises's statement about when it is appropriate to employ the ERE. He says:

. . . We can employ this problematic imaginary construction only if we never forget what purposes it is designed to serve. We want *first* of all to analyze the tendency, prevailing in every action, toward the establishment of an evenly rotating economy. . . . *Secondly*, we need to comprehend in what respects the conditions of a living world in which there is action differ from those of a rigid world. (pp. 249–50, italics added)

In this statement the two methods of understanding economic interaction come through loud and clear. The first is the method of economic teleology. The second is the method of contrasting images of functions.

Appendix 8

Menger on Rights and the Firm

That rights and markets are producible by entrepreneurs can be inferred from the writings of Carl Menger (1981) on "the general theory of the good." Menger says:

> . . . From an economic standpoint, . . . what are called clienteles, goodwill, monopolies, [firms, copyrights, trademarks] etc. are the useful actions or inactions of other people, or (as in the case of *firms*, for example) aggregates of material goods, labor services and other useful actions and inactions. (p. 55)

He goes on in the pages that follow to discuss the "causal connections between goods." Later in the same chapter, he speaks of "The Causes of Progress in Human Welfare." In his discussion, he makes the following remarks:

> . . . Assume a people which extends its attention to goods of third, fourth, and higher orders, instead of confining its activity merely to the tasks of a primitive collecting economy—that is, to the acquisition of naturally available goods of the lowest order (ordinarily goods of the first, and possibly second, order). If such a people progressively directs goods of ever higher orders to the satisfaction of its needs, and especially if each step in this direction is accompanied by an appropriate division of labor, we shall doubtless observe that progress in welfare which Adam Smith was disposed to attribute exclusively to the latter factor. (p. 73)

It is a logical extension of these ideas to say that if one wishes to identify and describe examples of how entrepreneurship contributes to specialization and·"wealth" in a market economy, one can investigate the type of actions that cause markets and rights to come into existence.

Appendix 9

The Political Nature of
Establishing Rights

Mises (1966) discusses the problem of external costs by pointing out that the absence of rights may be due either (1) to "a deliberate policy on the part of governments and legislators," or (2) to "an unintentional effect of the traditional wording of laws" (p. 656). He goes on to say:

> where a considerable part of the costs incurred are external costs from the point of view of the acting individuals or firms, the economic calculation established by them is manifestly defective and their results deceptive. But this is not the outcome of alleged deficiencies inherent in the system of private ownership of the means of production. It is on the contrary a consequence of loopholes left in this system. It could be removed by a reform of the laws concerning liability for damages inflicted and by rescinding the institutional barriers preventing the full operation of private ownership. (p. 658)

The issue that Mises does not consider here is the political nature of the process through which liability is determined. The inherently political nature of the process makes the presence of externalities a persistent characteristic of economic interaction in everyday life.

A person who believes he has been the victim of an external cost must obtain a judgment against the alleged offender. The questions faced by the judge are whether an action actually causes an external cost, the extent of the cost, and who incurs it. If the problem of making a correct judgment was a technological one, a robot could make it. A speedy judgment could be made and an offender could quickly be made liable for all the external costs. The problem, however, is not a technological one; it is one of value. To solve it, a judge must acquire an intersubjective understanding of plans and actions. The information needed to answer the aforesaid questions is largely in the minds of the plaintiff and defendant. Since each has an incentive to lie, the problem of applying law is reduced to the problem faced by the judge of sifting through the persuasion efforts of the plaintiff and defendant in an effort to get at the truth.

One could imagine a completely impartial judge and a courtroom situation in which the statements of both the plaintiff and defendant are equally effective in providing the judge with information. However, this is not the situation that exists in the image of a market economy. In that image all individuals—with their different degrees of expertise and wealth—are free to attempt to persuade others that their ideas and values are correct. Under these circumstances, those who devote more financial resources to persuading the judge are more likely to win their cases, regardless of the truth.

Thus, the process through which a judgment concerning whether an external cost has been caused is an inherently political one. As a result, other things being equal, those with wealth have an edge over those who are not wealthy. Moreover, if there are many joint contributors to the external costs and many who incur those costs, the cost of organizing a political collective becomes relevant. It follows that external effects are not only the consequence of defects and loopholes: They are also the consequence of the political nature of the process through which the principle of liability must be applied in the image of a market economy with incompletely specified rights. No reform of the laws concerning liability for damages and no "rescinding the institutional barriers preventing the full operation of private ownership" would be sufficient to transform this inherently political process into an economic one.

References

Alchian, Armen, and William R. Allen. 1983. *Exchange and Production: Competition, Coordination, and Control,* 3rd edition. Belmont, Calif.: Wadsworth.

Alchian, Armen, and Harold Demsetz. 1972. "Production and Economic Organization." *American Economic Review* 62:777–95.

Aspromourgos, Tony. 1986. "On the Origins of the Term 'Neoclassical.'" *Cambridge Journal of Economics* 10:265–70.

Block, Walter. 1980. "On Robert Nozick's 'On Austrian Methodology.'" *Inquiry* 23:397–444.

Caldwell, Bruce. 1982. *Beyond Positivism: Economic Methodology in the Twentieth Century.* Boston: George Allen & Unwin.

Chapman, Michael. 1986. "The Structure of Exchange: Piaget's Sociological Theory." *Human Development* 29:181–84.

Dennett, D. C. 1971. "Intentional Systems." *The Journal of Philosophy* 68:87–106.

Ebeling, Richard M. 1986. "Toward a Hermeneutical Economics: Expectations, Prices, and the Role of Interpretation in the Theory of the Market Process." in *Subjectivism, Intelligibility, and Economic Understanding,* edited by Israel Kirzner. New York: New York University Press.

Grinder, Walter E., and John Hagel III. 1977. "Toward a Theory of State Capitalism: Ultimate Decision-Making and Class Structure." *Journal of Libertarian Studies* 1:1.

Gunning, J. Patrick. 1986. "The Methodology of Austrian Economics and Its Relevance to Institutionalism." *American Journal of Economics and Sociology* 45:79–91.

———. 1989. "The Method of Imaginary Constructions." Department of Economics, Ohio University, Athens, Ohio. Unpublished manuscript.

————. 1989. *The Failure of the New Subjectivist Revolution: A Critique of Mises's Applied Economics and of Recent Developments in Subjectivist Economics*. Unpublished manuscript.

Gurzynski, Z.S.A. 1976. "Entrepreneurship—The True Spring of Human Action." *South African Journal of Economics* 44:1.

Haberler, Gottfried. 1981. "Mises' Private Seminar." *Wirtschaftspolitische Blatter* no. 4.

Hayek, F. A. 1931. "Reflections on the Pure Theory of Money of Mr. J. M. Keynes." *Economica* 11:270–95.

————. 1937. "Economics and Knowledge." *Economica* 4:35–54. Reprinted in *Individualism and Economic Order*. 1984. Ill.: University of Chicago Press.

————. 1973. "The Place of Menger's Grundsatze in the History of Economic Thought." In *Carl Menger and the Austrian School of Economics,* edited by J. R. Hicks and W. Weber. Oxford: Clarendon Press.

————. 1983. "The Keynes Centenary: The Austrian Critique." *The Economist* 287:39–41.

Hazlitt, Henry. 1959. *The Failure of the "New Economics."* N.J.: Princeton University Press.

Hoppe, Hans-Hermann. 1988. *Praxeology and Economic Science*. Auburn, Ala.: Ludwig von Mises Institute.

Kaufmann, Felix. 1933. "On the Subject-Matter and Method of Economic Science." *Economica* 13.

Kirzner, Israel. 1966. *An Essay on Capital*. New York: Augustus M. Kelley.

————. 1973. *Competition and Entrepreneurship*. Ill.: University of Chicago Press.

————. 1976. *The Economic Point of View: An Essay in the History of Economic Thought*. Kansas City: Sheed and Ward.

————. 1979. *Perception, Opportunity, and Profit*. Ill.: University of Chicago Press.

Kitchener, Richard F. 1981. "Piaget's Social Psychology." *Journal for the Theory of Social Behaviour* 11:253–78.

Lachmann, Ludwig M. 1943. "The Role of Expectations in Economic Science." *Economica*.

————. 1971. *The Legacy of Max Weber*. Berkeley, Calif.: The Glendessary Press.

————. 1976. "From Mises to Shackle: An Essay on Austrian Economics and the Kaleidic Society." *Journal of Economic Literature* 15:54–62.

————. 1977. "The Science of Human Action." In *Capital, Expectations, and the Market Process*. Kansas City, Mo.: Sheed Andrews and McMeel.

————. 1978. *Capital and Its Structure*. Mission, Kans.: Sheed Andrews and McMeel.

————. 1978. "Carl Menger and the Incomplete Revolution of Subjectivism." *Atlantic Economic Journal* 6:57–59.

————. 1982. "Ludwig von Mises and the Extension of Subjectivism." In *Method, Process, and Austrian Economics*, edited by Israel Kirzner. Lexington, Mass.: D. C. Heath.

————. 1983. "John Maynard Keynes: A View From the Austrian Window." *South African Journal of Economics* 51:368–79.

Lancaster, Kelvin. 1966. "A New Approach to Consumer Theory." *Journal of Political Economy* 74:132–57.

Menger, Carl. 1981. *Principles of Economics*. Trans. James Dingwall and Bert F. Hoselitz. New York: New York University Press. (Originally published under the title of *Grundstze der Volkwirthschaftslehre* in 1871.)

O'Sullivan, Patrick J. 1987. *Economic Methodology and Freedom to Choose*. London: Allen & Unwin.

Pareto, Vilfredo. [1900] 1953. "Sul Fenomeno Economico." *Giornale Degli Economisti*. Trans. reprinted as "On the Economic Phenomenon: A Reply to Benedetto Croce." *International Economic Papers* 3:180–86.

————. [1901] 1953. "Sul Principio Economico." *Giornale Degli Economisti*. Trans. reprinted as "On the Economic Principle: A Reply to Benedetto Croce." *International Economic Papers* 3:203–07.

Piaget, Jean. 1930. *The Child's Conception of Physical Causality*. New York: Harcourt, Brace and Company.

————. 1971. *Genetic Epistemology*. Trans. Eleanor Duckworth. New York: W. W. Norton & Company.

————. 1974. *Understanding Causality*. New York: W. W. Norton & Company.

————, and Barbel Inhelder. 1958. *The Growth of Logical Thinking*. New York: Basic Books.

Rothbard, Murray N. 1951. "Praxeology: Reply to Mr. Schuller." *American Economic Review* 41:943–46.

————. 1973. "Praxeology as the Method of Economics." In *Phenomenology and the Social Sciences*, edited by Maurice Natanson. Evanston, Ill.: Northwestern University Press.

Schuetz, Alfred. 1943. "The Problem of Rationality in the Social World." *Economica* 10:130–49.

————. 1953. "Common-Sense and the Scientific Interpretation of Human Action." *Philosophy and Phenomenological Research* 14:1–38.

Schumpeter, J. A. 1934. *The Theory of Economic Development*. Trans. R. Opie. Cambridge: Harvard University Press.

Selgin, G. A. 1988a. "Praxeology and Understanding: An Analysis of the Controversy in Austrian Economics." *Review of Austrian Economics* 2.

Shackle, G. L. S. 1966. *The Nature of Economic Thought*. London: Cambridge University Press.

———. 1969. *Decision, Order and Time*. London: Cambridge University Press.

———. 1970. *Expectation, Enterprise and Profit: The Theory of the Firm*. Chicago: Aldine Publishing Company.

———. 1972. *Epistemics and Economics*. London: Cambridge University Press.

Shand, Alex. H. 1980. *Subjectivist Economics: The New Austrian School*. The Pica Press.

Stonier, Alfred, and Karl Bode. 1937. "A New Approach to the Social Sciences." *Economica* 4:406–24.

Vaughn, Karen I. 1980. "Economic Calculation under Socialism: The Austrian Contribution." *Economic Inquiry* 18:535–54.

von Mises, Ludwig. 1966. *Human Action: A Treatise on Economics*. Chicago: Henry Regnery Company.

———. 1969. *The Historical Setting of the Austrian School of Economics*. New Rochelle, N.Y.: Arlington House.

———. 1978a. *The Ultimate Foundation of Economic Science*. Kansas City: Sheed, Andrews and McMeel.

———. 1978b. *Notes and Recollections*. South Holland, Ill.: Libertarian Press.

———. 1980. "Profit and Loss." In Ludwig von Mises, *Planning for Freedom*. 2nd ed. South Holland, Ill.: Libertarian Press.

———. 1981. *Epistemological Problems of Economics*. New York: New York University Press. (Originally published in 1933 as *Grundprobleme der Nationalkonomie: Untersuchungen ber Verfahren, Aufgaben, und Inhalt der Wirtschafts und Gesellshaftslehre*. Jena: Gustav Fischer.)

White, Lawrence H. 1984. *The Methodology of the Austrian School Economists*. Auburn, Ala.: The Ludwig von Mises Institute of Auburn University.

Williamson, Oliver E. 1985. *The Economic Institutions of Capitalism*. New York: The Free Press.

Subject Index

Index of Names

265